I0812286

THE GREAT AMERICAN FAMILY REUNION COOKBOOK

LORI NAWYN

FAMILIUS

Copyright © 2014 by Lori Nawyn

All rights reserved.

Published by Familius™ LLC, www.familius.com

Familius books are available at special discounts for bulk purchases for sales promotions, family or corporate use. Special editions, including personalized covers, excerpts of existing books, or books with corporate logos, can be created in large quantities for special needs. For more information, contact Premium Sales at 559-876-2170 or email specialmarkets@familius.com

Reproduction of this book in any manner, in whole or in part, without written permission of the publisher is prohibited.

Library of Congress Catalog-in-Publication Data

2014941562

pISBN 978-1-938301-99-5

eISBN 978-1-939629-50-0

Printed in the United States of America

Edited by Janna DeVore and Maggie Wickes
Cover design by David Miles
Book design by Maggie Wickes and David Miles

10 9 8 7 6 5 4 3 2 1

First Edition

TABLE OF CONTENTS

FOREWORD I

ACKNOWLEDGMENTS V

INTRODUCTION VII

WHY HAVE A REUNION? XI

MAKING YOUR REUNION GREAT XXI

APPENDIZERS, DIPS, SAUCES & BREADS 1

Roasted Garlic and Garlic Oil 2

Salmon Braid 3

Ice Box Rolls 4

Ann's Fresh Mexican Salsa 5

Brooke's Fruit Dip 6

Colorado Pear and Chicken Flatbread 7

Jones Family Farms Strawberry Salsa 8

Lima Bean Hummus 9

Delaware Shrimp Dip 10
Florida Zucchini Chips 10
Feta and Dill Dip 11
Jenna Kae's Peach-Mango Salsa 11
Bacon and Blue Dip 12
Kristy's Killer Barbecue Sauce for Wild Game 13
Pan Fried Jersey Tomatoes with Fresh Mozzarella and Basil 14
Jersey Fresh Fried Tomatoes 15
Southern Shrimp Dip 16
Piedmont Lexington-Style Dip 17
Sausage Grits Muffins 18
Lakota Fry Bread 19
Dakota Bread 20
Oregon Shrimp Dip 21
Fresh Green Onions 21
Grilled Green Onions and Thyme 22
Carolina Red Barbecue Sauce 22
Julia Bushree's Texas Caviar 23
Crockpot Pizza Dip 24
Baked Cinnamon Tortilla Chips with Fruit Salsa 25
Mustard Sauce for Ham 26
Spoon Bread 27

BREAKFAST & BRUNCH **29**

Salsa Scramble 30
Basil Tomato Frittata 31
Aebleskivers 32
Starbuck Inn Blueberry Pancakes 33

Pasta-Veggie Scramble 35
Sweet Crepes with Blueberry Sauce 36
DiMeo Farms Lemon Blueberry Pancakes 38
German Eggs 40
Bacon Onion Quiche Bites 41
Apple Au Gratin 42
Cheddar Dill Scones with Ohio Amish Cheese 43
Hazelnut Schnecken (Cinnamon Rolls) 44
South County Style Johnny Cakes 46
Lazy Morning Impossible Pie 47
Hootenanny with Raspberry Syrup 48
Memer's Dried Beef Gravy on Toast 49
Famous Farmhouse Bed and Breakfast Granola 50
Potato Hash and Baked Eggs 51
Carson Ridge Hashbrown Bake 52
Stuffed French Toast with Homemade Orange Syrup 53
Aunt Virgie's Danish Aebleskivers 54
Wildflower Inn Oatmeal-Buttermilk Pancakes 55

MAIN DISHES, SIDE DISHES & BURGERS 57

Lundy's Coconut Shrimp 58
Butterflied Spicy Coconut Shrimp 59
Famous Barbecue Chicken 61
Jane's Knouff's Beef Kabobs 62
Macaroni and Cheese with Cauliflower 63
Salmon Burgers 64
Arizona Arroz Con Pollo 65
Arizona Carnitas with Green Chiles 66

Arkansas Chicken-Cornbread Casserole ... 67
Colorado Summer Sauté ... 68
Rocky Mountain Macaroni Goulash ... 69
Coastal Tuna Loaf ... 70
Glazed Peaches and Pork ... 71
Peanut Crusted Chicken Strips ... 72
Reunion Spam Casserole ... 74
Easy Polynesian Chicken ... 74
Aloo Gobi ... 75
Prisco's Lasagna ... 76
Lori's Super Easy Oven Tacos ... 78
Chicago-Style Deep Dish Pizza ... 79
Indiana Pork Meatballs ... 80
Rosemary Roasted Reds ... 80
Corn, Ham, and Noodle Casserole ... 81
Kentucky Catfish Croquettes ... 82
Opelousas Baked Chicken ... 83
Natchitoches Meat Pies ... 84
Lobster Mac and Cheese ... 85
Gingery Shrimp Linguine ... 86
Maryland Lump Crab Cake on Creamed Corn with South Shore Butter ... 87
Maryland Crab Pizza ... 88
Aunt Grace's Boston Baked Beans ... 89
A Hot Dog Bar ... 90
Carol's Black Bean Burgers ... 91
Easy Pot Pie ... 92
Minnesota Tater Tot Hotdish ... 93
Minnesota Hotdish with Wild Rice ... 94
Mississippi Wild-Caught Gulf Shrimp and Eggplant Casserole ... 95

Missouri Crockpot Beef Brisket ... 96
Toni's Wild Woman Beans ... 97
Grilled Corn on the Cob ... 98
Buffet Casserole ... 99
Santa Fe Pasta ... 100
Chicken and Sour Cream Enchiladas ... 101
Chicken with Glazed Apples ... 102
Crispy Baked Sweet Potato Fries with Blue Cheese Dressing ... 103
Eastern North Carolina Chopped Turkey Barbecue ... 104
Swedish Meatballs ... 105
Hanky-Pankies ... 106
Cooperative Meatloaf for One Hundred ... 107
Dee's Spanish Chicken ... 108
Dillner Family Farm Broccoli Casserole ... 108
Charleston Red Rice ... 109
Roasted Garlic and Root Vegetables ... 110
June Halverson's Best Sloppy Joe's Ever ... 111
Real Texas Tamales ... 112
Simple Seafood Paella ... 114
Cornburgers ... 115
Coney Island Burgers ... 115
Tuna Fish Pie ... 116
Potato Wedges with Cilantro Lime Sauce ... 117
Cowboy Milk Can Dinner ... 118

SOUPS, STEWS, SALADS & SANDWICHES ... **119**

Brown Jug Soup ... 120
Taco Salad Bar ... 121

Fried Catfish Poor Boy Sandwich Minis 123
Tangy Coleslaw 123
Potato and Smoked Sausage Chowder 124
Healthy Summer Quinoa Salad 125
Slow Cooker Barbecue Chicken Sliders 126
Chicken Salad Sandwiches 127
Tuna Salad Sandwiches 127
Smoked Salmon Salad Sandwiches 128
Fran's Easy Vegetable Soup 129
Marinated Corn and Pea Salad 130
Six Bean Salad with Corn 131
Nancy's Holiday Salad 132
Potato Mac Salad 133
April Cardenas' Mango Curry Shrimp Salad 134
Mr. Maytag's Salad Dressing 136
Okra and Tomato Stew 137
Easy Kentucky Burgoo 138
Original "Hot Brown" Sandwich 139
Louisiana Sweet Potato Salad 140
Chicken and Dumplings 142
Dutch Oven Bison Stew 143
Berry Walnut Salad 144
Napa at the Waldorf 145
Minnie Jensen's Million-Dollar Duck Club Coleslaw 146
Traditional North Carolina Coleslaw 146
Tony Geary's Aunt's Stew 147
Sharee's Jell-O Salad Delight 148
Brunswick Stew 150

Grilled Shrimp and Scallop Salad with Dijon Lemon Vinaigrette 151
Hood River Salad 152
Apple Blue Cheese Slaw 153
Grandpa Hill's Favorite Fruit Salad 153
Pioneer Soup 154
Broccoli and Cranberry Salad 155

SNACKS, TREATS & DESSERTS **157**

Alaska Blueberry and Peach Crisp 158
Mor's Sur Flode Kager (Mother's Sour Cream Cookies) 159
Orange Cake 161
Grilled Bacon, Bananas, and Oranges 163
Easy Key Lime Pie 163
Dickey Farms' Sugar 'n' Spice Grilled Peaches 164
Georgia Sweet Potato Pie 165
Georgia Pecan Popcorn with Rosemary and Thyme 166
Idaho Honey Peach Ice Cream 167
Maytag Blue Cheese Cookies 168
Homemade Peanut and Molasses Popcorn 169
Oatmeal Cake 170
Sugar Cream Pie 171
Real Hoosier Sugar Cream Pie 172
Unbelievable Cookies 173
No-Bake Oatmeal Cookies 174
The Bluebird's Blueberry Lemon Cobbler 175
Traditional Smith Island Ten-Layer Cake 176
Fudge Brownie Pie 178
Aunt Thelma's Orange Carrot Cookies 179

Twirling Toffee Bars 180
Potato Chip Cookies 181
Biscochitos 182
Pennsylvania Dutch Soft Sugar Cookies 184
Pumpkin Spice Bars 185
Chocolate Raspberry Truffle Cake 186
Shoo-Fly Pie 188
Quick Coffee Cake 189
Cream-Filled Peach Brownie Cake 190
Fresh Raspberry Shake 192
Marguerites 193
The Most Delicious Cake I Ever Ate 194
Cranberry Pecan Cream Cheese Bars 195

THEMED REUNION MENUS **197**

State Fair 199
Corn Doggies 202
Iowa Girl Eats Clubhouse Turkey Burgers 203
Blue Ribbon Mandarin Chicken Salad 204
State Fair Bacon Corn 204
State Fair Raspberry-Lemonade 205
Grandma's Prize-Winning Cobbler 205
Homemade Eskimo Pies 206

Picnic Themed 207
Tuna Salad Coneys 209
Devil's Eggs 209
Rocky Road 210

Guys-Do-All-the-Work Cook Out 211

Grilled Sweet Soy Salmon 212

Grilled Cinnamon Sweet Potatoes 213

Sweet Addictions Crisps 214

Frontier 215

"Best of the West" Burgers 218

Kansas Corn Salad 218

Buffalo Chips 219

Blue-Buffalo Chicken Dip 219

Frontier Root Beer 220

Cow Pies 220

Mountain Campout 221

"Under the Stars" Dinner 223

Orange Peel Cupcakes 223

Mountain-Fresh Fruit Salad 224

Wilderness Pretzels 224

Happy Camper Trail Mix 225

Festival Themed 226

Gracehill Bed and Breakfast Wild Rice Pecan Waffles 230

Whole-Wheat Waffles 230

Chicken Pita Pockets 231

IDEAS & ACTIVITIES 233

ABOUT THE AUTHOR 247

ABOUT FAMILIUS 248

Foreword

BY EDITH WAGNER, EDITOR OF *REUNIONS MAGAZINE*

Family reunions are celebrations that bring families together for bonding and to maintain ties that can loosen when not tended regularly. Family reunions celebrate history, longevity, and a sense of belonging and place in the world.

Since food is so central to all we do, food at reunions can take on special significance. Fortunate are the families who have great food traditions that can be passed down, and reunions are just the place to do it—as long as Grandma is willing to share her secrets. Sharing recipes at reunions is a special tradition. Often for potlucks, members are asked to include copies of the recipe so others can duplicate a tasty dish. Even better is when meal preparation is done at the reunion and younger members can learn at the side of their elders. Reunion cookbook collections are prized mementos when filled with the favorite/secret/special recipes from aunts, uncles, and grandparents. These recipes are especially treasured when that older generation is no longer with us.

Reunion breakfasts for families who are cooking are usually easy. They are pretty consistently cold cereals, fruit, and sweets with no cooking except to make coffee. Lunch can follow that theme of easy, everyone for themselves, sandwiches, and condiments. Dinner, on the other hand, is generally pretty special.

Denise Heinze from Durham, North Carolina, planned an ocean beach reunion on Oak Island, North Carolina, in two adjacent rented houses for a family of seventeen. Adults signed up to cook one night and were responsible for buying, cooking, and serving the food. Meals included shrimp and chicken shish kabobs, spaghetti, beef and turkey tacos, and all-American hot dogs, hamburgers, and beer-soaked brats.

The Awaya Family Reunion reunites a Japanese-American family who includes teaching the younger generation the art of sushi making.

The Peters Family Reunion of more than forty is always on water, usually a lake or river, because they like water skiing. Meals are a highlight and can include barbecued spare ribs, chipotle pasta with chicken, and turkey chili for entrees and mussels, dips, spreads, and shrimp for appetizers.

A common reunion program starts with a Friday evening Meet and Greet, usually in a private room at the hotel or resort where members gather after they've registered. Friday night fish fries are common at these events. Many families have hors d'oeuvres or potluck that members bring for the occasion.

Picnics at reunions are another place where a potluck works nicely. Potlucks at family reunions are an opportunity for the aunts to share their prized dishes. Often, at the Banks Hill Outlaw Family Reunion that usually meets in Snow Hill, North Carolina, members fill groaning tables with side dishes and desserts while the menfolk are at the grill tending the meat. Men tending meat, women laying out groaning boards—it's a pretty typical reunion picture.

A fine food tradition at the Seidemann Family Reunion in Newburg, Wisconsin, is a Kuchen Contest. Kuchen means cake in German and the Seidemanns are a German family. Members bring cakes that are judged on several serious criteria. After the winners are announced, all of the cakes are auctioned off as a reunion fundraiser. It's a rigged auction! Kids can bid up for their parents until the winning cakes can bring several hundreds of dollars. The winner of the auction gets a cake with a small piece missing (eaten by the judges) and a stack of paper plates and forks!

Janet Park's family in Seattle, Washington, has an annual seafood reunion picnic on Puget Sound with crab, oysters, clams, and salmon right from their own waters. A nephew catches Dungeness crab in the bay and drops them right into pots. Then, Samish Bay oysters are grilled on a fire, while clams are made into a Northwest chowder. The rest of the courses (yes, there are more) are potluck with watermelon and s'mores ending the feast. Park says they walk around between courses!

Surveys by *Reunions Magazine* consistently find that the main purpose for family reunions is to maintain a connectedness that is found no place else. In fact most young parents see it as where their children will come to know their place in the world. Americans, particularly, tend to scatter, so family reunions become even more important to support the ties that bind!

A resident of Milwaukee, Wisconsin, Edith Wagner is founder, publisher, and editor of Reunions Magazine *and reunionsmag.com. She is author of* Reunions Workbook *and* The Family Reunion Sourcebook. *She is a speaker at reunion planning workshops for convention and visitors bureaus, and travels to write about reunion destinations.*

Acknowledgments

I am deeply grateful for my Grandma Esther who taught me that heartfelt compassion and understanding have the capacity to bridge emotional and generational distances. And for my Grandma Minnie who taught me that love and laughter are the glue that holds each day together.

Many thanks to those who shared recipes and insights for this book: Alison Arians of Anchorage's Rise & Shine Bakery for her kindness, spirit, passion, and enthusiasm—with people like Alison and her husband, Dan, Alaska is in good hands. Alabama residents Jane Knouff and her son Ricky for sharing Jane's beloved recipes for beef kabobs and her sought-after famous barbecue chicken recipe. Ellen Gutman Chenaux, of 8 Broads in the Kitchen, who rallied the broads in support of allowing me permission to include some of their fabulous recipes. Louisiana's Chef John Folse and Pennsylvania food writer Aliza Green who work diligently to refine food preparation into an art form. Many thanks, as well, to historians like Ethel Chachere Simpson for preserving the cultural heritage of food and recipes in their states. Thanks also to my dear friend Delone Bradford Glover who has spent her life fighting to preserve and promote the history of the Transcontinental Railroad, all the while caring for her children, grandchildren, and great-grandchildren and gathering decades of recipes that celebrate her love of food and family.

My heart and gratitude go out as well to the countless family farms across America that work to protect a heritage of nutritious foods and happy families. Thank you!

Introduction

My grandmother Esther Lucille made family mealtime unforgettable.

It wasn't that she created elaborate place settings. She didn't own crystal, china, or good silverware. Her napkins were paper, not cloth. On her kitchen table, the centerpiece (if you could call it that) was an assortment of glass jars filled with homemade pickles, jams, and jellies. The food Grandma prepared was, by most standards, nothing fancy and was often served straight from the pot or pan she cooked with. Though she prided herself on a standard of homespun excellence that manifested itself in all her meals, the details my grandmother felt were of most importance involved much more than aesthetics or appealing to the palate of hungry relatives.

Grandma Esther

With heartfelt wisdom, Grandma dished up ample servings of love and rich helpings of a heritage of belonging.

Whether the family gathering was a small assemblage of aunts, uncles, and cousins at her and Grandfather's rural Idaho farmhouse, or dozens upon dozens of relatives attending planned or impromptu reunions at the nearby church or legion hall, Grandma was a pillar of strength and goodwill. And, with her keen understanding of the importance of family ties, she was an ambassador for peace and unity.

Under Grandma's tutelage, preparing for meals was a shared occupation. Everyone took turns setting the table with a well-loved assortment of mismatched glasses, plates, and utensils. Cousins gathered eggs from the chicken coop. Uncles retrieved ingredients from the garden or cold room—a root cellar of sorts where anything that wouldn't fit in the refrigerator was stashed.

Younger children and aunts filled small serving bowls with olives, radishes, or carrot sticks. It was a privilege for older children to assist on the front lines of cooking, helping Grandma dredge chicken or elk steaks in flour, salt, and pepper; slicing potatoes; chopping cabbage; or stirring batter for a cake or cobbler.

Hidden in seemingly menial or mundane chores that sometimes caused a few of us to grumble (especially when it came to cleanup and washing dishes) was a treasure trove of shared responsibility that resulted in camaraderie. Grandma's network of individuals toiling collectively for the whole family afforded us the opportunity to overcome differences as we worked together for the common good. Her example of love and goodwill ensured day-to-day sorrows, complaints, and misunderstandings were interwoven with life lessons of forgiveness, compassion, tolerance, acceptance, and patience, as well as appreciation and adherence to the principles of gratitude and joy.

Once we sat down at the table—enjoying the food we'd all had a hand in preparing—stories and values were shared. Grandma told of her childhood, of growing up desperately poor in a family that nonetheless found itself brimming with thankfulness for one another and for life's simple blessings. My grandfather, a dry farmer as well as an avid outdoorsman, told of his adventures, like the fantastic machines he built—snow planes—that transported him into the frozen winter landscapes of Teton and Yellowstone National Parks. Uncles and aunts shared tales of both hardships and happiness, and of goals they had reached and dreams they were yet pursuing. We children, in addition to being able to relate our own hobbies and interests to the adults, learned of the worth of hard work and perseverance. We heard firsthand that trials and challenges can be successfully navigated and overcome, and that happiness is in the heart of the beholder—in how one chooses to perceive their circumstances.

My grandmother passed away in 2006, yet rarely a day goes by that lessons I learned from her don't benefit me. She was a practical woman who proffered practical wisdom, the kind that settles into your bones and becomes part of your own personal legacy. The kind that can bear you up and keep you moving forward despite whatever storms may come your way. The greatest wisdom she shared was of the power a family united in heart and purpose can have to help, heal, and sustain itself and strengthen and uplift its individual members.

Tapping into that power takes practice, work and effort, trial and error, and the determination to do it all over time and again.

When children are grown and moved away and when years and miles separate loved ones, harnessing that power can prove even more challenging. That's where family reunions play a vital role. Reunions provide a catalyst for teaching as they serve to extol the best of family relationships and breathe hope and energy into the future. The shared experiences in preparing for meals and enjoying food together as a family are an ideal place to begin to find common ground. Within our time together we discover that though families are made of diverse individuals, all struggling to find their place in the world, what keeps them together is simple, heartfelt love.

Getting the Most from This Book

At the heart of this book is a collection of family recipes from across America. Each state is represented with a number of dishes and examples of regional history. Insights into each state's most popular foods give a taste of local life and serve as springboards for incorporating your family's culture and heritage into your reunion celebrations. If you have limited time or short notice to plan your event, turn to the sample one-meal menus for themed family gatherings (see page 197). In addition, you'll find ideas for fast pull-together buffet-style meals, desserts, and snacks. Handy, don't-forget lists of kitchen supplies will help you remember what you need to make cooking and serving meals a success.

A brief planning guide provides an overview of how to get your reunion off the ground. Simple tips and activity ideas for making the most of family reunions of all sizes and durations help you round out the experience of shared togetherness. Even when only in planned annual or seasonal increments, sharing in meal preparation, eating, and associated post-meal cleanup is an ideal way to break the ice and build lasting relationships. With an emphasis on ensuring each family member feels his or her place as an integral and valued part of the whole, this book is also a tool that will assist you in finding and maintaining common interests and shared purpose with extended family members.

Why Have a Reunion?

My grandmother knew that family events need to be well thought out with attention to advance planning and preparation. As soon as one family meal was completed, Grandma would begin brainstorming the next, deciding what and who she could pull together to ensure success. As I learned from her, planning and preparation are best achieved when *purpose* is first addressed.

Reunions are stories in the making. A decade or so ago, when I began work as a writer for a local newspaper, one of my editor/mentors discussed the framework for gathering information for stories: the five Ws and one H. Who, What, When, Where, Why, and How. The same framework can be used to plan and prepare for a family gathering. For our purposes we'll put *why* first.

Why Have a Reunion?

The *why* of a reunion involves asking yourself a few questions to determine your reasons for holding a reunion and the specific purpose you want the reunion to serve. Following are examples of some of the most common motivations:

To get to know the relatives. Perhaps you didn't grow up around your extended family. You want to meet them and get acquainted.

To create a new tradition. Maybe your children have never had the chance to associate with their cousins. You want to forge a practice of annual get-togethers to help strengthen family ties.

To celebrate a special occasion. Do you have a grandparent with a milestone birthday coming up? Or are your parents approaching an important anniversary? You might want to involve the entire family in helping celebrate the important event.

In memory of an ancestor. Maybe your Great Uncle William was a famous figure in history. Involving his descendants in an event that will commemorate his accomplishments is a ideal way for family members to help each other learn more about his life and to educate younger generations about the value of bravery, courage, and hard work.

To explore family history. Learning more about your genealogy is a common reason to reunite with extended family. Sharing stories and insights into your roots helps you better appreciate your heritage and cultural customs.

In honor of an event. Is there an important date that has significance for your family? Whether tragedy or joy, getting together in honor of an event that has meaning for family members can deepen relationships and help foster understanding.

For a good cause. Maybe your family has a history of disagreeing with one another, yet you'd like to begin again and attempt to get everyone on the right track. If you have a family member facing severe illness, uniting everyone in a good cause can help you find common ground wherein seeds of compassion may be sown. One idea is to run a race together to help raise money to find a cure or to help raise funds to cover medical expenses. Likewise, pulling together for others who aren't even related to you can aid in healing family rifts. Pooling resources for victims of a disaster (making quilts, kits for school-age children, and so on) or helping another family devastated by personal loss are just two ideas.

For the simple fun of it. You don't have to have any reason to celebrate family, only a desire to make your time together memorable and fun!

Who's Invited?

Deciding *who* will be invited to the reunion involves determining the scope of your reunion. Depending on your *why*, or purpose (perhaps it's a combination of wanting to get to know the relatives *and* celebrating a birthday or anniversary), you'll need to determine who you'd like to invite. Your guest list could include:

- The immediate family you grew up in—your parents and your siblings.
- If your siblings have spouses and children, your brothers- or sisters-in-law and your nieces and nephews.
- If you're married and have children and/or grandchildren, your children and their spouses and children.
- Your grandparents and/or your great aunts and uncles.
- Your aunts and uncles and their children, your cousins, first cousins, second cousins, third cousins, and so on.

For some families, even simple combinations of the above can add up to quite a number! If it's your first reunion, and depending on your purpose, you may elect to try:

- A sibling reunion—a simple lunch or dinner together.
- A guys- or ladies-only reunion—a weekend away from spouses and children.
- A cousins-only reunion, with or without spouses and children—a carefree picnic in the park or a multi-course meal in a fine restaurant you've all dreamed of dining at.
- A reunion for the older members of your family—an event you and a few others host for elderly relatives to reconnect with other loved ones their age.

As you develop your guest list, determine how many adults will likely attend, how many children, and everyone's general age.

What Does the Reunion Entail?

The *what* of the reunion involves getting down to planning and preparing for the event. Ideally, especially if your reunion will be large, you'll want to enlist other family members to help. Form a planning committee that can easily stay in touch with one another. Your committee can include:

A ***chairman*** (usually you!) who keeps things moving forward, keeps the passion/purpose/goal/objective at the forefront of planning, schedules planning meetings with the committee, delegates tasks and assignments, and assists other committee members as needed in carrying out their responsibilities.

A ***secretary*** who compiles contact information for attendees, sends out invitations, and tracks RSVPs. A secretary could also create and maintain a family website, blog, or newsletter to keep everyone informed.

A ***finance chairperson/treasurer*** who helps keep track of budget and receipts, helps with needed fundraising efforts to cover costs for the reunion, gathers money from attendees for any per person or per family fees or deposits, and oversees other financial duties such as writing checks to the location, food, or activity coordinators to pay for expenses.

A ***location coordinator*** who helps pin down possible places to hold the reunion and makes reservations. This individual can also ensure adequate restroom facilities and garbage cans are available as well as comfort and convenience necessities, such as shade (for outdoor events), tables, chairs/seating, diaper changing stations, privacy for nursing mothers, and conditions that allow handicapped family members, babies and toddlers, and elderly family members to be comfortable.

A ***food coordinator*** who works with the chairman to oversee menu planning and shopping and delegates responsibility for decorations and food preparation and serving. This person also ensures that kitchens and cooking facilities are well stocked with necessary supplies and equipment (from refrigeration and stoves to basic kitchen tools) for the meals that will be cooked and served; that paper products such as paper plates and cups, napkins, utensils, etc., are purchased in proper quantities; and communicates with family members to become aware of special dietary needs or restrictions, such as food allergies, vegetarian diets, etc.

A ***setup, cleanup, and kitchen duty chairperson*** who delegates responsibility (in agreement with the location, food, and activity coordinators) for who will set up tables, chairs, shade awnings, and serving tables, as well as help with decorations. This person also helps assign food crews and teams and designates a crew for dishwashing, litter pickup, and all necessary cleanup of meals and activities.

An ***activities coordinator*** who plans and carries out (with the help of his or her own committee) special events, programs, activities, or family games. This person also provides certificates of award for contests, door prizes, thank-you gifts, and other honors and/or recognitions; plans for any crafts and makes sure needed supplies are obtained; considers the interests of all ages and attention spans; and delegates responsibility to others for photography or videography of the event, help with family history details, and the purchase and distribution of any souvenirs or t-shirts you might plan to have at the reunion.

A ***goodwill ambassador*** (or two) who, above all, has patience and a good sense of humor! This should be someone who is good at keeping the peace and promoting unity. He or she welcomes all those who attend, works with the chairman to make sure everyone is getting along and enjoying themselves, and looks for anyone who may feel left out and helps make them feel a part of things.

A ***medical specialist*** who has training as an EMT, or a family member who is a doctor or nurse. No one wants to think of accidents or illness at a family gathering, but from bug bites to sunburn, skinned knees to stomach upset and sunstroke, it's good to have a plan in place. Ensure you have a comprehensive first-aid kit, and someone well versed in treating common ailments and complaints like dehydration, aches, pains, sprains, blisters, minor burns, and abrasions, as well as how to address more major issues until help arrives.

How Long Will This Last?

Decisions about duration occur after you've presented ideas to your committee for *why* you'd like to hold a reunion and *who* you'd like to invite. In many eastern and southern states, some family reunions are traditional annual mainstays that involve elaborate planning with detailed schedules bridging multi-day events. Out west, reunions are generally more impromptu, shorter in duration, and fairly laid back.

You need to know if your reunion will last an hour, a day, or the entire weekend—or longer. If this is your very first reunion, a short and simple event is probably your best option—a get-together that is a half-day or day in length with only two or three meals so you can get the hang of planning and preparing for a crowd.

Whether you're a beginner or a seasoned pro, ask yourself these questions:

- Of those likely to attend, are the majority children, teens, young adults, middle aged, or older? Remember that babies and toddlers, pregnant moms, handicapped family members, and the elderly require special consideration.
- How well do reunion attendees know one another?
- What budget or travel constraints might there be?
- Are the majority of attendees fair-weather folks who will want to take it easy? Or are they the type who won't mind roughing it a bit?

Then consider if you'd like to have:

- A single meal: breakfast, brunch, lunch, or dinner.
- A daylong event with two or three meals and a few activities.
- An overnight event that will require meals, activities, *and* lodging.
- A multi-day event that requires intensive planning for many meals, several activities, and/or a main event, as well as lodging for two or more nights.

What Is the Feel and Theme?

It's important to know the general feel you want for the occasion. Will it be casual and carefree, or will it include fine dining? The ages and special needs of your guests can help you determine what's feasible. For example, if you'll have a lot of very young children in attendance, fine dining with nice glassware is likely not an option!

Decide (based on your purpose) if you want to incorporate a theme. Planning for reunions that are centered around a birthday or anniversary, that remember an ancestor, that honor an event or certain holiday, or that celebrate family history, heritage, or culture are pretty straightforward. Food and activities usually complement the function of the event. First-time reunions held for the purpose of getting acquainted with unfamiliar family members, or those held with the goal of promoting family unity, may need a boost to help get things moving. One advantage of deciding on a theme is that it helps you channel decisions about food and activities more easily and efficiently. A few sample themes include:

- Picnic*
- State Fair*
- Western*
- Think Pink (For breast cancer survivors in your group)
- Patriotic
- Hawaiian Luau
- Carnival
- Guys Do All the Cooking*
- Take Me out to the Ball Game
- Fiesta
- Family culture and heritage (Italian, German, Dutch, etc.)
- Campout*
- Festival*

**Sample menus and recipes for one full meal for these themed reunions are included towards the end of this book, starting on page 197.*

What Is the Budget?

With choices made for the duration and theme or feel of your event, you and your committee can get down to drafting a plan for how to pay for everything. Some families have annual events that are saved and budgeted for year-round. Fundraisers are held with the proceeds deposited into the reunion bank account, or each family contributes a predetermined amount. Some families have older members who pay into a reunion bank account to ensure that the tradition of hosting an annual gathering is maintained. Most often, however, reunion costs are split as equitably as possible among those who will be attending. With the help of your committee, settle on what kind of budget will be available and which costs will be split by attendees or shouldered by individuals and/or families. Along with food, lodging, and activities or events, you'll want to consider whether or not each family will be responsible for their own transportation costs to and from the reunion. With the exception of special guests, like an elderly parent or grandparent who cannot afford to pay his or her own way, most families cover their own transportation costs. It is worth discussing, however, how to best equalize these costs so no one is left with the burden of being the only family who has to pay exorbitant travel costs year after year. Changing the location from year to year is one option, as is, of course, making the event location as central to everyone as possible.

When to Schedule the Reunion?

Now it's time to set a date. Who would ever dream such a simple task could be so difficult? Start by determining what months are best for you. Correspond with heads of households to come up with a ballpark plan; break it down into options of months and days and come up with at least three or four alternatives. Depending on the size of your guest list, setting a date will likely need to be done a year or more in advance. Even then, it's nearly impossible for a large group to agree on one date that fits all needs and schedules. Some families plan reunions on specific holidays so everyone can anticipate the event and know how to schedule accordingly from year to year.

Reunions, and the planning that goes into them, demand flexibility: doing the best you can and making the best of everything. However, when it comes to setting a date, it's often best to choose a date when the majority can attend—and stick to it! After options have been discussed and debated, set a firm date and let individuals and families work toward being there. If you repeatedly change dates in an attempt to accommodate the whole group, you may find that after all your hard work many people decide they can't come anyway. Requiring that at least a small deposit be paid (six months or more in advance) for the facility you plan to rent and/or for food that will be purchased can help cement who indeed will attend.

Where to Hold the Reunion?

Location is based on all the choices you've already made. Together with *when* your reunion will be held, *where* is probably one of the most important choices you'll make. All the decisions you've made up until this point will help guide you as you search for the best location. Your location chairman can assist you in exploring the options.

No matter the length of your reunion—a few hours, an afternoon, or a weekend—when you begin to consider locations, remember the basic necessities: eating and proper hydration, rest room facilities, a shelter of some sort in case of extremes in weather, and, if you'll be spending the night, a good place to sleep. Whether your reunion meals are self-cooked or catered; your sleeping arrangements are four-star or under the stars; your attendees include the diaper set, energy-crazed youngsters, need-their-own-space teens, busy parents, empty nesters, or the older generation, make sure the place you choose to hold your gathering will accommodate everyone's needs. Factors unique to your family will need to be considered and prepared for, thereby lessening the stress and maximizing the enjoyment when the event rolls around.

If your reunion will last a day or so (or if there are those who must travel some distance to attend), lodging is a prime concern. Some families are fortunate to have a generous benefactor (Grandma, here we come!) who will offer his or her home, yard, or vacation property for the event. If not, a bit of sleuthing will help you locate accommodations that are economical, especially if family members are willing to split expenses. Once you've determined your destination, an Internet search using the words *family reunion lodging* will turn up scores of options.

In the past, my family has held annual reunions at a lodge in southeastern Idaho. The lodge, which normally serves as a church camp for girls for a few weeks each year, can sleep nearly seventy people. Divided between all the reunion attendees, the cost to rent the building averages around $10 per person per night—pleasing enough on pocketbooks that nobody squabbles over having to bring their own bedding or sleeping bag. The lodge contains several communal rest rooms and shower facilities, as well as complete kitchen facilities. Shared cooking and cleanup responsibilities ensure no one spends too much time working instead of enjoying other activities. You can check with local churches and groups in the area where you want to hold your reunion to find similar options. Be aware, however, that many may require you to book a year or more in advance. You can also check listings for town homes and condos that sleep several people, and research local motel and hotel options. Businesses are realizing the rewards of catering to large family activities, so be sure to explain the scope of your event and ask if they would be willing to offer family or group discounts.

If your family isn't afraid to rough it, consider a campground or dude ranch. Most dude ranches are geared toward family activities and provide a plethora of options. From barn dancing to ping-pong, helping out with ranch animals and chores to chuck-wagon dining and wild-west adventures, there's a little something for everyone.

Making Your Reunion Great

Adele M. Gill, in *USA Today*, describes the importance of family reunions in helping to "preserve fond memories, favorite recipes, stories, and, most importantly, relationships that will last for generations." Reunions and family celebrations, Gill writes, can also "provide family members with important values, strong and lasting bonds, and a deep sense of belonging that they can pass on to their children and their grandchildren" ("Importance of Family Reunions").

In a world where relationships seem increasingly transitory and without depth, belonging to the institution of family is an anchor in life's stormy seas. The main goal of a reunion is to celebrate family. To change or enhance family dynamics as a whole, you must remember your family is comprised of individuals who all need to feel loved and valued. That means extending patience, compassion, and understanding to others who may not always extend the same.

To help ensure each member feels his or her place and value, delegate responsibilities that are within the comfort zones of those attending. Give guests a chance to shine both as individuals and as part of the group. A teacher can use his or her skills to teach a class on family history, culture, and heritage. A chef can teach a class on methods of cooking family favorites. A sports fan or player can help children and teens learn to punt, pass, or pitch. A photo buff can lead a group in discovering how to enhance their photography skills. A budding artist can design invitations, programs, posters, and decor. Don't forget to involve children and teens as well. Teens are fantastic resources when it comes to helping the older set understand technology such as digital cameras and cell phones. Engage teens in helping in the kitchen and in making decisions about how to serve foods in a fun and interesting way. Even very young children can help set tables and assist with simple food preparation. Give jobs that will help guests feel they are important and take time to sincerely praise the efforts of everyone—including yourself!

Remember that flexibility is key. Do your best to plan for all eventualities and unforeseen conditions, but know that *every* gathering has a few rough spots. Smile and keep pressing forward! Determine to make the best of things, and remember to look for the silver living in every *crowd*.

How Will It All Come Together?

Now it's time to get down to specifics. What activities, contests, or games will best complement your reunion? (Check out page 227 for ideas.) What kinds of food will be served when and by whom? What does your purpose, guest list, duration, theme, and budget allow for? Will you eat meals at a restaurant or undertake cooking yourself? Will your food be potluck, catered, eat-out, or buffet? Do you want to involve the whole group in making breakfast and dinner but have everyone fend for themselves with their own sack lunches? Or will all meals be a group effort?

Decide how many breakfasts, lunches, brunches, and dinners you need. Don't forget about snacks and treats. To make things fun you might want to incorporate team cooking. For example, you could have a meal cooked by all the grandmas or grandpas, one prepared by all the dads, and another thrown together by all the kids.

Lydia Stucki, owner of Family-Reunion-Success.com, advises that if you wait until everyone is hungry to start fixing a meal, you've waited too long. Plan in advance to have meals ready on a predetermined schedule and let everyone know mealtimes. Cover attacks of the munchies by always having snack options set out.

Food Specifics

Budget. Lodging generally requires an advance deposit. For meals that will be catered, or those you will plan and prepare with the help of your food chairman and others, a deposit on the food may also be necessary. If you buy food for one hundred people and only fifty attend, you'll be stuck with the entire cost unless you have a plan in place. Putting down a deposit on the food gives your guests shared responsibility for the event and also makes it more likely they'll attend!

Let everyone know that you and your food chairman will endeavor to keep costs as low as possible but that planning for a group is difficult and expenses are bound to fluctuate. Even if you ask for an advance deposit on the food, let everyone know that additional expenses may crop up and that you'll divide them equitably at the end of the reunion when you reconcile receipts.

Lydia Stucki suggests adding up total food-related expenses (don't forget the cost of paper goods such as plates and cups, napkins, and utensils) and dividing it by the number of kids and adults in attendance, taking into consideration how much food each might consume, to determine a per-person cost. For example, if you spend $100.00 and there are fifteen people in attendance, and you have ten adults and five children, the charge for each adult should be greater than the charge for each child. Eight dollars per adult (10 x $8.00 = $80.00) plus $4.00 per child (5 x $4.00 = $20.00) would give you enough money to cover your food-related costs. Lydia's own preference for her family gatherings is to consider teenage boys, due to the amount most generally eat, as adults, and to stipulate that children under two years of age eat free.

Once you've established the basics for a budget, take into consideration the costs of various foods. What can you buy on sale? What fruits and vegetables will be in season when you hold the reunion?

Make a menu. Have your food chairman or secretary survey those who will be in attendance and take note of vegetarian or other special-needs diets. Incorporate family-favorite foods, like your aunt's macaroni salad everyone loves or the grilled dish your dad has made legendary. Fill in with recipes from this book to make complete meals.

Decide on recipes. Consider appointing one or two people whose sole duty it is to help you plan menus, purchase food, assign cooks, and acquire such items as paper plates, utensils, cups, napkins, and so on. Don't forget to consider how you'll keep cold foods cold and hot foods hot. Concise, advance menu planning and food storage ideas can prevent last-minute hassles and food borne illness.

If you're going to have two meals each day, and one will be time consuming to prepare, make certain the other will be a quick-fix. Likewise, if you have three meals to prepare each day, make two of them quick-fixes. Look for the quick-fix, buffet-style, and food-bar ideas that are mingled with the recipes from every state. Meals that can be prepared and frozen in advance are also helpful. Lydia Stucki recommends having enough food choices to satisfy everyone and appeal to every palate, but to be cautious that too many choices can tie up too much time in preparation.

For beverages, have your food committee check with local restaurants who may lease drink machines or prefilled coolers. Along with soda pop and other beverages, make sure there will be ample water (bottled or from another source) so everyone stays sufficiently hydrated.

Figure out portions. Websites such as Betty Crocker.com (http://www.bettycrocker.com/tips/tipslibrary/charts-timetables-measuring/amount-of-food-for-a-crowd) provide handy charts to help you figure out the amounts of certain foods needed to feed a crowd. There is, for example, a chart that explains how many chunks are in one cantaloupe. Use the Internet to search for other sites that provide info on average portion sizes.

Make a list. Using the recipes and menu you've created, make a master shopping list. Make copies of all the ingredient lists and recipes for those who will help with cooking.

Shop. Decide which ingredients can be purchased in advance (like dry goods and canned items) and which need to be purchased immediately before the reunion. Ensure you have provisions for storing food and leftovers.

Kitchen, Pantry, and Serving Supplies

If you're going to be cooking away from home, you'll want to be well prepared. The kitchen gadgets and supplies you take for granted each day because they're as close as your own cupboard, pantry, or cutlery drawer may not be found in the unfamiliar kitchen or cooking facility where you hold your reunion. After you've selected your menu, review the following lists to ensure you have the necessities. Depending on the number of people you'll be serving, you'll likely need some items in multiples. Make a master list of cooking equipment. A plastic storage bin with a snap-on lid that fits in the back seat or trunk of your car is ideal for transporting what you'll need. Mark your items by securing a piece of masking tape to them and writing your name on the tape in permanent marker.

If you're traveling by plane or otherwise cannot transport your own supplies, send a list of what you require to the owner of the kitchen or cooking facility you'll be using. Relatives who live close to the location where the reunion will be held can help as well.

Remember, choose only the items that apply to your menu:

- Can opener
- Bottle opener
- Cutting board
- Serrated knife and/or bread knife
- Paring knife
- Carving knife
- Pizza cutter
- Measuring spoons and cups
- Slotted spoon
- Wooden spoon
- Serving spoon
- Pasta rake
- Ladle

- Spatula
- Whisk
- Pastry blender or cutter (these are also great for chopping eggs or mashing bananas and other soft fruits)
- Electric hand mixer
- Various size bowls for mixing and serving
- Strainer or sieve
- Grater and/or zester
- Colander
- Apple corer/wedger
- Banana slicer (Plastic, horizontal banana slicers are relatively new, lost-cost, time-saving gadgets that make slicing bananas fast and easy. They are safe for kids to use as well!)
- Meat thermometer
- Vegetable peeler
- Potato masher (great for crushing cookies, crackers, or nuts without a food processor and for mashing avocados for guacamole or and mashing fruits or cooked vegetables for young children)
- Pancake turner
- Tongs
- Kitchen shears
- Ice cream scoop
- Rolling pin (for crushing nuts, spices, cookies, crackers, chips, or dried bread for bread crumbs)
- Serving fork
- Melon baller (for melon balls as well as for pitting stone fruits, hulling strawberries, coring pears and apples, scooping seeds or strings from melons or squashes or pumpkins, for removing seeds from tomatoes and zucchinis in preparation for stuffing them, and for portioning mini cupcakes, cookies, or meatballs)
- Baby wipes and/or sanitizing wipes (for wiping down surfaces and cleaning up)
- Pancake batter dispenser (a handy and economical gadget—it usually costs $15 to $25 at department stores—that's a sure-fire help for making pancakes on a griddle for a crowd)

- Cookie sheet
- Digital timer
- Slow cooker
- Paper towels
- Aluminum foil
- Waxed paper
- Plastic wrap
- Parchment paper
- Disposable baking and cooking pans
- Disposable pie tins or muffin tins
- Ziploc bags, other storage bags, containers for leftovers
- Muffin tin liners, paper snow cone cups, paper cups, popcorn bags, or little paper bags (for serving small snacks)
- Masking tape and fine tip permanent markers (for labeling kitchen tools so no one loses anything)
- Coolers for food storage
- Ice (check local sources to ensure its readily available and accessible, especially if you won't have traditional refrigeration)
- Aprons
- Hand sanitizer
- Serving gloves
- Plastic table cloths
- Paper and plastic bags
- Garbage bags
- Paper plates and napkins
- Styrofoam cups for hot drinks
- Plastic or paper cups for cold drinks
- Plastic utensils
- Hot pads or oven mitts
- Disposable scrubbing or scouring pads
- Dish soap, dish cloths, and dish towels

Pantry Basics

In addition to all the gear you'll need to prepare your meals—and clean up after them—you'll want to make sure not to forget basic pantry items, like condiments and seasonings, that make a big difference in taste, and flour and sugar in case you decide on a whim to make cookies or another treat. Here is a list of good pantry basics to bring along:

- Ketchup
- Mustard
- Relish
- Pickles
- Onions
- Olives
- Barbecue sauce
- Soy sauce
- Teriyaki sauce
- Honey
- Olive oil and/or vegetable oil
- Mayonnaise
- Salt and pepper
- Seasoning salt
- Spices
- Worcestershire sauce
- Horseradish
- Pesto
- Salsa
- Tabasco sauce
- Butter or margarine
- Peanut butter
- Jams and jellies
- Salad dressings
- Sugar
- Flour
- Sour cream
- Hot cocoa
- Coffee and teas
- Instant drink mixes

Kitchen and Camping Appliances

Longer reunions that include more than a meal or two also require more equipment. Make sure the accommodations for the reunion include appliances, such as:

- Coffee maker
- Toaster
- Blender
- Food processor
- Electric griddle
- Additional slow cookers
- Roaster
- Microwave

If you're roughing it outdoors, you'll also need to include all the equipment necessary for such an endeavor:

- Dutch ovens
- Charcoal briquettes for grilling
- Lighters
- Lanterns and/or flashlights
- Tents
- Shade/rain awnings or canopies
- Plastic wash basins or tubs (for washing utensils and kitchen equipment or supplies)
- Pots for heating water
- Firewood
- Length of rope and clothes pins (for hanging up wet dish towels and dish cloths to dry)
- Bug spray and sun screen
- Sufficient ice and coolers for storing food and drinks
- A comprehensive first-aid kit

Setting Up a Dining Area

Whether you're camping, renting a cabin or house, staying in separate hotel rooms, or just going to a local park, you'll need a place to serve all the food and to sit and enjoy it. If your venue includes a banquet room or a massive kitchen full of tables and chairs, you're likely set. If not, there are many ways to creatively build and arrange seating and dining areas in more rustic locations. Consider these ideas for seating:

- Logs
- Cinder blocks
- Benches made from large stumps and 2 x 6 x 10-foot slats of wood
- Bales of hay
- Plastic or wooden crates
- 5-gallon buckets
- Blankets and quilts

- Pillows
- Small bar stools
- Lawn chairs

Fun and Easy Serving Ideas

Sometimes it's easiest to be straightforward and serve up your meals on traditional platters or serving trays. But other times, you may want to be more creative—and give family members a way to show off their creativity and work together—and make even your serving utensils fit a theme or style. Here is a list of surprising implements you can turn into serving platters, trays, and containers:

- Sterile garbage can lids lined with parchment paper
- Cookie sheets
- Pizza tins
- Cake pans
- Galvanized buckets
- Terracotta pots
- Rectangular flower planters
- Plastic dollar-store beach pails (the shovel acts as a scoop!)
- Toy wagons
- Wooden crates
- Angel food cake pans
- Large glass canisters or candy jars
- Turkey roasting pans
- Berry baskets
- Mason jars (great for serving stalks of celery, carrot sticks, green onions, French fries, or breadsticks)
- Hollowed-out watermelon, cantaloupe, or honeydew melon halves (for fruit salads)
- Hollowed-out grapefruit, orange, or coconut halves (for small citrus or tropical salads)
- Hollowed-out avocados (for salsa or south-of-the border salads)
- Plastic gallon milk jugs with the handles still attached but tops removed to make a large

enough opening for easy access

- Cookie or candy tins
- Metal or wicker baskets and plastic bins or baskets (can be used for serving or to keep condiments together)

When setting out and organizing napkins, plates, cups, and utensils, group utensils by forks, knives, and spoons, or make individual sets for each guest tied together with ribbon or raffia. Place them in:

- Metal pails
- Wire baskets
- Terracotta pots or other flower pots
- Painted tin cans or paint cans
- Bread pans
- Cardboard drink holders (like those used at drive-ins)
- Old wooden soda-pop crates
- Enamel ware/spatter ware cups

Instead of using paper plates and conventional dishware, consider some of these items for plates:

- Pie tins
- Six-hole muffin tins (Individual slots can hold main dish, salad, fruit and vegetables, roll, and so on. You can even nestle a drinking cup or canned drink into one hole for easy carrying.)
- School lunch trays (check with local schools to see if they will rent theirs to you, or look for them online)
- Plastic deli food baskets (like the ones you see at your local deli or drive-in; these run around $1 to $2 each online. Line them with parchment paper or waxed paper. Printed dry wax tissue is available at http://www.papermart.com. Classic red and white checked sandwich sheets/basket liners/food wraps are available at http://www.jillybeankids.com.)

- Shallow wicker baskets lined with any of the above
- Dollar store Frisbees (wash well before using)
- Paper hot dog, burger, or fry trays and baskets (Plain white, fluted hot dog trays are available online from Walmart, as are poly-coated paper food trays and hot dog bags.)
- Hinged foam food containers
- Bread bowls (round loaves of bread with the center hollowed out for soups, stews, or casseroles)

To keep bottled water or other items needing refrigeration cold, fill any of the following with ice and serve your drinks, fruit cups, and other items straight from these:

- Ice chest or cooler
- Galvanized metal washtub
- Canoe, kayak, or small fishing boat
- Inflatable raft
- Kids' plastic swimming pool
- Wheelbarrow
- Wagon
- Large, hollowed-out watermelons or pumpkins
- Oversized flower planters
- Large turkey roasting pans
- Large picnic baskets, hat boxes, plastic storage bins, or old suitcases (lined with plastic)
- Tire or inner tube (lined with a large plastic bag)

For individual drink containers, the following make for fun substitutes to paper cups or plastic glasses:

- Mason jars (invert a cupcake liner or baking cup over the top, screw on the lid, and poke in a straw for insect and spill proofing)
- Clear milkshake or smoothie cups with straws and lids (from food supply stores or online)

To serve individual portions of chips, veggies, popcorn, pretzels, trail mix, or mini cookies, skip a bowl or sandwich bag and try filling one of these with a snack:

- Single-serve ice cream cups or cones
- Large paper cupcake liners or baking cups
- Large nut cups
- Snow cone cups
- Small jam jars or baby food jars
- Plastic margarita glasses
- Small mason jars
- Paper doilies rolled up like snow cone cups
- Small paper bags with sides folded down
- Popcorn bags or boxes (purchased from your local movie theater)

To hand out individual servings of vegetables or fruit chunks or slices, try:

- Bamboo skewers
- Large foil cupcake liners or baking cups
- Used, washed tin cans (ensure there are no sharp edges)
- Plastic cocktail cups
- White wire-handle take-out boxes (available from www.papermart.com)

Tips for Kitchen Success

Because nothing ever goes just as planned, keep in mind some of these tricks for problem solving in a pinch and early food prep:

- Use baking cups to drip-proof Popsicles. Simply poke the stick into the center of the baking cup and slide the cup up to the bottom of the Popsicle.
- Forgot the cupcake liners for muffins? Use squares of parchment paper to line cupcake or

muffin tins.

- Use muffin tins to serve condiments like diced onions, pickles, tomatoes, olives, mustard, ketchup, and relish.
- Use waffle cones for grab-and-go food and treats. For breakfasts, fill them with scrambled eggs or fruit slices. For lunch, fill them with pasta or fruit salad. For dinner, fill with chicken tenders, teriyaki beef, chicken, pork, or scalloped potatoes. For snacks, fill them with popcorn.
- For lighter, fluffier pancakes, waffles, biscuits, and rolls, substitute club soda for the liquid.
- For easier cleanup, pour club soda into still-warm pans to help loosen cooked foods.
- For the fluffiest rice, add a teaspoon of vinegar or lemon juice per every quart cooking water.
- Add pickles and boiled eggs to extend a premade potato salad.
- Add browned ground beef and onions to extend baked beans.
- Add a pinch of sugar to the water when boiling corn on the cob. It helps bring out the natural sweetness of the corn.
- Making a scalloped potato dish for a larger than expected crowd but don't have enough potatoes? Add sliced carrots.
- Before roasting marshmallows over the fire, first dip them in water to prevent them from burning.
- Leak-proof ice cream cones by putting a large marshmallow in the bottom of regular cones, a mini marshmallow in a sugar cone.
- Use non-stick cooking spray to coat your cheese grater for easy shredding.
- If you don't have a pancake batter dispenser, use a meat baster to dispense the batter.
- Use an empty glass bottle to double for a rolling pin if you forgot yours.
- Add a pinch of salt to the water when you hard boil eggs. It keeps shells from cracking.
- For easy potato wedges, use an apple slicer.
- Pour vinegar over meat to help it thaw quicker and to tenderize it. Rinse the meat before cooking if you're worried about the flavor.
- To extend the freshness of salad greens and herbs, prewash then layer or roll them up in damp paper towels. Place the layered or rolled-up greens or herbs in large Ziploc bags. Leave a half-inch opening in the zipper top to allow for air flow.

- Save butter wrappers for greasing pans.
- Squeeze lemon juice over fresh fruit chunks or slices to keep them from browning.
- Use cookie cutters to cut fun shapes from bread and melons for the kids.
- Give mayonnaise an extra punch by adding in ketchup, Dijon mustard, lemon or lime juice, Italian dressing, pesto, Sriracha sauce, Tabasco, red wine or cider vinegar, softened cream cheese, or herbs and spices.
- Premeasure spices, flour, sugar, baking soda, baking powder, and other dry ingredients for each meal into Ziploc bags. Stash all dry ingredients and canned items in plastic storage bins grouped by meal. Attach a recipe to each bin.
- Brown ground beef for sloppy Joes or tacos ahead of time and freeze.
- Fry bacon ahead of time. Layer it on paper toweling and slip it into freezer bags. Reheat on the grill when it's time for use.

A Quick Word about Germs

Finally, don't forget how important it is prevent the spread of germs. Always follow these guidelines in the kitchen:

- Keep hot foods hot and cold foods cold.
- Keep cold foods that will be cooked cold until you cook them.
- Keep your cooking area sanitary! Make sure everyone washes their hands and uses protective gloves when directly handling food.
- Wipe down work surfaces with disinfectant.
- Store meat, fish, and chicken away from other food. Keep drinks separate as well.
- Be sure to provide servings spoons, forks, or tongs so guests don't have to touch shared foods with their fingers.

APPETIZERS, *Dips,* SAUCES, *&* BREADS

Roasted Garlic and Garlic Oil

Created by Alison Arians, Rise & Shine Bakery, www.riseandshinebread.com

INGREDIENTS

Several heads of garlic, cloves separated and peeled

Olive oil

1 Put whole, peeled garlic cloves in a heavy, lidded pot. Cover the garlic cloves with olive oil.

2 Bring the oil and garlic to a simmer over medium heat. Give the garlic a stir, and then turn the heat down to the absolute lowest possible temperature, cover the pot, and simmer just at a bare bubble.

3 Stir the garlic occasionally and continue to cook until the garlic cloves are completely soft and tender, and you can easily squish one against the side of the pot with a wooden spoon. This will probably take an hour or more, but check after 45 minutes.

4 Uncover the pot and let cool. Strain the garlic from the oil.

5 Retain the oil and use for dipping crusty, artisan breads. The mashed, chopped, or minced garlic can be used to season a number of meat, vegetable, and pasta dishes, and in Alison's own wonderful Macaroni and Cheese with Cauliflower (see page 63).

Salmon Braid

INGREDIENTS

1 can (1 pound or about 2 cups) salmon, very well drained

1/4 cup dry bread crumbs

1 tablespoon chopped onion

3 tablespoons butter, melted

1/4 cup chopped black olives

2 tablespoons Worcestershire sauce

2 tablespoons Tabasco or chili sauce

2 eggs, well beaten

1 can (8 ounces) refrigerated seamless dough sheet

1 egg, beaten

2 teaspoons Parmesan cheese (optional)

1 Preheat oven to 375 degrees.

2 Combine salmon, crumbs, onion, butter, olives, Worcestershire sauce, Tabasco or chili sauce, and eggs until well blended.

3 Unroll dough on a 10 x 14-inch section of parchment paper; roll into a 8 x 12-inch rectangle 1/4-inch thick. Spread salmon mixture lengthwise evenly over the middle 1/3 of dough.

4 Using a pizza cutter or kitchen scissors, cut outer sides of dough into 3/4-inch sections to within 1/4-inch of salmon mixture. Alternate folding strips of dough across salmon at an angle with ends overlapping; press dough to seal. Brush top of braid with egg and sprinkle with optional Parmesan cheese.

5 Bake for 18-22 minutes or until golden brown. Slice crosswise and serve warm.

Serves 12.

Ice Box Rolls

Created by Margaret Holloway Glass, from the collection of her daughter Margaret Glass Simpson

INGREDIENTS

1 cup boiling water

6 tablespoons shortening

6 tablespoons sugar

1 teaspoon salt

1 cup whole milk, scalded

1 envelope (2 1/4 teaspoons) active dry yeast

4 1/2–5 cups all-purpose flour

Makes 2 dozen rolls.

1 In a large bowl, pour boiling water over shortening, sugar, and salt. Mix until shortening is melted. Stir in milk.

2 In a separate bowl, combine yeast and flour. Add 4 cups of the flour-yeast mixture into the warm milk mixture and mix well. Add additional flour a few tablespoons at a time until dough is moist but stiff, about 5 minutes if using the dough hook of an electric stand mixer. If mixing by hand, knead dough 6–8 minutes. Leave dough in the bowl and cover with plastic wrap. Place in the refrigerator overnight.

3 Remove chilled dough and let it sit at room temperature for 1 hour.

4 Preheat oven to 350 degrees. Coat two 9-inch round cake pans with cooking spray and set aside.

5 Remove the dough from the bowl with a rubber spatula or pastry scraper and divide into 24 even pieces. Shape each piece into a ball and place in prepared pans, using 9 rolls in the outer circle of each pan and 3 rolls in the middle.

6 Cover with a clean towel or plastic wrap and let rise until doubled in size, about 1 hour.

7 Bake 20–25 minutes, until golden brown. Serve warm.

Several years ago, Ethel Chachere Simpson assisted in collecting Arkansas-related cookbooks for the Department of Special Collections at the University of Arkansas Libraries in Fayetteville. In her search, she also rediscovered a number of old family recipes, passed down through the years.

Family reunions are the perfect time to pull out Grandma's recipe books and try some old family favorites. You may have to make some adjustments, of course—the culinary arts have come a long way in the past century. But the chance to pass on shared food memories is priceless. Simpson eagerly shared this recipe from her family's collection. It was written in a family member's own hand and has been updated for use here.

Ann's Fresh Mexican Salsa

Created by Ann Rohrer

INGREDIENTS

- 1 cup chopped green chiles
- 1/2 cup chopped onion
- 3 cloves of garlic, minced
- 2 cups diced tomatoes (canned or fresh)
- 1 tablespoon sugar
- 1/4 teaspoon oregano
- 1/4 teaspoon cumin
- 1 teaspoon salt
- 2 tablespoons apple cider vinegar or lemon juice

1 Blend ingredients and serve.

Makes about 4 cups.

If you let it sit for an hour, flavors will marry well and taste even better.

Sometimes all a big gathering needs is lots of snacks, especially if the emphasis is on outdoor activities and fun in the sun. Chips and salsa make a great snack that everyone loves. And making the salsa could be its own group activity. This great recipe draws on the flavors of America's neighbor to the south and is sure to please young and old alike.

Brooke's Fruit Dip

Created by Brooke Perry Sepulveda

INGREDIENTS

1 package (8 ounces) cream cheese, softened

1 jar (7 ounces) marshmallow cream

2 teaspoons lemon juice

2 teaspoons orange juice

1/2 teaspoon lemon zest

1/2 teaspoon orange zest

1. With an electric mixer, beat cream cheese and marshmallow cream until creamy and smooth.
2. Add juices and zests.
3. Mix well.
4. Serve with your favorite fruits.

Makes about 2 cups.

Colorado Pear and Chicken Flatbread

Created by Chef Jason K. Morse, C.E.C., Owner, 5280 Culinary LLC, www.5280culinary.com

INGREDIENTS

1/4 teaspoon chopped fresh garlic

4 tablespoons olive oil

1/4 teaspoon dried herbs de Provence

1 piece naan (flatbread)

2 fresh Colorado pears, peeled, seeded, and diced

5 grape tomatoes, cut in half

1 cup diced cooked grilled chicken

1/4 cup shredded Italian blend cheese

1/4 cup crumbled smoked blue cheese

1. Preheat outdoor grill to 350 degrees.
2. Mix the garlic, olive oil, and herbs de Provence together.
3. Spread mixture on the flatbread. Top with pears, tomatoes, chicken, and cheeses.
4. Cook on grill until cheese is melted and flatbread is toasted.
5. Cut into 1- or 2-inch strips.

Serves 2.

Colorado has a relatively short growing season, and pears don't last long. They are usually available in August and September, sometimes into early October. Since pears will rot if left on the tree to ripen, they're picked and ripened off tree. Choose pears that are firm and plump. Avoid those with damaged skin, soft spots, or dull color. They should give gently to pressure at the neck/stem area when ready to eat. Prior to use, store them in a cool, dry place, and handle with care to avoid bruising them.

This recipe makes one flatbread, which can be sliced into pieces to serve 2. Double, triple, even quadruple, as needed!

Each month the Colorado Department of Agriculture features a different commodity to highlight the variety and quality of products grown in the state. Visit www.coloradoagriculture.com for a complete list of recipes.

Jones Family Farms Strawberry Salsa

Used by permission of Jean Jones
Courtesy David Oxford, Jones Family Farms and Winery

INGREDIENTS

1 serrano chili or jalapeño chili pepper, seeded and finely chopped

1 quart strawberries, hulled and finely chopped

1 yellow bell pepper, stemmed, seeded, and finely chopped

1 red bell pepper, stemmed, seeded, and finely chopped

4 tablespoons chopped fresh cilantro

3 tablespoons fresh lime juice

1/2 teaspoon salt

1/2 teaspoon sugar, if desired

1. Gently toss all ingredients together.
2. Set aside 15-30 minutes to allow flavors to combine.
3. Serve.

Makes approximately 7 cups.

In southwestern Connecticut, nearly a dozen miles east of Long Island Sound, is a working 400-acre New England farm where it is said memories are always in season. Over 150 years ago, Philip James Jones founded Jones Family Farms. To date, seven generations have contributed to the success of the pristine farm that annually draws scores of visitors who can now harvest their own Christmas trees, pumpkins, blueberries, and strawberries.

May is a crucial month on the farm; frost can destroy the entire strawberry crop. Round-the-clock care must be taken of the delicate strawberry blossoms. Doing so is a labor of love, as is ensuring that generations of farm guests have the opportunity to learn about the patience, care, and pride that goes into the process of growing and harvesting all the crops the farm produces.

Strawberries are the first fruits of summer. Every June, families and guests to the farm spend a few short weeks harvesting the brilliant red berries for use in jams, pies, and other desserts—or to enjoy them straight off the vine.

Jones Family Farms Strawberry Salsa is wonderful with corn tortilla chips, pita chips, or served over grilled fish or chicken.

Lima Bean Hummus

Created by Elizabeth Gilbert

1 If using dry lima beans, cook in salted water until tender, approximately 20 minutes. Drain well and set aside.

2 In a sauté pan, heat 2 tablespoons olive oil over medium heat. Sauté garlic and onions in hot oil until tender.

3 Place all ingredients, including remaining olive oil, into food processor and process until smooth. Place hummus in serving bowl.

4 If desired, garnish with additional herbs and/or lemon zest.

5 Serve with pita chips or tortilla chips. Keeps 3 days covered in the refrigerator.

Makes approximately 3 cups.

INGREDIENTS

2 cups (16 ounces) lima beans, dry, canned, or frozen

1/4 cup olive oil

4 cloves of garlic

1/4 cup roughly chopped white onion or sweet Vidalia onion

Juice of 3 lemons

Zest of 1 lemon

2 tablespoons fresh chopped thyme

1 tablespoon chopped fresh mint

Salt and pepper to taste

Sometimes referred to as butter beans, lima beans are planted on more acres than any other vegetable crop in Delaware; the state's lima bean acreage—11,500 acres—is number one in the USA. Lima beans are an excellent source of protein, manganese, and iron.

Delaware resident Beth Gilbert's ready-in-minutes lima bean hummus recipe is popular at local farmer's markets. "This is a recipe you can have fun with when the various herbs come into season," says Beth. "I happen to love thyme and rosemary, so they are always in my refrigerator. Mint gives it that refreshing taste, but is not always available. I have been thinking of trying it with a roasted red pepper, cilantro, and lime."

DELAWARE

Delaware Shrimp Dip

INGREDIENTS

2 cups mayonnaise

1 package (8 ounces) cream cheese, softened

Pinch salt

2 tablespoons snipped fresh parsley

2 tablespoons fresh grated onion

1 teaspoon Worcestershire sauce

2 cans (4 ounces each) small shrimp, drained

1 Combine all ingredients and mix well.

2 Refrigerate several hours or overnight.

3 Serve with veggie sticks or crackers.

Makes 4 cups.

FLORIDA

Florida Zucchini Chips

Created by Chef Justin Timineri
Courtesy Fresh from Florida

INGREDIENTS

1/4 cup dry bread crumbs

1/4 cup freshly grated Parmesan cheese

1/4 teaspoon seasoned salt

1/4 teaspoon garlic powder

1/8 teaspoon freshly ground black pepper

2 tablespoons fat-free milk

2 1/2 cups medium Florida zucchini, sliced 1/4-inch thick

1 Preheat oven to 425 degrees.

2 Whisk together bread crumbs, Parmesan, salt, garlic powder, and pepper in a medium bowl. Pour milk into a shallow bowl. Place an ovenproof wire rack coated with cooking spray on a foil-lined baking sheet.

3 Dip zucchini slices in milk and then dredge in bread crumb mixture. Put coated slices directly onto the prepared wire rack.

4 Bake 30 minutes, or until browned and crisp.

5 Serve immediately with Feta and Dill Dip (see recipe on opposite page).

Makes approximately 4 dozen chips.

FLORIDA

Feta and Dill Dip

1 Mix together all ingredients and serve.

Makes 1 cup.

INGREDIENTS

1 cup plain low-fat yogurt

1 tablespoon fresh Florida dill, chopped

1 tablespoon crumbled feta cheese

HAWAII

Jenna Kae's Peach-Mango Salsa

Created by Jenna Kae Whiting

INGREDIENTS

2 ripe mangos

6 fresh, ripe peaches (or bottled or canned)

1/4 medium red onion, chopped

1 teaspoon garlic powder

2 tablespoons cilantro (dried or fresh), chopped

1 tablespoon lime juice

1 Peel, pit, and chop mangoes and peaches and place in a large bowl.

2 Stir in remaining ingredients.

3 Either serve immediately or chill for later. Serve with tortilla chips.

Makes 6–7 cups.

Bacon and Blue Dip

Courtesy Lindsay Petermeir

INGREDIENTS

1 package (8 ounces) cream cheese, softened

1/2 cup sour cream

1/4 cup mayonnaise

4–8 ounces Maytag Blue Cheese, to taste

1 teaspoon lemon juice

1/2 teaspoon horseradish

1/2 cup grated carrot

1/2 cup grated radishes

1/4 cup finely chopped pimentos

1/4 cup finely chopped green onion tops

2 tablespoons fresh parsley or dill, chopped

1/2 cup cooked bacon, crumbled

1 Combine cream cheese, sour cream, mayonnaise, and Maytag Blue cheese. Blend until smooth. Add other ingredients. Chill well.

Makes 4 1/2–5 cups.

Kristy's Killer Barbecue Sauce for Wild Game

Kristy Crabtree, www.NevadaFoodies.com

INGREDIENTS

1 yellow bell pepper

1 red bell pepper

1 onion

7–8 cloves of garlic

Olive oil to baste vegetables

1 jar (21.6 ounces) plain barbecue sauce

1 teaspoon cumin (optional)

1 teaspoon salt (optional)

1 teaspoon pepper (optional)

1 Option 1: Dice up all vegetables large enough to skewer for roasting OR

Option 2: Dice up all vegetables and put everything on a sheet of tinfoil and put straight on the grill.

2 Grill until all vegetables become browned, not burned, and remove from heat.

3 Place all ingredients in a blender and blend on high speed until smooth. Remove from blender and pour into a bowl for serving.

Makes approximately 6 cups.

You can also keep the sauce in an air tight container for up to 2 weeks in the refrigerator.

Las Vegas, Nevada, may now be home to an array of ultimate buffets, filled with more food than anyone could ever eat, but the state didn't start out with much to offer in terms of cuisine. In her book Taste of the States: A Food History of America, *author Hilde Gabriel Lee writes, "The land, basically desert, was so poor that it could barely support its Shoshone Indians. . . . Nomads with no permanent villages, the Shoshones lived off the land collecting berries seeds, and nuts. . . . The Indians of Nevada ate very little meat since it was rarely available in this desert.*

"One of the first settlements in Nevada was formed by a group of Mormons who came from Salt Lake City in 1850 and built Mormon Station, a crude trading post. . . . During the next decade Brigham Young sent more Mormons to establish settlements along well-traveled trails so that the stream of gold seekers could get food and supplies. . . . Mormon grapes, melons, potatoes, corn, wheat, and squash helped Nevada mining camps survive the days of boom and bust."

Today, the same crops grow abundantly in Nevada, and cattle dot the range. Food blogger Kristy Crabtree uses her barbecue sauce on grilled elk, venison, or antelope skewers. It's also great on more common meats like grilled chicken, steaks, or burgers.

Pan Fried Jersey Tomatoes with Fresh Mozzarella and Basil

Created by Aliza Green for her book Starting with Ingredients
Courtesy Aliza Green and the Philadelphia Inquirer

INGREDIENTS

1/2 loaf firm white sandwich bread

1 cup all-purpose flour

2 eggs, lightly beaten

2 teaspoons kosher salt

1/2 teaspoon freshly ground black pepper

1/4 teaspoon cayenne

1 pound large tomatoes sliced 1/2-inch thick

2 cups peanut or canola oil for frying

1/2 pound fresh mozzarella, drained and cut into slices

Large leaves from 1 bunch basil

1 Cut off and discard crusts from bread. Process bread to make fine crumbs. Set up three bowls: one with flour; one with eggs seasoned with salt, black pepper, and cayenne; one with the fresh bread crumbs.

2 Dip tomato slices into flour, then eggs, then coat with the crumbs. Place in a single layer on a wax-paper-lined tray and chill until ready to cook.

3 Heat 1 cup of oil in heavy skillet till shimmering but not smoking. Gently place tomato slices in pan without crowding. Pan fry till edges are golden, then turn, using large fork or tongs, and brown other side. Drain tomatoes on paper towels and continue with another round of tomatoes. Add remaining oil as needed.

4 Preheat oven to 400 degrees. Arrange fried tomatoes in a baking pan, top with mozzarella. Bake 10 minutes, or until cheese starts to melt. Serve immediately, carefully removing the fragile tomatoes from the pan with a spatula. Top with fresh basil leaves just before serving.

Serves 6.

Cookbook author, journalist, and pioneering chef Aliza Green looks forward to tomato season. "I get tomato fever and eat them in abundance. These pan-fried tomatoes," she claims, "are simple, seasonal, and absolutely delicious."

As Aliza aptly points out, it's hard to imagine anything better than this simple dish of pan-fried, vine-ripe tomato slabs topped with sliced, milky-fresh mozzarella that is melted and bubbling right from the oven. To get the crispiest coating, she advises frying the slices in an old-fashioned cast-iron skillet. She adds that the recipe is best made with large beefsteak tomatoes.

Jersey Fresh Fried Tomatoes

Created by Hackett's Farm Market

INGREDIENTS

8 plum tomatoes (such as Roma)

Dried crab boil seasoning

Cornmeal

New Jersey is called the Garden State for a reason: its rich soil fosters the growth of all sorts of plants and vegetables. Jersey Tomatoes—the official state vegetable—really do taste better than commercially grown tomatoes from elsewhere.

Complaints about the bland, lackluster flavor of modern-day tomatoes promoted researchers at Rutgers New Jersey Agricultural Experiment Station to attempt to rekindle old-time Jersey Tomato varieties. They were successful in bringing back favored tangy, old-time varieties like the Ramapo Tomato—an iconic New Jersey favorite—which, along with the Moreton variety, can be grown successfully in other states.

1. Wash and slice tomatoes crosswise into 3/8-inch thick rounds.
2. In a non-stick pan, add a scant tablespoon of vegetable oil and fill with the sliced tomatoes. Sprinkle the seasoning on the top side, then sprinkle cornmeal on the tomato. Turn and sauté over medium heat until crisp. Before turning, add the seasoning and cornmeal to the other side and crisp again. If plum tomatoes are not handy and you use ripe, round tomatoes, add a pinch of sugar to balance the acidity. Use more sugar with green tomatoes.

Serves 4–6.

Variations: Whisk together 1 egg and 2 tablespoons milk (or buttermilk). Dip tomatoes in mixture, then coat with bread crumbs before frying. Or coat slices with flour only. Substitute Creole seasoning for crab boil seasoning.

Some people insist a good fried tomato must be fried in bacon grease—which brings with it the added option of making a really good BLT. Simply layer the bacon, crisp green lettuce, and fried tomatoes on thick slices of sourdough.

Lori's Tip: Crab boil seasoning is generally made from a blend of spices: salt, mustard seeds, peppercorns and pepper flakes, celery seeds, dried chives, and bay leaves. If you can't locate it at your local market, try the Internet for sources or recipes to make your own.

Southern Shrimp Dip

Created by Forrest Clark

1 In a medium-sized mixing bowl, combine sour cream, cream cheese, mayonnaise, Worcestershire sauce, parsley, onion powder, celery salt, garlic powder, and hot sauce (if desired).

2 Mix well.

3 Fold in drained shrimp.

4 Cover and chill at least 4 hours, to allow flavors to blend.

Makes approximately 4 1/2 cups.

INGREDIENTS

1 container (8 ounces) sour cream

1 package (8 ounces) cream cheese, softened

1 1/2 cups mayonnaise

1 tablespoon Worcestershire sauce

3 tablespoons dried parsley

1 1/2 teaspoons onion powder

1 1/2 teaspoons celery salt

1 pinch garlic powder

1 tablespoons of hot sauce (optional)

2 cans (4 ounces each) small shrimp, drained

Piedmont Lexington-Style Dip

Created by and used by permission of Jim Early, president and CEO, The North Carolina Barbecue Society

1 Combine all ingredients in a small saucepan and bring to a simmer. Cook, stirring, until the sugar dissolves.

2 Remove from heat.

3 Spoon or brush sauce over barbecued meats.

Makes 3 cups.

Jim Early, president of the North Carolina Barbecue Society (www.ncbbqsociety.com), has made it his group's mission to "preserve North Carolina's barbecue history and culture and to secure North Carolina's rightful place as the Barbecue Capital of the World." Jim says, "Our goal is to promote North Carolina as the Cradle of Cue and embrace all that is good about barbecue worldwide." He generously shares one of his favorite recipes.

INGREDIENTS

1 1/2 cups distilled white or cider vinegar

10 tablespoons tomato ketchup

Salt to taste, if desired

1/2 teaspoon cayenne pepper

Pinch crushed hot red pepper flakes

1 tablespoon sugar

1/2 cup water

Freshly ground pepper to taste

Sausage Grits Muffins

Created by Forrest Clark

INGREDIENTS

3 cups water

1 cup yellow grits (not instant) or Bob's Red Mill Grits/Polenta

1/4 cup Kraft Colby Jack and Monterrey Cheese

1 cup milk

2 large eggs

1 teaspoon pepper

1 teaspoon salt

6 large strips bacon, cooked and crumbled

8 ounces hot/spicy sausage, browned and crumbled, not drained

1 Preheat oven to 415 degrees. Spray mini-muffin tins with non-stick cooking spray.

2 Bring water to a boil in a medium sauce pan. Add grits and cook at a low boil on medium heat for about 6 minutes, or until they thicken. Stir frequently to ensure they don't burn to the bottom of the pan.

3 When thickened, remove the pan from the heat. Add cheese and mix until completely melted. Stir in milk, eggs, pepper, salt, bacon, and sausage.

4 Fill each muffin tin 3/4 full. Bake 30 minutes, or until centers are set.

Makes 36 mini-muffins.

The muffins are ideal as appetizers or for a brunch and, Forrest asserts, best when served with a creamy, white sauce or his Southern Shrimp Dip (see page 16).

Lakota Fry Bread

Used by permission of Deb Painte, Native American Training Institute

INGREDIENTS

2 cups all-purpose flour

2 teaspoons baking powder

1/4 cup sugar

1/2 cup instant nonfat dry milk

1/4 teaspoon salt

1 cup water

Vegetable oil (for deep frying)

1 In a large bowl, mix the flour, baking powder, sugar, dry milk, and salt together. Stir in the water until you have a sticky dough.

2 Turn the dough out onto a floured surface and sprinkle with flour. Roll out to a 16 x 12-inch rectangle, about 1/2-inch thick. Cut the dough into twenty-four 2-inch squares. Cut a 1/2-inch slit in the middle of each square.

3 Add enough oil to a deep cast-iron skillet or a deep fat fryer to reach a depth of 1-2 inches and heat the oil to 350-365 degrees. (The oil is ready when a piece of dough sizzles as soon as it is placed in the pan.)

4 In batches, fry the squares of dough, turning once, until browned on both sides, about 3 minutes total. Transfer to paper towels to drain.

Serves 4–6.

Fry bread is a traditional Native American bread made with flour, sugar, and water, and then fried. One taste, and you'll know why it is so well loved.

Fry bread can be eaten plain or topped with butter and honey or cinnamon, or like a taco with browned meat, shredded cheese, and lettuce.

Dakota Bread

From the North Dakota Wheat Commission

INGREDIENTS

1 package active dry yeast

1/2 cup warm water

2 tablespoons sunflower oil

1 egg + 1 egg white

1/2 cup cottage cheese

1/4 cup honey

1 teaspoon salt

2–2 1/2 cups bread flour

1/2 cup whole wheat flour

1/4 cup wheat germ

1/4 cup rye flour

1/4 cup oats

Cornmeal

1 Sprinkle yeast in warm water; stir to dissolve.

2 In a large bowl, mix sunflower oil, egg, cottage cheese, honey, and salt. Add dissolved yeast and 2 cups bread flour, beating until flour is moistened. Gradually stir in whole wheat flour, wheat germ, rye flour, and oats, plus enough bread flour to make a soft dough.

3 On a floured surface, knead dough, about 10 minutes or until dough is smooth and elastic.

4 Place dough in greased bowl and cover loosely with oiled plastic wrap. Let rise in warm place until doubled in size, about 30 minutes. Punch down dough. Shape into one round loaf. Place in a greased glass pie pan sprinkled with cornmeal. Cover with oiled plastic wrap and let rise until doubled in size, about 1 hour.

5 Preheat oven to 375 degrees. Brush loaf with egg white and sprinkle with wheat germ, sunflower kernels, or oats. Bake 30–40 minutes. If too dark, cover loosely with foil the last 10-15 minutes of baking. Remove from pie pan and cool on a wire rack.

Makes 1 loaf.

In her book Taste of the States: A Food History of America, *Hilde Gabriel Lee writes that "North Dakota has had an agricultural economy since the time the territory became a state. . . . The pioneers who came to Dakota in wagons brought potatoes, squash, rice, preserves, pickles, and eggs. The fragile items such as eggs were packed in cornmeal for the rough journey. However, the supply of both eggs and cornmeal was usually exhausted at journey's end. In 1812 a small group of Scottish Highlanders established a settlement in the Red River Valley and ignored the eating habits of the area, which were primarily based on the food of the Indians. The Highlanders had brought with them salt pork and beef from England, as well as oatmeal for porridge, salt fish, and shortbread." The recipe on this page celebrates North Dakota's most popular crop—wheat. This hearty bread would be the perfect topic for a workshop at your family reunion. Pull the family together and teach them how to make homemade, whole-grain bread.*

OREGON

Oregon Shrimp Dip

Courtesy Brooke Perry Sepulveda

INGREDIENTS

1 carton (16 ounces) of sour cream

1 can (4 ounces) shrimp, drained & smashed

1 cup mayonnaise

2 tablespoons chopped onion

1/2 package (0.2 ounces) ranch dressing mix

2 tablespoons grated parmesan cheese

1/4 teaspoon pepper

1 Mix all ingredients together and chill well.

2 Serve with veggie sticks, chips, or crackers.

Makes about 3 1/2 cups.

PENNSYLVANIA

Fresh Green Onions

Created by Jane Dillner, Dillner Family Farm

INGREDIENTS

1 cup chopped or sliced green onions and scallions

1 tablespoon butter

1 tablespoon olive oil

1 Wash and trim green onions and scallions.

2 Chop or slice. Sauté-braise green onions and scallions in butter and olive oil.

3 Cook slowly until softened and slightly golden. As the onions cook, the flavor mellows, yet intensifies.

Makes 1 cup.

Wonderful with meat or vegetable dishes.

Grilled Green Onions and Thyme

Created by Jane Dillner, Dillner Family Farm

INGREDIENTS

6–8 green onions

Juice from half a lime

1/2 teaspoon dried thyme

Salt and pepper to taste

1 Wash and trim green onions. Place on a sheet of aluminum foil.

2 Squeeze the lime juice over onions. Sprinkle with dried thyme, and salt and pepper to taste. Seal foil around onions.

3 Place on the grill, on the side away from direct heat or over low coals. Grill 30 minutes. Serve with other grilled foods.

SOUTH CAROLINA

Carolina Red Barbecue Sauce

INGREDIENTS

1 1/2 cups apple cider vinegar

1/2 cup ketchup

1 tablespoon brown sugar, packed

1 teaspoon salt

1/2 teaspoon crushed red pepper flakes

1 Combine all ingredients in a small bowl and stir until sugar is dissolved.

2 Cover with plastic wrap and refrigerate until ready to use.

Makes 2 cups.

Can be prepared 2–3 days in advance. If the flavor is too tart for your taste, add additional ketchup or brown sugar.

South Carolinians don't have a preference for a specific barbecue sauce, but they do prefer a specific meat. In fact, most South Carolinians will tell you that the word barbecue means pork! Saying barbecue pork would be redundant. Saying barbecue chicken or barbecue beef would not.

This recipe can be used with any slow-and-low cooked pork roast. Pull the pork with two forks and serve with the sauce.

Julia Bushree's Texas Caviar

Julia Bushree, Georgetown, Texas

INGREDIENTS

1 large jar picante sauce (hot or medium)

2 cans (16 ounces each) black eyed peas, drained

1 can (16 ounces) white hominy, rinsed and drained

1 cup diced green bell pepper

1/2 cup diced red bell pepper

1 cup diced sweet white onion

1 cup chopped fresh red juicy tomatoes

Few dashes Tabasco sauce

1/2 cup chopped fresh cilantro

1/4 cup seeded and chopped jalapeño peppers

1 cup chopped scallions, including greens

1 tablespoon sugar

Salt and freshly ground black pepper, to taste

2 tablespoons ground cumin

1 Stir all ingredients together in a large bowl. Refrigerate 24 hours.

2 To serve, place a pretty bowl of Texas Caviar over a larger bowl filled with crushed ice. Serve with tortilla chips or crackers.

Makes about 14 cups.

Texas Caviar isn't actually what it claims to be, but it is a celebrated dish throughout the state. According to food critic Joyce Senz Harris of the Dallas Morning News, "Texas Caviar is simply a jazzed-up version of black-eyed peas—a marinated, make-ahead salad that can be eaten with a fork or scooped up in a tortilla chip."

The dish had its beginnings in the 1950s at Neiman Marcus in Dallas. Famed cookbook author and consultant for food services at Neiman Marcus, Helen Corbitt, noticed how much Texans seemed to love their black-eyed peas. So, writes Harris, "[Corbitt] tried something different: She pickled the peas in a vinaigrette marinade and served them for New Year's Eve at the Houston Country Club. Only later, when she took her pickled black-eyed peas to Austin's Driskill Hotel, did the dish get the nickname of Texas Caviar."

Crockpot Pizza Dip

Created by Kristin Thompson

INGREDIENTS

1 package (16 ounces) cream cheese, cubed

1 jar (16 ounces) pizza sauce

1 package (8 ounces) pepperoni, chopped or mini

2 cups shredded mozzarella

1 Place all ingredients in a slow cooker. Cook on low for 2–3 hours or until melted.

2 Serve with Ritz Crackers of Club crackers.

Makes 7 cups.

Baked Cinnamon Tortilla Chips with Fruit Salsa

Created by Jenna Kae Whiting

INGREDIENTS

1 kiwi, peeled and diced

1 Golden Delicious apple, peeled, cored, and diced

4 ounces raspberries

8 ounces strawberries, diced

1 tablespoon white sugar

1/2 tablespoon brown sugar

1 1/2 tablespoons fruit preserves, any flavor

10 small (7- or 8-inch) flour tortillas

4 tablespoons melted butter

2 cups cinnamon sugar (1/4 cup white sugar to 1 tablespoon cinnamon)

1 Preheat oven to 350 degrees.

2 In a large bowl, thoroughly mix kiwis, apples, raspberries, strawberries, white sugar, brown sugar, and fruit preserves. Cover and refrigerate at least 15 minutes.

3 Coat one side of each tortilla with melted butter. Sprinkle tortillas with desired amount of cinnamon sugar. Use a pizza cutter to cut each tortilla in half and then cut each half into 4 wedges. Arrange in a single layer on a large parchment-lined, rimmed baking sheet.

4 Bake 8–10 minutes. Cool approximately 15 minutes. Serve with chilled fruit salsa. Best served the same day the salsa is prepared.

Serves 5–6.

Mustard Sauce for Ham

Created by Laura Baker

INGREDIENTS

2 beef bouillon cubes

1 cup sugar

6 tablespoons all-purpose flour

1 cup prepared mustard

1 cup vinegar mixed with 1/2 cup water

2 cups hot water

1/2 cup butter

6 egg yolks, well beaten

1 Combine all ingredients in the top of a double broiler placed over a pot of simmering water. Cook, stirring, until thick. Serve with ham.

Serves 12–16.

Note: Spiral hams have a continuous helix cut that makes them super easy to serve—a bonus when you're in a hurry to feed a large crowd. Just warm the ham and you're ready. Be aware, however, that spiral hams can be pricey. With your budget in mind, shop sales and educate yourself on the available options. With the exception of canned, most types of ham can be frozen for at least 1–2 months before you use them.

Coastal Virginia is rich with fresh seafood of all kinds: shrimp, oysters, flounder, crab, and more. As you move inland, more succulent flavors are added to the mix: hams from Smithfield, the world's largest pork processor and hog producer; crisp, sweet apples from the hills neighboring Thomas Jefferson's Monticello; hearty Brunswick stew from its namesake county in Southern Virginia; and savory cornbread and beans from the Blue Ridge Highlands in Appalachia.

Virginia resident Jenny Oaks Baker is a Grammy-nominated concert violinist. For seven years, Jenny performed as first violinist with the National Symphony Orchestra, and her eleven albums have consistently charted on Billboard. She's also the mother of four who enjoys gatherings with her large extended family, which is scattered throughout the country. Here, she shares her late mother-in-law's recipe for Mustard Sauce. Paired with a Virginia ham, this sauce is a family favorite. Jenny calls the recipe "a Baker family tradition and treasure."

Spoon Bread

Adapted from The Old-Fashioned Cookbook, *West Virginia Department of Agriculture*

INGREDIENTS

2 cups water

1 cup white cornmeal

1 tablespoon butter

1 teaspoon salt

2 cups whole milk

3 large eggs

1 teaspoon baking powder

1 Preheat oven to 350 degrees.

2 Generously grease a 1-quart baking dish.

3 Add water to a large, heavy-bottomed pot. Whisk in cornmeal. Over medium-high heat, bring mixture to a boil stirring constantly for about five minutes or until mixture is thickened.

4 Remove from heat and add butter, salt, and milk. Mix well.

5 Beat eggs lightly; add to mixture; sift in the baking powder; mix well.

6 Pour into prepared baking dish and bake 30 minutes until puffed and brown and knife inserted in center comes out clean. Serve hot with butter on top.

Serves 4–6.

Slaw dogs: hot dogs slathered with coleslaw. Ramps: a unique version of wild onion. Fried bologna sandwiches. Biscuits and gravy Pepperoni rolls: pepperoni blanketed and baked inside of soft white bread. Invented by Giuseppe Argiro, the rolls first came into being in Fairmont, West Virginia, as a lunch item for coal miners.

West Virginia's official state fruit is the Golden Delicious Apple; Clay County hosts an annual festival to celebrate the fruit. The event includes a pig roast and Golden Delicious baking contest.

West Virginia Spoon Bread is a traditional pudding-like dessert with Native American roots. It has a light, fluffy, custard-like texture and requires a spoon to eat.

If your ancestors hail from southern states, try this recipe to give family members a taste of the old South.

BREAKFAST & Brunch

Salsa Scramble

Created by David Worthington

INGREDIENTS

1 can (11 ounces) Mexi-corn, drained

2 cans (15 ounces each) black beans, drained

2 bunches green onions, chopped

2 cans (10 ounces each) Ro*Tel tomatoes

2 tomatoes, chopped

1 bunch fresh cilantro, chopped

Salt and pepper, to taste

1 Combine all ingredients in a medium bowl. Cover and refrigerate overnight.

2 The next day, add as little or as much as you prefer to your raw scrambled eggs and cook until eggs are done.

Makes about 12–14 cups.

The South is often associated with the simple life. Magnolia Springs, Alabama, near the coastal waterways of southern Alabama, is a modern example of simplicity.

At the Magnolia Springs Bed & Breakfast, innkeeper David Worthington relies on simple ingredients and simple preparation for guest breakfasts and brunch. His Salsa Scramble is a guest favorite. To accommodate those who don't like salsa combined with their eggs, David suggests serving the salsa on the side. It's also great with chips, taco salads, and other south-of-the-border dishes.

Basil Tomato Frittata

Created by Carol Beazley, Beazley House Bed & Breakfast Inn

INGREDIENTS

6–8 eggs

3/4 cup cottage cheese

3/4 cup plain yogurt

1 teaspoon dried basil

1 teaspoon granulated onion

1 can (14.5 ounces) Italian tomatoes, drained

3 tablespoons sundried tomatoes

8 ounces Italian cheeses, shredded

Feta cheese, crumbled

Dash Mrs. Dash garlic herb blend

Dried basil

Cherry tomatoes, halved (optional)

Fresh basil leaves (optional)

1. Preheat oven to 350 degrees.
2. Combine eggs, cottage cheese, yogurt, basil, onion, Italian tomatoes, and sundried tomatoes in a blender or food processor; pulse just until blended.
3. Coat a 10-inch pie plate or 8 small ramekins with non-stick vegetable spray. Distribute shredded Italian cheeses in the bottom of the pie plate, or divide equally between ramekins. Pour egg mixture over cheese. Sprinkle crumbled feta over top; finish with a sprinkle of Mrs. Dash Garlic Herb Blend and dried basil.
4. Bake 35–45 minutes, or until knife inserted comes out clean. For ramekins and mini-frittatas, increase oven temperature to 375 degrees and bake 10–15 minutes or until center is set.
5. If desired, garnish with cherry tomatoes and fresh basil leaves.

Serves 6–8.

Napa Valley's first bed and breakfast inn, the Beazley House, opened in 1981. The establishment, a circa 1902 mansion located in historic Old Town Napa, is well known for its delicious breakfasts, exquisite gardens, comfortable rooms, and gracious hosts, Jim and Carol Beazley. Carol's Basil Tomato Frittata is a favorite among guests.

Frittatas are commonly cooked in a skillet and finished in the oven. Carol's method combines the wonderful flavor of the egg dish with welcome ease of preparation—a great feature for a family brunch! Instead of ramekins, you can also divide the mixture into muffin tins for mini-frittatas.

Aebleskivers

Adapted from a recipe by Lyla G. Solum from For Danish Appetites

INGREDIENTS

4 eggs

2 cups buttermilk

4 tablespoons unsalted butter, melted

2 cups all-purpose flour

1 1/2 teaspoons baking powder

1/2 teaspoon baking soda

1/4 teaspoon salt

2 tablespoons sugar

Extra virgin olive oil or melted butter

1 Separate the eggs; whisk together yolks, buttermilk, and butter. In a large bowl, sift together the dry ingredients. Add to egg mixture and blend well.

2 Beat egg whites until just stiff, approximately 2–3 minutes; fold into other mixture.

3 Put one teaspoon olive oil or melted butter in the bottom of each aebleskiver pan cup; heat until oil or butter bubbles. Pour in about 2 tablespoons of the batter into each cup (or enough to fill). As soon as they get bubbly around the edge, turn quickly. Danish cooks like to use a long knitting needle for this, but a fork or wooden skewer works well.

4 Turn the aebleskivers as necessary to keep them from burning, and continue cooking approximately 3–4 minutes or until golden brown and a toothpick (or knitting needle!) comes out clean when stuck in the center. Serve with hot with syrup or jam and powdered sugar.

Makes approximately 3 dozen.

Late September brings Danish Days to Solvang, California. Sights, sounds, and tastes immediately transport visitors to Old World serenity and deeply rooted traditions. Each year, a maid is chosen to spread good will to visitors who have the opportunity to be "Dane for a day." She rides parade floats and makes aebleskivers (Danish pancake or pastry balls) every morning during the three-day celebration.

Aebleskivers, or Danish pancake balls, are a traditional, highly favored food passed down generation to generation. To fry them you'll need a aebleskiver pan or Danish cake pan.

This recipe would be ideal for a Danish ancestry themed reunion or gathering. Try a batch of aebleskivers in advance of your event so you understand the process and cooking time. When everyone tastes the results, your reunion attendees are sure to want to attend time and time again!

CONNECTICUT

Starbuck Inn Blueberry Pancakes

Courtesy Peter Starbuck

INGREDIENTS

2 tablespoons cooking oil

2 cups buttermilk pancake mix

1 1/2 cups half and half

2 eggs, beaten

1/2 cup fresh picked blueberries

1. Heat large skillet with oil over medium-high heat. Combine pancake mix, half and half, and eggs. Fold in blueberries.
2. When the middle of the pancake bubbles, flip over and cook until golden brown.

Serves 12–18.

Near the western edge of Connecticut, where it borders New York, picturesque Kent is home to the famed Starbuck Inn, which specializes in emphasizing "physical and emotional comfort, the lost art of lounging around, and excellent food."

KENTUCKY

Corn Muffins

INGREDIENTS

1 cup all-purpose flour

1 cup yellow corn meal

2 tablespoons sugar

3 teaspoons baking powder

1/2 teaspoon salt

1 egg, beaten

1 cup milk

1/4 cup melted butter

1. Preheat oven to 350 degrees.
2. In a large bowl, sift together flour, sugar, baking powder, and salt.
3. Combine egg, milk, and butter. Add to dry ingredients. Stir just enough to moisten.
4. Fill 12 prepared muffin tins 2/3 full. Bake for 20–25 minutes.

Makes 12 corn muffins.

Swedish Bread

INGREDIENTS

2 1/2 cups milk, divided

1 envelope (.25 ounces) active dry yeast

5–6 cups all-purpose flour

1/2 cup butter

2/3 cup sugar

1 egg, well beaten

1/4 teaspoon salt

1 teaspoon almond extract

1–2 tablespoons melted butter

1/3 cup brown sugar

1/2 cup slivered almonds

1 egg white, beaten

1 tablespoon milk

1. Preheat oven to 350 degrees.
2. Add yeast to 1/4 cup warm (not hot) milk. When dissolved, add 1/2 cup flour, beat thoroughly, cover, and let rise.
3. When light, add remaining milk and 4 1/2 cups flour; cover, let rise again, then add remaining ingredients and enough flour to make a soft dough. Knead. Cover and let rise until double in bulk.
4. Roll out into rectangle. Brush with melted butter. Sprinkle dough with brown sugar and slivered almonds. Roll up jelly roll style and join ends together to form a ring. Or braid dough. Let rise again, about 45 minutes.
5. Whisk together egg white and milk; brush ring or braid with milk mixture. Bake at 350 degrees for 25–30 minutes or until golden brown.

Serves 10–12.

While Kansas has no official state food, Kansas City is a barbecuing mecca. European immigrants left their mark on the state's food heritage. Savory sausages, jerky, and other meat products hailing from Kansas are among the very best in the county.

Swedish and German settlers to the state brought cuisine from their native countries, namely sweet breads and pastries. Today, Kansas is known for its wheat and is often referred to as the Breadbasket.

Pasta-Veggie Scramble

Recipe reprinted by permission of Pete & Gerry's Organics and the American Egg Board. *All rights reserved.*

1 Coat a 10-inch omelet pan or skillet with non-stick cooking spray. Add zucchini, onions, and red pepper.

2 Cover and cook over medium heat until zucchini is crisp-tender, about 3 minutes.

3 Meanwhile, beat together whole eggs and whites, cheese, and seasonings. Pour over vegetables. Add fettuccine and tomatoes.

4 As egg mixture begins to set, gently draw an inverted pancake turner completely across bottom and sides of pan. Continue until eggs are thickened but still moist. Do not stir. Serve immediately.

Serves 2.

INGREDIENTS

1/2 cup (about 2 ounces) thin zucchini slices, halved

2/3 cup chopped green onions with tops

1/3 cup julienned sweet red pepper

2 whole organic eggs

4 organic egg whites

2 tablespoons grated parmesan cheese

1 teaspoon garlic salt

3/4 teaspoon Italian seasoning

1/8 teaspoon ground red pepper

4 ounces fettuccine or linguine, cooked and drained

4 cherry tomato halves

New Hampshire's short growing season hasn't stopped farmers and agricultural experts from putting the state's bounty—beef, milk, maple syrup, berries, apples, pumpkin, corn, and other vegetables—to good use. In the heart of the state's White Mountains, Pete and Gerry's Organic Eggs (www.peteandgerrys.com) is a family farm that has been producing eggs for four generations. They share this recipe, which is full of veggies and readily available ingredients that make a delicious breakfast or brunch for hungry reunion goers.

Sweet Crepes with Blueberry Sauce

Created by Ellen Gutman Chenaux

INGREDIENTS

Crepes

1 cup all-purpose flour

1/4 teaspoon salt

1 tablespoon sugar

2 medium eggs

1 1/4–1 1/2 cups milk

1/2 cup butter, melted

1 recipe Crepe Filling

1 recipe Blueberry Sauce

1. Mix the flour, salt, and sugar together. Stir eggs and mix with the milk. Whisk the egg-milk mixture into the flour until smooth. Whisk in the melted butter. Add extra milk if the batter is too thick. The batter should be thinner than pancake batter. Cover and let the batter rest for at least 15 minutes before cooking.
2. Heat an 8-inch crepe or frying pan over medium-high heat. Brush the pan with a small amount of oil, just enough to glaze the pan.
3. Spoon about 1 1/2 ounces of the batter into the pan and tip the pan to coat the bottom. Cook for about 30 seconds. Flip the crepe and cook the other side for about 10–15 seconds. They should be golden but not brown. Slide each crepe onto a square of waxed paper.
4. Spoon 1 1/2 tablespoons Crepe Filling on to each crepe. Smooth with a knife or off-set spatula. Roll into a somewhat flat egg roll shape.
5. At this point, the blintzes can be refrigerated or frozen in layers separated with parchment paper. When ready to serve, top with blueberry sauce.

Makes 8–10 crepes.

Crepe Filling

1 Mix the cream cheese, egg yolk, and sugar together until smooth.

Blueberry Sauce

2 Combine the blueberries, sugar, and lemon juice in a medium-size pot. Mix the cornstarch with water, eliminating all lumps, and set aside. Bring berry mixture to a boil over medium heat. Add the cornstarch mixture. Continue cooking, stirring constantly, until the sauce has thickened.

Filling

1 package (8 ounces) cream cheese, softened

1 egg yolk, beaten

1 tablespoon sugar

Blueberry Sauce

2 cups blueberries, fresh or frozen (preferably the small wild blueberries)

1 cup sugar

Juice of half a lemon

1 tablespoon cornstarch

1 tablespoon water

Ellen Gutman Chenaux is the innkeeper and proprietor of Birchwood Inn in Lenox, Massachusetts. Her New Jersey roots provided her with a passion for baking and cooking. She learned to bake from her grandmother and aunt. "I grew up," she says, "with possibly the only Jewish mother who wouldn't cook, and a father with a legendary sweet tooth." Ellen's wonderful sweet crepes are beloved by her guests.

"Nearly all Jewish grandmothers were known for their blintzes (thin pancakes)," says Ellen, "and it now appears to be a lost art. It needn't be because they really are easy—it's all in the wrist—and amazingly flexible. If the first one doesn't come out right, that's fine. Most of us have problems with the first one.

"At Birchwood Inn we often double or triple the recipe, and it does just fine. Put the batter into two bowls, leaving one in the refrigerator until needed as you don't want the batter to get too warm. To freeze, place wax paper in between each crepe and place carefully in a plastic bag."

If you're a beginner at making crepes, be aware there's a learning curve when it comes to getting the pan to just the right temperature and successfully cooking the crepes—but practice makes perfect and the results are well worth the effort. Once you have the method down, making Ellen's Sweet Crepes is sure to be a tradition you'll want to keep.

DiMeo Farms Lemon Blueberry Pancakes

Created by Mildred DiMeo of DiMeo Blueberry Farms, Hammonton, New Jersey

INGREDIENTS

1 1/2 cups part-skim ricotta cheese

1/4 cup melted butter

4 organic egg yolks

1/2 cup all-purpose flour

1/4 cup sugar

2 teaspoons grated lemon peel

8 organic egg whites

2 1/2 cups fresh blueberries

1. In a medium-sized bowl, combine ricotta cheese, melted butter, and egg yolks until all blended.
2. In a small bowl, stir together the flour, sugar, and lemon peel.
3. Stir dry ingredients into ricotta mixture. In a medium-sized bowl, beat egg whites until they form soft peaks. Fold egg whites and then blueberries into batter.
4. Over medium heat, form cakes by spooning 1/4 cup of batter per blueberry pancake onto a hot, lightly greased griddle or skillet.
5. Cook, turning once, until blueberry pancakes are browned, about 4 minutes.

Makes 24 delicious old-fashioned blueberry pancakes.

In addition to tomatoes, New Jersey produces a large number of blueberries, cranberries, corn, and peaches. For your family reunion breakfasts, try these lemony blueberry pancakes.

Easy Massachusetts Cranberry Corn Muffins

1. Preheat oven to 425 degrees. Grease muffin tins.
2. In a large bowl, cream together shortening and sugar.
3. In a separate bowl, stir together cornmeal, flour, baking powder, and salt.
4. Blend dry ingredients into shortening-sugar mixture. Blend in milk and egg and beat for 1 minute. Fold in cranberries. Fill muffin cups 1/2 full. Bake 15 minutes.

Makes 12 large muffins.

INGREDIENTS

1/4 cup shortening

2 tablespoons sugar

1 cup cornmeal

1 cup flour

4 teaspoons baking powder

1/2 teaspoon salt

1 cup milk

1 egg, beaten

1 cup dried chopped cranberries

German Eggs

Created by Patti Wiles, Owner/Innkeeper, At Cumberland Falls Bed and Breakfast Inn

INGREDIENTS

1 dozen eggs*

1/3 pound Monterey Jack cheese, shredded

1/3 pound sharp cheddar, shredded

1/3 pound cream cheese, softened

1/3 pound parmesan, substituted for any of the above cheeses (optional)

2 cups cottage cheese

1/4 cup all-purpose flour

1 teaspoon baking powder

1/2 cup butter (do *not* use margarine), melted

1 Preheat oven to 350 degrees.

2 Combine all ingredients; mix well. Bake in well-greased ramekins, or any well-greased baking dish that is suitable for the amount of the eggs you are cooking. If you are making this for one, you can use a custard cup. Bake ramekins for about 20 minutes; a 9 x 13-inch pan for 35–40 minutes.

Serves 12.

Patti's Tip: Any spice can be added to this egg dish to vary the taste. Some of those we use At Cumberland Falls include tarragon, basil, cilantro, oregano, chile pepper, lemon pepper, and garlic. Nearly anything that you like would be excellent provided it is a good mix with eggs.

**You can reduce amount of eggs in the dish, contingent upon your needs, but you will also need to reduce all the elements in the recipe.*

Just fifteen minutes from the breathtaking Blue Ridge Parkway in Ashville, North Carolina, is a state treasure: George Vanderbilt's 1895 Biltmore Estate. Visiting the estate is like taking a step back in time. Nearby, at Cumberland Falls Bed & Breakfast Inn, innkeeper Patti Wiles welcomes guests of the Biltmore, as well as guests coming from all over the world to visit the beautiful Blue Ridge Mountains. Patti serves up all sorts of fabulous dishes at the inn but says this is her most popular egg dish. It is versatility at its finest, coordinating very well with many kinds of veggies.

Patti's German Eggs recipe represents just one of the hundreds of ways eggs can be used in all sorts of food. In North Carolina, the egg industry is among the top ten commodity receipts and home to such specialty brands as Eggland's Best.

This recipe, from the North Carolina Egg Association, may be "mini" in name, but it's packed with impressive flavor and perfect for a brunch table or passed as hors d'oeuvres.

Bacon Onion Quiche Bites

Courtesy Jan Kelly, North Carolina Egg Association

1 Preheat oven to 375 degrees.

2 Place shells on parchment-lined baking sheet. In a mixing bowl, beat together the eggs, half and half, cheese, bacon, and onion. Spoon 2 teaspoons of filling into each shell.

3 Bake until quiches puff and turn slightly brown, about 15–20 minutes.

4 If desired, garnish with fresh chive.

Makes 30 mini quiches.

INGREDIENTS

30 mini phyllo shells, 1 1/2 inches in diameter

3 eggs

1/3 cup half and half

3/4 cup shredded cheddar cheese

2 tablespoons cooked and crumbled bacon pieces

1 teaspoon dried minced onion

Fresh chives for garnish (optional)

Apple Au Gratin

Created by Donna Schlabach

INGREDIENTS

2 pounds Granny Smith apples, peeled and sliced

1/2 cup raisins

1/2 teaspoon cinnamon

1/4 cup lemon juice

3/4 cup brown sugar, packed

1/2 cup all-purpose flour

1/8 teaspoon salt

1/4 cup butter, softened

1 cup grated sharp cheddar cheese

1 Preheat oven to 350 degrees. Butter a 1-quart casserole dish or similar pan.

2 Arrange apples in prepared dish. Sprinkle with raisins, cinnamon, and lemon juice. Stir together the brown sugar, flour, salt, butter, and cheese. Sprinkle this mixture over the apples. Bake 30 minutes, or until apples are tender.

Serves 4–6.

Berlin, Ohio, resident Donna Schlabach, the innkeeper at Donna's Premier Lodging, has created an apple recipe that would make Johnny Appleseed proud. Her Apple Au Gratin is great served warm and can be enjoyed with any meal—her favorite is brunch. The recipe is similar to an apple crisp, but includes cheddar cheese which adds a distinctive flavor.

Cheddar Dill Scones with Ohio Amish Cheese

Created by Yvonne Martin, The White Oak Inn

1. Preheat oven to 375 degrees.
2. In a food processor or with a pastry blender, combine flour, baking powder, salt, parsley, dill, and butter. Process until mixture resembles oatmeal.
3. Pour mixture into a large bowl and mix in cheddar cheese.
4. Beat eggs with half and half. Make a well in the dry ingredients and pour in egg mixture.
5. Using a fork, stir together until just combined.
6. Turn out onto a lightly floured board and knead about 8 times. Divide dough into two pieces. Pat each piece into a circle, about 3/4-inch thick.
7. Cut into 8 wedges. Place on a lightly greased or parchment-lined cookie sheet and bake until tops are golden, about 15 minutes.

Scones will be even better if you can chill them for 15–30 minutes before baking.

INGREDIENTS

2 1/2 cups of all-purpose flour

1 tablespoon baking powder

1/2 teaspoon salt

1/4 cup chopped fresh parsley or 2 tablespoons dried

2 tablespoons chopped fresh dill weed or 2 teaspoons dried

3/4 cup butter, cut into pieces

1 cup shredded sharp cheddar

2 large eggs

1/2 cup half and half

Makes 16 scones.

Yvonne Martin (member of 8 Broads in the Kitchen and owner of The White Oak Inn in Danville, Ohio) loves the Amish influence in her home state, especially the Amish cheese. "Because the Amish don't have electricity," Martin says, "their raw milk cannot be properly chilled on the farm. For that reason it can't be sold for drinking purposes, but since the cheese making process destroys harmful bacteria, it can be used to make cheese. "

Yvonne's scone recipe combines two of her favorite flavors: dill and Amish cheddar cheese. "The scones themselves are best served warm from the oven," she says. "They make a great accompaniment to soups or salads, or a nice change from sweeter breakfast pastries when the main course is also going to be sweet."

Hazelnut Schnecken (Cinnamon Rolls)

Courtesy Polly Owen, Oregon Hazelnut Marketing Board

INGREDIENTS

Dough

3 1/3 cups bread flour

3 tablespoons sugar

1/2 teaspoon salt

1/4 ounce fast rise yeast or 1 tablespoon fresh yeast

1/3 cup unsalted butter

1/2 cup + 2 tablespoons milk

2 large eggs

Syrup

1/2 cup + 1 tablespoon unsalted butter

2 tablespoons turbinado sugar (brand Sugar in the Raw)

4 tablespoons maple syrup

3 tablespoons light corn syrup

1 cup hazelnut pieces

Dough

1. Butter a 12-cup muffin pan.
2. Line a roasting pan or baking pan with parchment paper (for turning the sticky buns onto later) large enough to cover muffin pan.
3. Combine flour, sugar, salt and yeast in a large mixing bowl.
4. Melt butter in the milk over very low heat and beat in eggs.
5. Stir milk/butter mixture into the dry ingredients to make the dough. Knead for 10 minutes or for 5 minutes with a dough hook. When it is springy and satiny, form a ball and put in a greased bowl. Turn to coat and cover with plastic wrap. Leave in a warm place for 1 hour or until doubled in size.

Syrup

1. Using an electric mixer, cream butter until soft and smooth, and add sugar. Beat in syrups and then divide mixture among the muffin cups and top with hazelnuts (about a tablespoonful in each sticky-based waiting cup).

Assembly

1 Preheat oven to 350.

2 Knock dough back, knead once or twice and then roll out to a large rectangle (approximately 12 x 24 inches) with the long side nearest you. Beat egg and add milk; glaze the dough using a pastry brush or your fingers.

3 Mix the filling ingredients in a little bowl and sprinkle onto the dough. Now, roll up from the long side and away from you, carefully and firmly (not too tight) keeping a firm sausage shape.

4 Cut into 12 even slices, and lie each slice spiral-swirly cut side up, on top of the nuts and syrup in the muffin cups.

5 Leave to rise for about 20 minutes then put into the oven and bake for 20–25 minutes until golden.

6 Place roasting pan or baking sheet on top and turn the whole thing the other way up. Remove the muffin tray and dislodge any nuts that are still stuck in it, adding them, along with any residual syrup, to the upturned buns.

7 Cool, then enjoy!

Makes 12.

Glaze

1 large egg

2 tablespoons milk

Filling

3 tablespoons sugar

1/2 cup light brown raw sugar (demerara) or 1/2 cup turbinado sugar (brand Sugar in the Raw)

1 tablespoon cinnamon

South County Style Johnny Cakes

Courtesy Paul Drumm, Kenyon's Grist Mill

INGREDIENTS

1 cup Kenyon's White Johnny Cake Cornmeal or other white cornmeal

1/2–1 teaspoon sugar to taste

1/2 teaspoon salt

1 1/4–1 1/2 cups boiling water

1 Combine dry ingredients in a bowl and mix thoroughly. Gradually add boiling water to make a gloppy consistency that will drop off the end of a spoon. By the spoonful, drop onto a well-greased, medium hot griddle or fry pan (350–380 degrees) for 6 minutes, or until you see a dark brown ring form around the outside edge.

2 Drizzle with oil then flip and cook for an additional 5–6 minutes. Don't be afraid to press them down.

Serves 2–4.

Rhode Island boasts a number of foods unique and beloved to the state. The official beverage, for example, is coffee milk—milk mixed with coffee syrup. Like most New England states, clam chowder is a favorite in Rhode Island. But in addition to Manhattan or New England style chowder, local restaurants serve up Rhode Island Clear Chowder—a clam chowder made with clear broth. The state also has its own favorite version of hot dogs and pizza. Gaggas are small hot dogs in their natural casing that are covered in mustard, meat sauce, onions, and celery salt and served in a steamed bun. Pizza strips are rectangular strips of dough covered in a spicy pizza sauce, no cheese included. Folks in South County Rhode Island even insist on eating their Johnny Cakes differently from the rest of us—without maple syrup.

Kenyon's Grist Mill in Usquepaugh, Rhode Island, has been grinding white cornmeal and flours since 1696. Their Johnny Cake Meal is a stone ground white meal, suitable for making any kind of Johnny Cake. Here, they share the South County version, meant to be thick and eaten with butter only.

Lazy Morning Impossible Pie

Contributed by the Triangle Ranch Bed and Breakfast, adapted from Midwest Living *magazine, used by permission of Lyndy Ireland*

INGREDIENTS

- 1 pound bulk ground pork sausage*
- 1 large onion, chopped
- 1 cup grated American cheese
- 2 eggs, lightly beaten
- 1 cup milk
- 1/2 cup all-purpose baking mix, such as Bisquick

1. Preheat oven to 400 degrees. Grease a 9-inch pie pan.
2. In a large skillet, brown sausage and onion over medium heat. Drain off fat and layer into bottom of prepared pie pan. Top with the grated cheese.
3. Whisk eggs, milk, salt, and baking mix until combined. Pour over the meat/cheese mixture.
4. Bake 25–30 minutes, until inserted knife comes out clean. Garnish each serving with a drizzle of salsa, a small spinach leaf, and a dollop of sour cream.

Serves 6.

**Lyndy's Tip: For vegetarians, substitute sausage with 2–3 cups lightly salted and steamed broccoli florets.*

The Triangle Ranch Bed & Breakfast near Badlands National Park has been family owned and operated for more than 100 years. Lyndy Ireland's great-grandfather traded a good team of driving horses and buggy for the original homestead in 1903. The Spanish-style ranch house is on the National Register of Historic Places. A favorite at the ranch is this recipe, which really is perfect for lazy mornings.

Hootenanny with Raspberry Syrup

Created by Dixie Burbidge, Stone Canyon Inn

INGREDIENTS

Hootenanny

6 eggs

1 cup milk

4 dashes salt

1 cup all-purpose flour

3 tablespoons butter

Powdered sugar, for garnishing

1 pint fresh raspberries

1 recipe Raspberry Syrup

Raspberry Syrup

2 cups pure maple syrup

1/2 cup frozen raspberries

1 Preheat oven to 450 degrees. Coat 6 small pie tins (about 4.5 inches in diameter) with cooking spray.

2 In a blender combine eggs, milk, salt, and flour; blend until smooth.

3 Add 1/2 tablespoon butter to each prepared pan. Place tins in oven and melt butter until it bubbles, about 3 minutes.

4 Immediately pour batter into each tin, filling to within a 1/2 inch to 1/4 inch of the rim. Bake about 18 minutes. Hootenannies will puff up and take on a beautiful golden-brown color. Slide finished hootenannies onto plates and sprinkle with powdered sugar. Serve with fresh raspberries and raspberry syrup.

Serves 6.

Raspberry Syrup

1 Warm pure maple syrup and berries in a small pan over medium heat until berries are thawed and heated through.

Utah cooks have a long tradition of food preservation based on seasonal, farm-to-table fruits and vegetables. It's common to find rows of home-canned peaches, pears, applesauce, tomatoes, salsa, and more on many pantry shelves in the state.

Dixie Burbidge runs the Stone Canyon Inn in the stunning red-rock formations that make up Bryce Canyon National Park. At the Inn, she serves up new versions of old family recipes her children grew up with, putting a modern twist on old-fashioned comfort food. She shares her version of individual hootenannies—a type of pancake with a richer taste—here. Kids will get a kick out of watching these bake if you want to show them some magic in the kitchen.

Memer's Dried Beef Gravy on Toast

INGREDIENTS

5 slices salt pork, sliced thin

1 medium onion, chopped

4 cups whole milk

1/2 cup flour

1 jar (5 ounces) dried beef, chopped

1/4 teaspoon pepper

1 bunch fresh asparagus, cut into 2-inch sections

3 hard-boiled eggs, peeled and sliced

1 In a very large pan, fry salt pork slowly on low heat until crispy. Add onion and sauté until translucent.

2 Remove salt pork and add milk.

3 Over medium heat, gradually mix the flour in, scraping bottom of pan to prevent sticking.

4 When mixture thickens, add dried beef, pepper, and asparagus; fold in sliced eggs.

5 Serve hot on toast or mashed potato.

Serves 6.

Lori's Tip: In Memer's recipe, the salt pork adds flavor to the white sauce. Salt pork is not bacon—it is not smoked or cured and has a totally different flavor that is much saltier and fattier than bacon. Both the Hormel Foods Corporation and John Morrell & Company produce salt pork, which is commonly carried by many small and specialty grocers.

My friend Sharon's paternal great-grandmother, Memer Champagne, was born in Vermont and was of French Canadian descent. When she was raising a family in the 1930s, times were rough and money tight. Memer spoke very little English, but she was a talented cook who managed to keep her family well fed. Her recipe for Dried Beef Gravy on Toast was a staple during the Depression Era. Asparagus for the dish was picked alongside a local Vermont river bank. The recipe, passed down through the generations, remains a family favorite. Sharon lovingly remembers her grandmother as simply Memer, which is French (mémère) for grandma.

Famous Farmhouse Bed and Breakfast Granola

Created by Janie Gabelein, Farmhouse Bed and Breakfast

INGREDIENTS

1 cup canola oil

1 1/2 cups honey

1/4 cup water

1 tablespoon vanilla

10 cups old fashioned oats

2 cups shelled sunflower seeds

1 1/2 cups sesame seeds

1 cup shredded coconut

1 cup wheat germ

1 tablespoon cinnamon

2 cups sliced almonds

4 cups Grapenuts cereal

1 1/2 cups raisins

1. Preheat oven to 325 degrees.
2. Coat a turkey roasting pan with cooking spray.
3. Combine canola oil, honey, water, and vanilla and add to the pan. Place the pan in oven to warm.
4. In a large bowl, combine all the dry ingredients except for the raisins.
5. Remove the warmed pan from the oven and stir in the combined dry ingredients. Return to oven.
6. Bake, stirring often, until grains look dark golden brown, about 25 minutes. Remove from the oven when done and stir in raisins.
7. Cool overnight. Store in zipper-top bags in the refrigerator or freeze.

Makes about 2 gallons of granola.

Washington's Whidbey Island is the northern boundary of Puget Sound. Near the south end of the island, about 35 miles north of Seattle, is The Farmhouse Bed and Breakfast. For the past fourteen years, owners Gary and Janie Gabelein have taken pride in making The Farmhouse—once their family home—a place where visitors feel peace and love. As such it seems appropriate that the homey establishment is located on Sunshine Lane. When the sun comes up in the morning guests are treated to Janie's Famous Farmhouse Granola.

Potato Hash and Baked Eggs

Created by Judith Burbrink, Villa Heidelburg Bed and Breakfast

1 Preheat oven to 350 degrees.

2 Heat skillet with olive oil over medium-high heat and brown potatoes and yams. Add diced shallots and peppers and cook until limp.

3 Spray four Au Gratin dishes with cooking spray and divide potato mixture between them. Sprinkle with half of the grated cheese. Break 2 eggs into each dish. Top eggs with cream. Sprinkle with remaining cheese.

4 Bake approximately 20 minutes or until eggs are set to desired texture. Garnish with dill.

Serves 4.

INGREDIENTS

Extra virgin olive oil

6–8 red or Yukon gold potatoes, diced with skins on

1 sweet potato or yam, peeled and diced

1/4 cup diced shallots

1/4 cup diced red peppers

1 cup shredded Parmesan cheese

8 eggs

1/2 cup cream or half and half

Dill weed for garnish

For the vegetarians in your family, or those who are gluten intolerant, Judith Burbrink of West Seattle offers up a delectable egg and potato entree. The innkeeper of the acclaimed Villa Heidelberg Bed and Breakfast, Judith enjoys creating new dishes for her customers.

Carson Ridge Hashbrown Bake

INGREDIENTS

6 eggs

3/4 cup milk

3/4 cup mayonnaise

1 tablespoon Italian seasoning

1 teaspoon seasoning salt

1/2 tablespoon seasoning pepper

1/2 tablespoon Mrs. Dash

Worcestershire sauce for flavor

6 cups frozen hash browns, thawed

1/4 cup melted butter

3/4 pound maple ground sausage links

1 sliced red pepper or tomato

3/4 cup shredded mixed cheddar and provolone cheese

1. Preheat oven to 350 degrees.
2. In a medium-sized bowl beat together eggs, milk, mayonnaise, and seasonings. Set aside. In a large skillet over medium-high heat, fry hash browns with butter until golden brown.
3. Add the egg mixture and fry until eggs are slightly cooked. In a separate pan, break ground sausage into bite sized-pieces and cook thoroughly.
4. Place hash brown and egg mixture into a greased 9 x 13-inch casserole dish. Arrange the pieces of ground sausage and peppers or tomatoes on top.
5. Sprinkle with the cheese and bake 20–25 minutes.

Serves 8–10.

Pastoral Carson, Washington, is home to Carson Ridge Luxury Cabins where owners Pete and Latisha Steadman offer tranquil respite for couples, groups, and families. An hour from Portland, towering pine forests, and rolling meadows with exquisite views of Wind River Mountain, the Cascade Mountain Range, and the Columbia River Gorge are the backdrop for the cabins, which are snuggled within three acres of natural gardens.

Carson Ridge Luxury Cabin's scrumptious hash brown bake is a wonderful start to any morning. Accompanied by sliced fresh fruit and a selection of breakfast juices, you'll have a perfectly simple and delectably satisfying breakfast or brunch.

Stuffed French Toast with Homemade Orange Syrup

Created by Joyce Schulte, Chambered Nautilus Bed and Breakfast Inn

1 Cut across the top-crust side of the bread and cut a pocket in each slice. In a small mixing bowl stir together the softened cream cheese and the orange marmalade. Mixture should not be soupy. Spoon about 1 tablespoon of the cheese mixture into each pocket. In a mixing bowl, beat eggs, milk, vanilla, cinnamon, and nutmeg until combined. Dip stuffed bread slices into egg mixture.

2 Heat butter or margarine on a griddle, and place stuffed bread slices on greased griddle. Fry over medium heat until golden brown, turning once. Serve with warm orange syrup and garnish with orange slices and/or strawberries, and powdered sugar.

Makes 8 slices.

Orange Syrup

1 In a small saucepan combine sugar, butter, and frozen orange juice concentrate. Place over low heat until butter is melted. Do not boil! Remove from heat and cool 5–10 minutes. Beat until slightly thickened and serve warm. Orange Syrup will keep in the refrigerator for several weeks.

Makes 1 1/2 cups.

Seattle's Chambered Nautilus Bed and Breakfast Inn is owned and operated by Joyce Schulte, a proud member of 8 Broads in the Kitchen. Joyce's amazing Stuffed French Toast is a sure-fire winner for a breakfast and brunch favorite!

INGREDIENTS

Stuffed French Toast

8 slices (1 inch thick) French bread

4 ounces cream cheese, softened

1/4 cup orange marmalade

3 eggs

3/4 cup milk

1/4 teaspoon vanilla

1/8 teaspoon cinnamon

Dash ground nutmeg

2 tablespoons butter or margarine

1 recipe Orange Syrup

Orange slices

Strawberries

Powdered sugar

Orange Syrup

1 cup granulated sugar

1 cup butter

1 can (6 ounces) frozen orange juice concentrate

Aunt Virgie's Danish Aebleskivers

Created by Virginia Hill

INGREDIENTS

3 eggs, separated

1 cup light cream

1 cup all-purpose flour

4 teaspoons baking powder

1/2 teaspoon salt

1. Separate egg yolks and whites. Beat yolks until light. Add cream.
2. Sift together flour, baking powder, and salt. Whisk into egg mixture.
3. Beat egg whites until stiff, then gently fold into batter. Heat aebleskivers pan and put 1/2 teaspoon melted butter into each cup; get it really hot. Pour batter into cup until 1/2 full. Turn with ice pick as they brown. When pick comes out dry, they are done. Roll in powdered sugar and serve hot.

Makes approximately 2 dozen.

My Aunt Virgie's recipe for aebleskivers uses cream instead of buttermilk. Her method of preparing the dessert incorporated a small kitchen ice pick. Aunt Virgie's mother, Ane Emile Christopherson, was an expert cook of Danish pastries.

Wildflower Inn Oatmeal-Buttermilk Pancakes

Created by Sherrie Jern

INGREDIENTS

Pancakes

2 cups old-fashioned oatmeal

2 1/2 cups buttermilk

2 eggs, lightly beaten

1/4 cup butter or margarine, melted and cooled

1/2 cup all-purpose flour

2 tablespoons sugar

1 teaspoon baking powder

1 teaspoon baking soda

1/4 teaspoon salt

Strawberry Butter

1 cube unsalted butter, softened

3 tablespoons strawberry jam

1 Combine the oats and buttermilk. Cover and allow to sit at room temperature for 15–30 minutes. Stir in eggs and butter. Add flour, sugar, baking powder, baking soda, and salt. Stir gently until combined. Re-cover and let rise for 10 minutes.

2 Cook on a medium hot grill. Serve with warm maple syrup or strawberry butter.

Serves 4.

Strawberry Butter

1 Combine butter and jam. Shape into a log. Roll up log in a piece of plastic wrap. Twist ends to seal. Chill well.

2 When butter has hardened, unroll from plastic wrap and slice into rounds.

Wyoming's Grand Teton National Park is a favorite spot for family gatherings. Hiking, horseback riding, floating, fishing, and golfing are just a few of a multitude of options to keep everyone entertained. Just miles away The Wildflower Inn offers western-style hospitality. Inn owner Sherrie Jern notes that this recipe for oatmeal-buttermilk pancakes is her most requested.

MAIN DISHES, *Side Dishes,* & BURGERS

Lundy's Coconut Shrimp

Created by Lundy Pridgen Wilder

INGREDIENTS

Shrimp

1 1/2 pounds (45–47) raw large shrimp, deveined and peeled, tail on

1/2 cup all-purpose flour

1/2 cup cornstarch

1 tablespoon salt

1/2 tablespoon pepper

2 tablespoons vegetable oil, plus more for frying

1 cup ice water

2 cups sweetened flaked coconut

Marmalade Dipping Sauce

1/2 cup orange marmalade

1/4 cup Dijon mustard

1/4 cup honey

1/4 teaspoon hot pepper sauce

1 Pat shrimp dry on paper towels and set aside.

2 For batter, mix together flour, cornstarch, salt, and pepper. Add the 2 tablespoons vegetable oil and the ice water. Stir to blend well.

3 Pour the coconut into a shallow bowl. Hold shrimp by tails and dip one at a time into the batter and in coconut, rolling the shrimp to coat all sides.

4 Heat several inches of oil in a large pot over medium-high heat to 350 degrees. Place shrimp in batches (depending on the size of your pot) in heated oil. Don't overcrowd the pot. Fry the shrimp until golden brown, about 2–3 minutes.

5 Serve with prepared Marmalade Dipping Sauce.

Marmalade Dipping Sauce

1 Combine the marmalade, mustard, honey, and hot sauce in a small bowl. Mix well.

Serves 6–8.

Fried green tomatoes. Collard greens. Okra. Boiled peanuts. Cornbread. Buttermilk pie. Seafood gumbo. Fried catfish. Grits. Gulf-coast shrimp. Traditional Alabama fare is savory and satisfying. A resident of Gulf Shores, Alabama, Lundy Pridgen Wilder is an avid gardener and featured speaker on perennials and gardening at Memphis Botanic Garden. She shares two recipes for fried coconut shrimp, each with its own tangy dipping sauce. Lundy emphasizes her preference for using USA wild-caught shrimp.

Butterflied Spicy Coconut Shrimp

Created by Lundy Pridgen Wilder

1 Split shrimp lengthwise down to tail with a sharp knife, but do not sever tail; set aside. Combine lime juice, salt, curry powder, and ginger in a small bowl. Add shrimp; cover and marinate in the refrigerator at least 2 hours.

2 Preheat oven to 375 degrees. Spread coconut on a baking sheet and toast lightly, 3–5 minutes. Set aside. In a medium bowl, mix beer, flour, salt, white pepper, sugar, and paprika.

3 Heat oil in heavy skillet over medium-high heat to 350 degrees. Dip shrimp in batter and fry until brown. Roll immediately in toasted coconut.

4 Serve with Apricot Dipping Sauce.

Apricot Dipping Sauce

1 Combine and cook apricot preserves, both vinegars, paprika, Tabasco, salt, pepper, and sugar in a small saucepan over medium heat for 3–4 minutes, stirring several times. Heat until thoroughly blended.

Serves 4–6.

INGREDIENTS

Shrimp

35 raw large shrimp, deveined and peeled, tail on

1/4 cup lime juice

1/2 teaspoon salt

1 1/2 teaspoons curry powder

1/2 teaspoon ground ginger

1 1/2 cups grated fresh coconut

12 ounces beer, flat

2 1/2 cups all-purpose flour

1/2 teaspoon salt

1/2 teaspoon white pepper

1–2 tablespoons sugar

1 teaspoon paprika

Vegetable oil, for frying

Apricot Dipping Sauce

1 cup apricot preserves

1/4 cup raspberry vinegar

1/4 cup sherry vinegar

1 teaspoon paprika

Dash Tabasco sauce

1–2 teaspoons salt

1/2 teaspoon pepper

1 tablespoon sugar

Southern-Style Green Beans

INGREDIENTS

8–10 slices bacon

1 medium onion, diced

1–2 cloves of garlic, minced (optional)

Red pepper flakes to taste

4 cups chicken broth

4 pounds (64 ounces) fresh green beans, washed, ends snapped, and trimmed into 2-inch sections

8–10 small new red potatoes, sliced

Salt and pepper, to taste

1 Cut bacon into 1-inch sections. In a large skillet, cook bacon over medium heat until browned. Remove bacon from pan. Drain the fat from the skillet, leaving a tablespoon or so in the pan.

2 Use remaining bacon fat to sauté the onions, garlic, and red pepper flakes until the onion is translucent. If needed, add a little butter so onions don't stick.

3 Add bacon and onions to a large pot or slow cooker. Add chicken broth, beans, and potatoes. Stirring occasionally, cook on low for 2–3 hours or until beans and potatoes reach desired tenderness. Add salt and pepper to taste as cooking time progresses. Check to ensure there is sufficient broth to cook beans and potatoes; add more broth or water if necessary.

Makes 12–15 servings. Freezes well for a make-ahead meal.

**Optional: If green beans aren't in season, use canned. Large cans of green beans commonly come in 50 and 101-ounce sizes. Adapt the recipe for the size of can you choose, adding the canned green beans once the potatoes have started to become tender. Adjust cooking time accordingly.*

For large crowds, 2 or 3 cans (10.7 ounces each) of cream of celery soup help extend the recipe.

Famous Barbecue Chicken

Used by permission of Jane Knouff

1 Preheat oven to 500 degrees.

2 Prepare chicken. In a large skillet over medium heat, whisk together remaining ingredients. When heated through, add chicken and coat thoroughly with sauce.

3 Add chicken to a foil-lined 9 x 13 baking dish. Cover with a second sheet of foil and seal. Bake for 15 minutes. Reduce heat to 350 degrees and continue baking until done, approximately 1 hour and 15 minutes.

Serves 6.

INGREDIENTS

1 large chicken, cut into pieces

2 tablespoons vinegar

2 tablespoons ketchup

1 tablespoon lemon juice

2 tablespoons Worcestershire sauce

3 tablespoons brown sugar

4 tablespoons water

1 teaspoon mustard

2 tablespoons butter

1/2 teaspoon salt

1 teaspoon chili powder

1 teaspoon paprika

A nine-year tradition in Lawrence County, Alabama, The Alabama Chicken and Egg Festival once drew scores of visitors. Late in 2013, the decision was made to cease holding the event. However, the recipe for the festival's famous barbecue chicken—once featured in Reader's Digest*—lives on, destined to be a favorite for generations to come.*

Alabama native Jane Knouff, who celebrated her 84th birthday in 2014 and who is the mother of three, grandmother of three, and great-grandmother of one, is often credited with creating the sought-after chicken recipe. Her son, Ricky, explains the recipe actually came from one of Jane's best friends. "My mother received this recipe when my oldest sister was born over sixty years ago. Mother was twenty-three at the time. She has used this recipe all my life at family gatherings, during the holidays, when company came and sometimes when it was just the family. She would double and even triple the recipe when there were community functions."

Jane Knouff

Jane's Knouff's Beef Kabobs

Created and used by permission of Jane Knouff

INGREDIENTS

2 1/2 pounds sirloin steak, cut into 1-inch cubes

1/4 cup soy sauce

1/4 cup oil

1 tablespoon vinegar

1 tablespoons ground ginger

2 1/2 tablespoons brown sugar

1 1/2 tablespoons granulated sugar

1 tablespoon garlic salt

Green pepper wedges

Onion wedges

Bacon pieces, uncooked, cut into bite-sized sections

Tomato wedges (optional)

Mushrooms (optional)

1. In a small bowl, whisk together soy sauce, oil, vinegar, ginger, brown sugar, sugar, and garlic salt. Pour marinade over steak cubes, cover, and refrigerate for two hours.
2. Drain off and reserve marinade. Place beef on skewers, alternating with green pepper, onion, bacon, and optional tomato and mushrooms. Brush skewers with marinade.
3. Grill skewers until steak cubes are cooked through, frequently basting with marinade.

Makes 8–10 kabobs.

Jane's Tip: To cook in the oven, place skewers on broiler pan, brush with marinade, and place four inches from heat. Broil 15–20 minutes, frequently basting with marinade.

Macaroni and Cheese with Cauliflower

Created by Alison Arians
Adapted from a Mark Bittman recipe in Runner's World

1 Preheat oven to 375 degrees. Grease a 9 x 9-inch baking dish.

2 Bring 4 quarts water with 1 tablespoon salt to a boil over high heat. Cook cauliflower in boiling water until quite tender.

3 While the cauliflower cooks, grind bread slices in a food processor (you'll want about 1 1/2 cups bread crumbs) and then combine the crumbs in a small bowl with the Parmesan cheese and set aside. Scoop the cauliflower out of the boiling water with a slotted spoon and put it in the food processor. Do not pour out the boiling water.

4 Cook pasta in the boiling water until tender, about 9–10 minutes. Drain pasta and set aside in a large bowl. Process cauliflower with vegetable stock, mustard, nutmeg, optional roasted garlic, salt, and pepper, working in batches if necessary, until smooth. Taste the puree and adjust seasonings if necessary. It should be quite well seasoned, since it will be flavoring the pasta as well. Pour sauce over the pasta, sprinkle the cheese in, stir to combine, and spread evenly in the prepared dish. (Continued on next page.)

INGREDIENTS

1 large cauliflower, cored and cut into 1-inch florets

3–4 slices whole-grain bread

1/4–1/2 cup grated Parmesan cheese

8 ounces whole-wheat elbow macaroni or spiral pasta

1 1/2 cups vegetable stock

1–2 tablespoons Dijon mustard

1/8 teaspoon ground nutmeg

3 or 4 cloves of garlic, roasted (optional—see recipe on page 2)

Sea salt or kosher salt and black pepper to taste

1/2 cup grated sharp cheddar—maybe a bit more!

Alison's macaroni and cheese makes a delicious accompaniment for grilled meats or a wonderful stand-alone vegetarian main dish (pair it with a simple salad and a roll). She adapted the recipe to make it healthier than many of its cream or butter-filled counterparts and calls the dish "great comfort food." After it has had time to mellow in the refrigerator, the flavors are even better. Alison advises making a double batch and freezing it in bread pans ahead of time. Although the roasted garlic is an optional ingredient, you won't want to skip it. Rather than roasting the garlic in the oven, Alison uses olive oil on the stove top. Her recipe for roasted garlic is on page 2.

Dan and Alison Arians both underwent a good deal of soul-searching while looking for the perfect occupations. They wanted to experience a sense of accomplishment and fulfillment. In 2007, they made the decision to build and operate their own bakery.

Now, the Rise & Shine Bakery is one of Anchorage's premier bakeries.

5 If you're going to freeze some of it, make it to this point, then cover and freeze. If you're making the dish from frozen, make sure to give the macaroni and cheese plenty of time to thaw—it takes a long time.

6 Cover the pan with foil and bake about 30 minutes or so, testing with a knife or an instant read thermometer in the middle of the dish to make sure the casserole is hot all the way in the center. When the dish is piping hot, spike the heat to 450 degrees, cover the noodles with the bread crumbs and Parmesan, and put the dish back into the oven, uncovered, until the bread crumbs are browned, about 5–10 minutes.

Serves 4.

Salmon Burgers

INGREDIENTS

1/2 cup chopped onion

2 tablespoons butter

1 can (1 pound or about 2 cups) salmon, well drained, 1/3 cup liquid reserved

1/3 + 3/4 cup dry bread crumbs

2 eggs, beaten

1/4 cup fresh chopped parsley

1 teaspoon dry mustard

1/2 teaspoon fine sea salt

Olive oil, for frying

6 Kaiser rolls

1 In a large skillet, cook onion in butter until translucent.

2 Flake salmon and place in a medium-sized bowl. Blend in reserved 1/3 salmon liquid, 1/3 cup bread crumbs, eggs, parsley, mustard, and salt. Form mixture into 6 patties.

3 Place 3/4 cup crumbs in a shallow dish or pie plate. Press patties into crumbs, coating well. Fry in olive oil for 3–4 minutes per side or until browned. Serve on Kaiser rolls with mayonnaise, lettuce, pickles, or other condiments as desired.

Serves 6.

Favored Alaskan salmon species include: King (Chinook), Silver (Coho), Red (Sockeye), and Pink (Humpy). King and Red have the richest flavor. This recipe gives a quick option for using canned salmon.

Arizona Arroz Con Pollo

1 Add chicken cubes, 2 1/2 tablespoons butter, garlic, salt, black pepper, cayenne pepper, onion, and red pepper to a large skillet. Cook until onions are tender and chicken is browned and centers of cubes are no longer pink.

2 Add remaining butter, rice, chicken broth, cumin, tomatoes, and cilantro. Simmer tightly covered until rice is tender and liquid is absorbed.

3 To serve, sprinkle with cheese and garnish with sliced onions and sour cream.

Serves 6–8.

Arizona is home to Grand Canyon National Park. The state flower is the saguaro cactus blossom. One of the most common trees in the state is the drought-tolerant Mesquite tree, which produces seed (or bean) pods that can be ground into flour. The pods were once a mainstay in the diet of indigenous peoples. Now Arizona-famous foods include all types of native plants and animals: cactus pads and flowers, fresh chiles, figs and dates, citrus fruits, kale, arugula, artisan romaine lettuce, grass-fed beef, and natural pork and poultry.

INGREDIENTS

2 1/2 pounds raw chicken breasts, cubed

3 1/2 tablespoons butter

2 cloves of fresh garlic, finely minced

1/2 teaspoon fine sea salt

1/4 teaspoon ground black pepper

1/8 teaspoon cayenne pepper

1/2 cup onion, diced

1/4 cup red bell pepper, diced

2 cups uncooked long grain brown rice

2 1/2 cups chicken broth

Dash of cumin

1/2 cup canned crushed tomatoes, undrained

5-7 stems cilantro, chopped

Shredded Monterey Jack cheese

Green onions, sliced

Sour cream

Arizona Carnitas with Green Chiles

Courtesy Pamela Johnson, National Pork Board

INGREDIENTS

3 tablespoons olive oil

2 1/2 pounds boneless pork shoulder, cut into bite-sized pieces

1/2 teaspoon salt

1/8 teaspoon ground black pepper

1 large yellow onion, cut into thin slivers

1 can (4 ounces) diced green chiles, undrained

2 cloves of garlic, minced

1/2 cup chicken broth

Flour or corn tortillas

Cheddar cheese, shredded

Tomato, chopped

1 Preheat oven to 350 degrees.

2 Heat 2 tablespoons of the oil in a heavy ovenproof pot over high heat. Add half of the pork cubes; sprinkle with half of the salt and half of the black pepper.

3 Cook pork until it starts to brown, stirring often. Remove pork. Repeat with remaining pork cubes and salt and black pepper, adding more oil if necessary.

4 Remove pork and set aside in a medium bowl. Drain drippings from pot. Heat remaining 1 tablespoon oil in the same pot over medium heat.

5 Cook onion in hot oil until tender. Stir in undrained chiles and garlic; cook for 2 minutes.

6 Return pork to pot. Add chicken broth. Cover and bake 1 hour.

7 Serve pork in tortillas topped with cheddar cheese, tomato, and sour cream if desired.

Serves 8–10.

This delightfully spicy dish will really help you get in the Arizona spirit. It's a wonderful make-ahead-and-freeze dish; but you can still involve a cooking team in reheating and setting up to serve the carnitas on warmed tortillas.

Arkansas Chicken-Cornbread Casserole

Created by Nikki Schaefer, Woodruff County Extension, University of Arkansas Division of Agriculture

INGREDIENTS

4 cups prepared, crumbled cornbread

1/4 cup chopped onion

1/4 cup chopped celery

1 1/2 cups cooked, coarsely chopped chicken

1 can (10.75 ounces) fat free condensed cream of chicken soup

1 1/2 cups light chicken broth

Sage to taste (optional)

1 Preheat oven to 350 degrees. Butter a 2-quart baking dish. Combine cornbread, onion, and celery, and mix well. Place half of mixture in prepared baking dish. Spread chicken over cornbread layer.

2 Combine soup and chicken broth, pour over chicken.

3 Place remaining cornbread mixture over chicken and press mixture down. Let rest for 20 minutes and then bake for 45 minutes.

Serves 8–10. Easily converted for larger crowds.

Nikki's Tip: Freeze leftovers in meal-sized portions. Defrost in refrigerator.

Most states have symbols: birds, trees, flowers, and even foods. But Arkansas has its own state cooking vessel: the Dutch oven. Down home southern cooking in Arkansas includes fried catfish, fried peas, fried pies, and fried chicken, savory chicken and dumplings, chicken and rice, slow cooked pork and beef, coleslaw, biscuits hot from the oven, and, of course, cornbread!

Colorado Summer Sauté

Adapted from a recipe by Chef Kevin Clarke, Colorado Mountain College Culinary Institute

INGREDIENTS

1 tablespoon olive oil

1 medium clove of garlic, minced

1/2 cup white onion, diced

2 cups diced summer squash, peeled or unpeeled

2 cups diced zucchini, peeled or unpeeled

2 cups canned or frozen and thawed sweet corn

1 cup canned pinto beans, drained

1 can (4.5 ounces) chopped green chiles, well drained

1 medium fresh ripe tomato, diced (optional)

Salt and freshly ground black pepper to taste

3 tablespoons cheese (crumbled cotijo cheese recommended)

1. Add olive oil, garlic, and onion to a large skillet. Cook over medium heat until onion is tender.
2. Add summer squash and zucchini. Sauté until lightly browned. Stir in corn, beans, and chiles. Continue to cook until all ingredients are hot.
3. Season with salt and pepper. Garnish with cheese just before serving.

Serves 4–6.

Onions: Nothing to Cry About—Kind Of!

Once you understand which onion goes with what, life is much simpler.

Yellow onions *have a wonderful flavor for general cooking, but the high sulfur content can indeed lead to your eyes watering. Try chilling them first to lessen the effect.*

White onions *are generally milder in flavor and great for use in Mexican dishes.*

Sweet onions*, such as Vidalia and Walla-Wallas, are great on sandwiches and in salads.*

Red onions *are generally used in non-cooked dishes like salsas and salads.*

Rocky Mountain Macaroni Goulash

1. Add ground beef, onions, and consommé or broth to a large slow cooker. Cook on high for 6–8 hours, or until beef is fully cooked. Stir every hour or so, breaking up the meat into crumbles as it cooks. If cooking liquid seems scant, add a little water.
2. As beef nears the end of cooking time, cook the macaroni; rinse with water and drain. Pour the butter over the cooked macaroni and stir to combine.
3. Season beef with salt and pepper. Stir in tomatoes, tomato sauce, and soup. Combine macaroni and beef mixture. Return the goulash to the slow cooker, or pour into baking dishes.
4. Toss together bread crumbs with cheese. Top goulash with crumb mixture and bake at 350 degrees for 30 minutes until heated through and cheese is melted.

Serves approximately 24.

Pair this home-style goulash with a simple green salad and rolls, and you'll have a filling meal for a crowd.

INGREDIENTS

8 pounds lean ground beef

3–4 large onions, chopped

1 can (50 ounces) beef consommé or beef broth

2 pounds elbow macaroni

8 tablespoons butter, melted

2–3 teaspoons salt, to taste

1–2 teaspoons pepper, to taste

2 cans (28 ounces each) tomatoes

1 can (15 ounces) tomato sauce

1 can (50 ounces) tomato soup

1–2 cups buttered bread crumbs

2–3 cups grated cheese

Coastal Tuna Loaf

1 Preheat oven to 350 degrees.

2 Rinse and drain tuna. Flake tuna and mix with rice, 1/2 cup dry bread crumbs, onion, and parsley in a large bowl. Add milk, salt, paprika, lemon juice, and eggs. Mix well to combine.

3 Form mixture into a loaf and place in a prepared loaf pan. Sprinkle on 1/4 cup bread crumbs and dot with butter.

4 Bake for 35–40 minutes. If desired serve with white sauce.

Makes 6 servings.

INGREDIENTS

Tuna Loaf

2 cups canned tuna

1 cup cooked white rice

1/2 + 1/4 cup dry bread crumbs

1–2 tablespoons grated fresh onion

1 tablespoon minced fresh parsley

3/4 cup milk

1 teaspoon salt

1/2 teaspoon paprika

1 tablespoon lemon juice

2 eggs, beaten

1–2 tablespoons butter

White Sauce

1 Melt butter in a sauce pan over low heat. Whisk in flour and seasonings. Stirring constantly, heat until mixture is smooth and bubbly.

2 Whisk in lemon juice. Gradually whisk in half and half. Bring to a boil, stirring constantly, for 1 minute or until thickened. Reduce heat and stir in shrimp, lobster, or crab and optional paprika or cayenne.

Sauce

2 tablespoons butter

2 tablespoons flour

1/4 teaspoon salt

1/8 teaspoon pepper

1/2 teaspoon lemon juice

1 cup half and half

1/2 cup cooked or canned shrimp, lobster, or crab meat (optional)

1/4 teaspoon paprika or 1/8 teaspoon cayenne (optional)

Glazed Peaches and Pork

From Peachy: A Harvest of Fruity Goodness *by Lori Nawyn*

INGREDIENTS

2 jars (18 ounces each) peach jam or preserves

2 bottles (8 ounces each) Russian dressing

2 packages (2 ounces each) dry Lipton Onion Soup mix

4 pounds pork loin pieces

2 cans (29 ounces each) sliced peaches, drained

1. Stir together jam or preserves, Russian dressing, and soup mix.
2. Add loin pieces to slow cooker.
3. Pour marinade over the pork and cook on medium heat for 4–5 hours; stir at least every 30 minutes. Add peaches during final hour of cooking.
4. Serve over rice.

Makes 12–15 servings.

Peanut Crusted Chicken Strips

Created by TerryAnn Moore, Oaklyn, New Jersey

1. Preheat oven to 400 degrees.
2. Dredge chicken strips in flour. Blend together egg white, peanut butter, and Vidalia onion salad dressing; dip chicken in mixture.
3. Whisk together bread crumbs, peanuts, and chili powder; roll chicken in mixture until well coated.
4. Place strips on a greased cookie sheet and bake until cooked through, about 20–25 minutes.
5. Serve with Peanut Onion Sauce.

Serves 2–3.

Peanut Onion Sauce

1. Mix the peanut butter and dressing until smooth.
2. Stir in the remaining ingredients.
3. Mix well and chill until serving time.

INGREDIENTS

Chicken

1 pound boneless, skinless chicken breasts, cut into 1/2 x 2-inch strips

1 cup all-purpose flour

1 egg white, beaten

2 teaspoons peanut butter

1 tablespoon purchased Vidalia onion salad dressing

3/4 cup dry bread crumbs

3/4 cup salted peanuts, finely chopped

1/2 teaspoon chili powder

Sauce

3 tablespoons peanut butter

1/3 cup Vidalia onion salad dressing

1/2 teaspoon soy sauce

1 tablespoon snipped parsley

1/2 cup sour cream or yogurt

The peanut became the official state crop of Georgia in 1995. Georgia is the number one producer of peanuts in the United States, providing 45 percent of America's peanut crop each year. It's estimated that Americans eat more than one million pounds of roasted peanuts every day, and one acre of peanuts yields 30,000 peanut butter sandwiches! Peanuts are actually legumes, not nuts.

These tasty baked chicken strips were delectable enough to get TerryAnn Moore a nod from the judges in the Plains Georgia Peanut Festival Recipe Contest.

Honey-Almond Chicken

INGREDIENTS

3 pounds chicken drumsticks and thighs

1/2 cup butter, melted

1/2 cup olive oil

1–1 1/2 cups slivered almonds

3/4 cup honey

1 Preheat oven to 375 degrees.

2 Line a rimmed baking sheet with foil. Spray foil with non-stick spray. Whisk together butter and olive oil in a medium bowl.

3 Pulse almonds in food processor until they reach the consistency of crumbs, but don't over process. Place almonds in a shallow dish or pie plate.

4 Dip each chicken piece in butter/oil mixture until saturated. Roll chicken in almonds and coat well. Place chicken on baking sheet. Bake for 25 minutes.

5 While chicken is cooking, heat honey in a medium sauce pan over low heat until runny.

6 Remove chicken from oven. Baste with honey. Return to oven and continue baking 15–20 minutes more until chicken reaches internal temperature of 165 degrees.

Serves 6.

According to the National Chicken Council, Georgia is top producer of broilers. If chicken is on the menu for your reunion, try this crunchy-sweet dish. And for dessert? A Georgia sweet potato pie like the one on page 165, or oh so yummy grilled peaches.

Reunion Spam Casserole

1 Preheat oven to 350 degrees.

2 Whisk together sour cream, soup, milk, and salt and pepper.

3 Layer half of the noodles in a well-buttered 9 x 13-inch baking dish. Add half of Spam, half of the soup mixture, and one-third of the cheese.

4 Repeat layers topping with remaining cheese.

5 Bake for 25–30 minutes or until heated through and cheese is bubbly.

Serves 8–10.

INGREDIENTS

1 carton (8 ounces) sour cream

1 can (10.75 ounces) cream of mushroom soup

1 cup milk

Salt and pepper to taste

3 cups cooked egg noodles, elbow macaroni, or large shells

1 can (12 ounces) Spam, cut into small cubes

2 cups shredded cheddar cheese

Easy Polynesian Chicken

INGREDIENTS

8 cups cubed raw chicken

1 small red onion, chopped

1 large can (20 ounces) chunk pineapple, drained, juice reserved

2 tablespoons cornstarch

1 can (12 ounces) frozen orange juice concentrate, thawed

4 tablespoons lemon juice

2 tablespoons soy sauce

1/4 cup brown sugar

1 can (15.25 ounces) sliced peaches, undrained

1 Place chicken, onion, and pineapple chunks in a 4–7 quart slow cooker.

2 Whisk cornstarch into reserved pineapple juice. Blend in orange juice concentrate, lemon juice, soy sauce, and brown sugar. Pour mixture over chicken.

3 Cover and cook on low for 4–5 hours or until chicken is fully cooked. Add peaches during last hour of cooking. Serve over rice.

Serves approximately 10–12.

Aloo Gobi

Recipe courtesy the Idaho Potato Commission and Karl Bendix, Executive Chef, Colorado State University, Fort Collins, CO

INGREDIENTS

1/4 teaspoon soybean oil (or substitute safflower or canola oil)

1 medium yellow onion, diced

1/4 teaspoon ground cumin

1/4 teaspoon ground coriander

2 teaspoons ground turmeric

1/2 teaspoon ground ginger

1/2 teaspoon granulated garlic

1/4 cup green chili peppers, pre-diced (canned, not drained)

2 cups diced tomatoes (canned, not drained)

1 teaspoon salt

3 Idaho potatoes, diced with skins on

1 head fresh cauliflower, cored and broken into small florets

1 cup red kidney beans (canned, not drained)

1/4 cup tap water

2 teaspoons garam masala (prepared the day before if you make your own)

1 Heat oil in skillet over medium-high heat. Add onions and cumin. Stir together and cook until onions become soft, golden, and translucent.

2 Add coriander, turmeric, ginger, garlic, chiles, tomatoes, and salt. Let simmer 5 minutes.

3 Add potatoes, cauliflower florets, beans, and water. Ensure that the potatoes are covered with the sauce.

4 Cover and allow to simmer for 20 minutes or until potatoes are tender and cooked. (Ensure that dish reaches an internal temperature of 140 degrees for 15 seconds.)

5 Add garam masala and stir. Cover and hold at least an hour at temperature before and while serving.

Makes 8 1/2-cup servings.

When most people think about Idaho foods, the first thought that comes to mind is potatoes, and rightly so. The Idaho Legislature proclaimed the potato as the state vegetable in 2002. Potatoes grow very well in the state's climate and fertile volcanic soil. And thanks to Gilligan's Island star Dawn Wells (Mary Ann) the vegetable enjoys rock-star status in a potato peeling video (produced by IdahoPotato.com) that has millions of views.

This Idaho-themed recipe is actually an Indian dish that uses Idaho's famous potatoes as a central ingredient. Garam masala refers to a blend of ground spices that can include cinnamon, cloves, nutmeg, cumin and/or coriander seeds, peppercorns, and cardamom pods.

If you'd like to make your own, consult the Internet for recipes. You can also buy a premade version, such as Simply Organic or McCormick, in most grocery stores.

Prisco's Lasagna

Courtesy Rob Prisco

INGREDIENTS

1 pound ground chuck

1 pound bulk Italian sausage

1/4 cup finely chopped onion

1 can (15 ounces) tomato puree

2 cans (6 ounces each) tomato paste

5 cups water

1 clove of garlic, minced (garlic powder may be used)

3 tablespoons chopped parsley, divided

1/2 teaspoon dried basil

3 teaspoons salt, divided

1/2 teaspoon pepper, divided

Pinch oregano, or to suit your taste

1 pound dry lasagna noodles

1 1/2 pounds ricotta cheese

2 beaten eggs

1 pound sliced or shredded mozzarella cheese

1 pound link Prisco's Italian Sausage, browned (optional)

1/2 cup imported Romano grating cheese (or flavor of your choice)

1 In a large pot over medium-high heat, brown the ground chuck and sausages. Add onions and allow them to soften and brown slightly. Once onions have softened, stir in puree, tomato paste, and 5 cups water. Season with minced garlic, 1 tablespoon of the chopped parsley, basil, 1 teaspoon salt, 1/4 teaspoon pepper, and a pinch of oregano. Simmer the sauce for 2 hours. It should be somewhat thicker than the sauce for spaghetti.

2 While sauce simmers, prepare the ricotta filling by combining ricotta, remaining 2 tablespoons chopped parsley, 2 teaspoons salt, and 1/4 teaspoon pepper. Set aside until sauce is ready.

Prisco's Fine Foods dates back to 1926 when Italian immigrants, Tony and Mary Prisco, opened a neighborhood grocery store on the south side of Aurora, Illinois. The store was located on the first floor of their home. From that location and with their "Store on Wheels," they reached out to the city's diverse neighborhoods with a blend of personal service, humor, hard work, and compassion that made them some of the most beloved figures of their day. Eighty years later, customers keep coming back for Prisco's selection of award-winning meats and sausages, homemade deli products, fresh produce, fine wines, and Italian and ethnic specialties.

This flavorful lasagna recipe is destined to become a hit with your family. Engage a team of willing, hungry chefs to help.

3 About 20 minutes before sauce is finished simmering, preheat oven to 375 degrees. Butter or spray a 9 x 13-inch baking pan. Cook lasagna noodles according to package directions. Drain and rinse noodles in cold water and drain again. Layer half the lasagna noodles side by side and overlapping in the bottom of the pan. Spread with half the ricotta mixture and then cover with half the sliced mozzarella cheese. Ladle half of the meat sauce over the sliced cheese. Repeat the entire process—lasagna noodles, ricotta, mozzarella, and sauce. If using, slice and arrange the sausage links over the top of the sauce.

4 Sprinkle grating cheese over the top. Bake 30 minutes or until hot and browned. Let stand for about 10 minutes before cutting into squares. This allows the eggs and cheeses to hold the lasagna together and it will not slide apart when served.

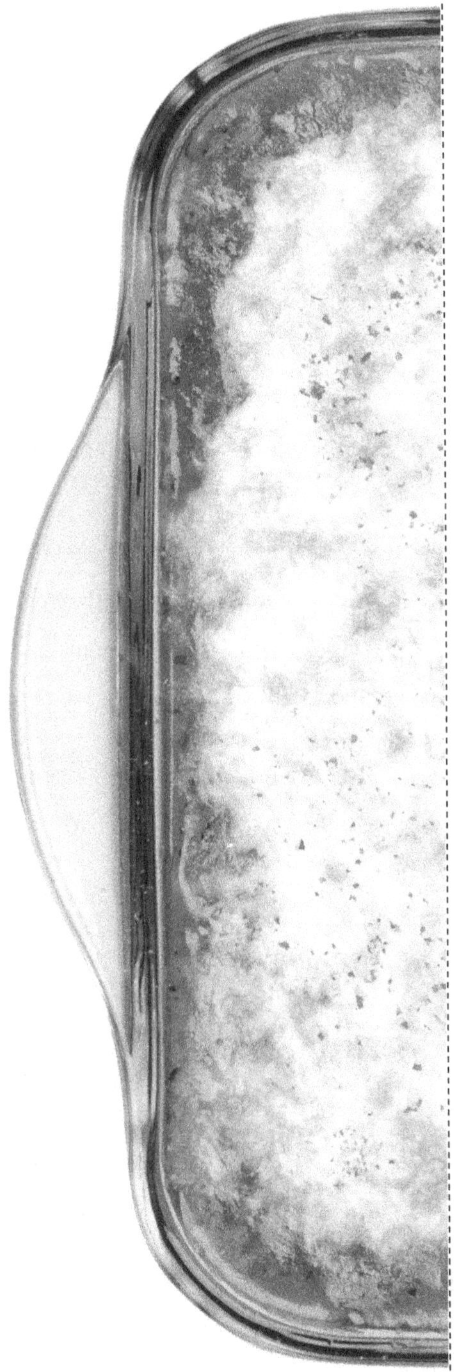

Serves 8.

Prisco's Tip: Warm Italian garlic bread is always a favorite served with lasagna. Or try dinner rolls or crescent rolls for variety. You may want to prepare meatballs from the ground meat. If so, slice them and put one layer in the middle and another layer on the top of the lasagna. Then sprinkle with grating cheese.

Lori's Super Easy Oven Tacos

Created by Lori Homeyer, www.primnpurdyblog.com

INGREDIENTS

2 pounds ground beef

1 jar mild salsa

1 packet taco seasoning mix

1/4 cup water

Soft tortilla shells

Shredded cheddar or Monterrey Jack cheese

Shredded lettuce

Sour cream

1. Preheat oven to 375 degrees.
2. Brown ground beef and drain off fat. Mix in salsa, taco seasoning mix, and water.
3. Spoon the beef-salsa mixture into the soft shells and place shells in a 9 x 13-inch pan.
4. Stack the shells horizontally so that there is a soft fold (like a regular taco). Keep doing this until all the beef-salsa mix has been used.
5. Top with as much shredded cheese as desired.
6. Bake until shells are lightly browned, about 10–15 minutes.
7. Let cool for a few minutes and add your own toppings: lettuce, sour cream, etc.

Makes 12–16 tacos.

The best of traditional Illinois fare can be found in the most unexpected of places—small family-run establishments scattered throughout the suburban landscape that make everything from scratch.

Illinois resident Lori Homeyer describes herself as a "country-lovin', boot stompin', farm girl with a strong Christian faith, Midwestern dreams, and Southern charm." She and her family live about a dozen miles from Harvard, Illinois—home of Milk Days, an annual gala celebration of milk.

"When all the kids were living at home (three teenagers, two of them boys)," says Lori, "I needed fast, easy recipes that were also crowd pleasers. When my two boys were in high school, they played varsity football and each family took a turn cooking for the entire varsity football team. I made these tacos (three pans full) at one of the dinners; we didn't have any leftovers!"

Chicago-Style Deep Dish Pizza

INGREDIENTS

1 can/tube (11 ounces) refrigerated crusty French loaf dough

2 cups shredded mozzarella cheese

1/2–1 cup pepperoni slices

8 ounces browned sausage, crumbled

1 small white onion, chopped

Mushroom, fresh diced tomatoes, bell peppers, or red peppers in desired amounts (optional)

1 can or jar (8 ounces) pizza or thick spaghetti sauce

1 Preheat oven to 350 degrees.

2 Generously oil one 9-inch glass pie plate or 9-inch round metal cake pan. Unroll dough and spread across pie plate, forming dough to bottom and sides. The edges of the dough should lap over the side, leaving enough dough to fold back toward the center.

3 Spread cheese over bottom of crust. Layer in pepperoni, sausage, onions, and any other desired toppings. Top with sauce. Fold edges up toward center of toppings and pinch together to seal.

4 Bake 40–45 minutes or until deep golden brown. Cut into wedges to serve.

Makes 8 servings.

Among the many beloved foods in the state of Illinois are its famous Chicago hot dogs and fries, deep dish pizzas, and piquant Mexican dishes, all of which and much more can be found at the annual Taste of Chicago Festival held Sunday to Sunday the week of the Fourth of July.

Chicago-style pizza is deep and pie-like. Though the pizza itself is thick topping-wise, the crust is not and tends rather to be on the thin to medium side in thickness. Due to the necessity of a longer baking time for the thickness of ingredients, topping order is reversed so the cheese doesn't burn. An assembly line of family members will be able to quickly generate enough pizzas to feed a crowd.

Indiana Pork Meatballs

Adapted from an Indiana Pork recipe

INGREDIENTS

4 pounds ground pork

4 tablespoons dried onion flakes

3 cups corn flakes, crushed

1 teaspoon salt

1 teaspoon freshly ground black pepper

5 eggs, beaten

1 cup ketchup

3/4 cup brown sugar

4 teaspoons dry mustard

1 Preheat oven to 375 degrees.

2 In a large bowl, combine pork, onion, corn flakes, salt, pepper, and eggs.

3 In a small bowl, stir together ketchup, brown sugar, and dry mustard.

4 Combine 8 tablespoons of the ketchup mixture with the pork. Coat 24 muffin tins with non-stick spray. Form 24 meatballs from the pork mixture and put into muffin tins.

5 Divide remaining ketchup mixture evenly and spoon on top of each meatball. Bake for 30 minutes until internal temperature reaches 160 degrees.

Makes 24 meatballs.

Rosemary Roasted Reds

Courtesy Black Gold Farms

1 Preheat oven to 400 degrees.

2 Toss all ingredients together and place on 2–3 rimmed baking sheets.

3 Roast for 25–35 minutes until fork tender. Stir once or twice during roasting time.

Serves approximately 20.

INGREDIENTS

5 pounds red potatoes, washed and cut into chunks, unpeeled

5 tablespoons olive oil

5 tablespoons fresh rosemary leaves, minced or 1 teaspoon dried rosemary

2 1/2 teaspoons salt

1 1/4 teaspoons freshly ground black pepper

Corn-Ham-Noodle Casserole

Created by Shirley Wynn

INGREDIENTS

4 tablespoons minced fresh onion

2/3 cup butter

1/2 cup all-purpose flour

1 teaspoon salt

1 teaspoon celery salt

1/4 teaspoon pepper

2 teaspoons Worcestershire sauce

4 cups milk

2 cups shredded cheddar cheese

2 cups chopped cooked ham

4 cups whole kernel corn, drained

2 cups cooked noodles, such as medium-width egg noodles, corkscrew pasta, large shells, or elbow macaroni

1. Preheat oven to 400 degrees.
2. Cook onion in butter for 2–3 minutes.
3. Over medium-low heat, stir in flour, salt, celery salt, pepper, and Worcestershire sauce. Gradually add milk and cheese. Stir and heat until mixture is smooth and bubbly.
4. In a shallow 1 1/2-quart baking dish, alternate layers of meat cubes, corn, noodles, and cheese sauce. Arrange meat triangles on top. Bake 15 minutes.

Serves 8.

Kentucky Catfish Croquettes

INGREDIENTS

4 cups cooked catfish, flaked

2 tablespoons grated onion

4 eggs, beaten

4 tablespoons chopped fresh parsley

2 cups dry bread crumbs

1 teaspoon celery salt

1/2 teaspoon pepper

2 cans (10.75 ounces each) cheddar cheese soup

4 tablespoons + 1/2 cup milk

Olive oil, for frying

Dash paprika

1 Combine fish, onion, eggs, parsley, bread crumbs, celery salt, pepper, 1 cup soup, and milk. Divide and form into 12 cakes.

2 In a large skillet, fry in 1/8-inch olive oil over medium-high heat for 3–5 minutes until browned. Gently turn and fry an additional 3–5 minutes until the opposite side is browned. Remove to paper towel to drain.

3 Whisk together remaining soup with milk and paprika and heat through. Spoon over croquettes.

Serves 12.

Opelousas Baked Chicken

Contributed by Ethel Chachere Simpson

INGREDIENTS

1 whole chicken

2 tablespoons olive or other vegetable oil

1 tablespoon salt

3 teaspoons mild paprika

1 teaspoon ground black pepper

1 teaspoon garlic powder

1 tablespoon finely minced green onion tops or chives

2 tablespoons finely minced parsley leaves

1/2 teaspoon powdered thyme or powdered sage

Liquid pepper sauce to taste, about 1/4 teaspoon

2 tablespoons Worcestershire or other dark seasoned sauce

1. Preheat oven to 275 degrees.
2. Wash a whole chicken carefully inside and out and pat it dry with paper towels.
3. Mix all remaining ingredients and rub thoroughly into the skin of the chicken. If any is left over, place it in the cavity of the chicken.
4. Bake in a roaster or in a foil-covered pan until a thermometer inserted in the thickest part of the thigh reaches 160 degrees.
5. Toward the end of the cooking time, remove the covering and baste chicken with the pan juices to brown the bird. The chicken should be quite dark, thanks to the paprika and Worcestershire sauce.

Serves 6.

Beginning in 1802, the Chachere family of South Louisiana held a family reunion on the Sunday nearest the feast of St. Louis, a king of France in the thirteenth century and the patron saint of this French Catholic clan. They referred to the reunion as the Saint Lou-ee, giving the name an English-French pronunciation that reflected their heritage and their new identity as Americans.

Author Ethel Chachere Simpson grew up in southwestern Louisiana in a family of talented cooks, including Tony Chachere, the first inductee into the Louisiana Chefs Hall of Fame. The Chacheres' hometown, Opeslousas, founded in 1720, has a rich food history that includes elements of African, French, Spanish, and Native American cuisine. This recipe is all about the Opelousas cooking style: long, slow cooking, and a signature mixture of herbs and spices.

Natchitoches Meat Pies

Created and used by permission of Chef John Folse

INGREDIENTS

1/2 cup vegetable oil

1/2 pound ground beef

1/2 pound ground pork

1/2 cup diced onions

1/2 cup diced celery

1/4 cup diced green bell pepper

1/4 cup diced red bell pepper

1 tablespoon minced garlic

2 cups beef stock

Salt and cracked black pepper to taste

Two 9-inch unbaked pie shells

1 egg

1/2 cup water

1 Preheat oven to 400 degrees.

2 In a heavy-bottomed sauté pan, heat oil over medium-high heat. Sauté beef and pork until golden brown. Stir until all juices have evaporated. Add onions, celery, bell peppers, and garlic. Sauté 3–5 minutes or until vegetables are wilted. Allow meat and vegetables to cook 1 hour. Add beef stock as necessary to prevent sticking. Season with salt and pepper. Remove from heat and allow to cool.

3 Cut pie crusts in half. Spoon a generous portion of meat mixture onto each piece of dough. In a small bowl, combine egg and water. Brush egg wash around edge of shell, fold over, and press edges with a fork. Place on a greased cookie sheet or pan. Make small slits in dough to vent steam. Brush egg wash over each pie and bake 30 minutes. Pies may also be deep fried.

Yields 4 servings.

Natchitoches, Louisiana, is the oldest permanent settlement from the Louisiana Purchase and home to the oldest and largest Creole settlement outside of New Orleans. Meat pies, a Christmas Eve tradition, were probably brought to Louisiana by the Cajuns upon their exile from Nova Scotia in 1755.

Chef John Folse's take on meat pies is a tasty treat, and the recipe can be easily adapted for large groups. These would also go well with a State Fair themed reunion.

Lobster Mac and Cheese

Adapted from a recipe by Ina Garten

1 Preheat oven to 375 degrees.

2 Bring 4 quarts of water to a boil over high heat, salt, and add pasta. Cook according to package directions, drain well, and set aside.

3 Warm the milk in a small saucepan, but do not let it boil.

4 In a large pot, melt 6 tablespoons of butter and add the flour. Cook over low heat for 2 minutes, stirring with a whisk. Whisk in the warm milk and cook, stirring, until thickened and smooth, about 2 minutes.

5 Remove from heat. Add the Gruyère, cheddar, salt, pepper, and nutmeg. Add the cooked macaroni and lobster and stir well. Place the mixture in a 2-quart casserole dish.

6 Melt the remaining 2 tablespoons of butter, combine them with the fresh bread crumbs, and sprinkle on the top. Bake 30–35 minutes, or until the sauce is bubbly and the macaroni is browned on the top.

Serves 6–8.

INGREDIENTS

1 pound elbow macaroni

4 cups milk

6 tablespoons + 2 tablespoons unsalted butter, divided

1/2 cup all-purpose flour

4 cups grated Gruyère cheese

2 cups grated extra-sharp cheddar

1 tablespoon salt

1/2 teaspoon freshly ground black pepper

1/2 teaspoon nutmeg

1 1/2 pounds cooked lobster meat

1 1/2 cups fresh white bread crumbs (about 5 slices bread)

Of course, when most people think of Maine, it's Maine Lobster that first comes to mind. Reunions held near a beach make the perfect setting for a feast of seafood. Consider a clam bake, crab cakes, or this easy lobster mac and cheese.

Gingery Shrimp Linguine

Created by Danielle Hanscom, Brampton Bed and Breakfast Inn

INGREDIENTS

1 1/2 pounds large fresh or frozen raw shrimp, shells on

Zest and juice of 2 limes

2 tablespoons extra virgin olive oil

1-inch piece of fresh ginger, peeled and finely chopped

1 can (8 ounces) unsweetened canned coconut milk

Salt and pepper to taste

4 tablespoons finely chopped fresh cilantro

Linguine for 4, cooked al dente and kept hot

1 If shrimp are frozen, defrost under cold water; pat dry with paper towels. If they are fresh, rinse under cold water and pat dry with paper towels. Zest the limes before squeezing the juice. Set both aside.

2 In a large wok or frying pan, add olive oil and heat until hot but not smoking. Add ginger and sauté until fragrant. Add shrimp, lime zest and juice, and sauté until shrimp turn pink, about 3–4 minutes.

3 With a slotted spoon, remove just the cooked shrimp and keep warm. Return the pan with the ginger and lime juice to the stove. Add coconut milk and cook for 2–3 minutes or until slightly reduced. Add salt and pepper to taste.

4 While the sauce is cooking, peel the shrimp and return to the pan. Remove sauce from heat, adjust seasoning to taste, add chopped cilantro, and serve over hot pasta.

Serves 4.

Here Brampton Bed and Breakfast Inn owner Danielle Hanscom, another member of 8 Broads in the Kitchen, shares an ideal Maryland meal that's quick and delicious.

Maryland Lump Crab Cake on Creamed Corn with South Shore Butter

Created by Restaurant Local, Courtesy Holly Smith, Managing Editor, Maryland Life

1 Combine crabmeat, egg yolk, lemon juice, mayonnaise, mustard, bread crumbs, salt, and pepper in a large mixing bowl and form into six cakes.

2 In a sauté pan, heat butter. Brown cakes on both sides, and finish in a 375-degree oven until warm.

3 Prepare Creamed Corn and South Shore Butter.

4 To serve: Put a pool of the creamed corn in the center of a plate or bowl. Place a crab cake in the center of the corn. Top with the South Shore Butter and garnish with fresh chopped chives.

Makes 6 appetizer-sized portions.

Creamed Corn

1 Combine all ingredients in a saucepan and simmer 5–7 minutes. Put two-thirds of this mixture into a blender and puree until smooth. Add puree to remainder of corn mixture and season to taste with salt and pepper.

South Shore Butter

1 In a small saucepan over medium heat combine wine, shallots, and seasoning. Cook until reduced by three-fourths. Slowly whisk in butter on low heat until completely emulsified. Season with salt, pepper, and lemon juice to taste.

INGREDIENTS

Crab Cake

1 pound Maryland jumbo lump crabmeat

1/4 cup egg yolk

2 tablespoons fresh lemon juice

1/4 cup mayonnaise

3 tablespoons whole-grain mustard

1/4 cup fresh bread crumbs

Salt and pepper to taste

2 tablespoons butter

Creamed Corn

2 cups fresh corn taken from the cob

1/4 cup heavy cream

1/4 cup water

1 teaspoon granulated sugar

South Shore Butter

2 cups dry white wine

1/4 cup chopped shallots

2–3 teaspoons Old Bay Seasoning

1/2 pound cold butter, coarsely chopped

Fresh lemon juice

Maryland Crab Pizza

Nila Mechali, Mama Vida, Randallstown, Maryland

INGREDIENTS

1 premade, 12-inch thin pizza crust

1 cup Toto's Blue Crab Salsa

1 1/2 cups shredded mozzarella cheese

1–1 1/2 cups fresh crab meat

1/4 cup diced red bell pepper

1/4 teaspoon oregano flakes

Crushed red pepper flakes to taste

Parmesan cheese to taste

1. Preheat oven to 400 degrees.
2. Top pizza crust with Toto's Blue Crab Salsa.
3. Evenly coat the crust with mozzarella cheese, crab meat, red pepper, and oregano flakes.
4. Place pizza directly on oven rack. Bake 13–16 minutes or until cheese is bubbly and turning golden brown.
5. Remove from oven, top with red pepper flakes and parmesan cheese to taste. Slice and serve!

Serves 2–3.

Located in Randallstown, Maryland, Mama Vida's produces several brands of all-natural gourmet food products and sauces. Owners Toto and Miki Mechali were immigrants (he's from Morocco; she's from Israel) who followed other family members to Baltimore and founded a food-packaging plant. The company is named after Toto's mother. Miki's mother, a Holocaust survivor, was an inspiration as well. "She really pushed them to open the business," says Toto and Miki's 32-year-old daughter, Nila Mechali, the company's director of marketing. "She felt that if you could do anything, you could do it in America." Nila's recipe relies on Maryland's famous blue crabs and her family's line of Blue Crab Salsa. If you don't have access to Toto's Blue Crab Salsa, substitute your favorite salsa and increase the amount of crab used. Or, go online to mamavida.com and order online.

Aunt Grace's Boston Baked Beans

Created by Grace Kling

INGREDIENTS

- 2 large cans (20–30 ounces) pork and beans
- 1 medium onion, grated
- 6 tablespoons ketchup
- 6 heaping tablespoons brown sugar
- 3 tablespoons molasses
- 2 teaspoons dry mustard
- 8–10 slices bacon

1. Preheat oven to 325 degrees.
2. Drain beans slightly. Mix all ingredients except bacon together.
3. Place in a baking dish and cover with bacon slices. Bake 1 1/2 hours or until bacon is well cooked.

Serves 10.

No visit to Boston, Massachusetts, is complete without a taste of the city's namesake dishes—Boston Baked Beans and Boston Cream Pie. Add in some clam chowder, fish and chips, a cranberry corn muffin, and a Boston brownie, and you've captured the heart of Massachusetts cuisine.

Boston Baked Beans are traditionally flavored with pork (most often bacon) and molasses. My aunt's twist on an easy version has been a family favorite for years. They are ideal for family gatherings.

A Hot Dog Bar

Upstate New Yorkers claim the michigan as their own signature food. That's right, michigan with a lower case m. *Most Michiganers have probably eaten something similar to a michigan but would never call it that. Instead, Michiganers are likely to call the food a Coney Island Hot Dog or maybe a Texas Red Hot (talk about a food with an identity crisis). Wherever it comes from, there's no disputing the robust flavor of a good michigan—a steamed hot dog in a steamed bun smothered with meat sauce and topped with onions. The meat sauce is also called michigan sauce, again with the lower case* m, *and its origins are equally murky, but it is said to have been created by a native Michiganer who brought the secret recipe with him to New York (either Coney Island or Plattsburgh) in the 1920s.*

The michigan's origins may be unknown, but its flavors are famous and evoke childhood memories of carnivals and hot dog stands. For your reunion, think outside the box and be inspired by the michigan: create a hot dog bar instead of the more traditional potato or taco bars. Hot dogs are a fast and easy fix for a crowd. And if you do it the michigan way, any number of toppings can be spread out in front of your guests. Beforehand, let guests—especially the kids—contribute ideas for hot dog toppings. Or have a hot dog cook-off to compete for the title of Grand Champion Hot Dog Master! Who knows, maybe your creation can be named after your home state but become famous in another state. Here are some ideas for putting on the dog:

Canned or prepared chili

Grilled onions

Diced fresh green onions

Chopped jalapeños

Feta cheese

A mustard bar with assorted mustards

Diced onions

Dill, stacker, or bread and butter pickles or pickle spears

Sliced tomatoes

Sliced, fried bacon

Cucumber spears

Sweet relish

Corn relish

Barbecue sauces or wing sauce

Stewed or grilled apples

Sauerkraut

Swiss cheese

Thousand Island dressing

Sliced avocado

Grilled green peppers

Mango salsa

Coleslaw

Chipotle sauce

Melted Velveeta cheese

Green olives

Fried eggs

Pork and beans

Carol's Black Bean Burgers

Courtesy Keith Charak, from the Sherwood Forest Bed and Breakfast Cookbook

INGREDIENTS

1 tablespoon canola oil

1/2 small yellow onion, chopped

1/2 red bell pepper, seeded and chopped

2 cloves of garlic minced

1/2 teaspoon salt

1 can (15 ounces) black beans, rinsed and drained

1/2 cup cooked brown rice

1/4 cup chopped pecans

1 green onion, thinly sliced

1 teaspoon ground cumin

1 tablespoon tomato paste

1 tablespoon red wine vinegar

1 small jalapeño pepper (seeds removed), diced

2 eggs, lightly beaten

1 cup fresh whole-grain bread crumbs

1 In a frying pan, heat 1/2 tablespoon of the canola oil over medium heat. Add the onion and sauté until soft and translucent, about 4 minutes. Add the bell pepper and the garlic and sauté until they begin to soften, about 3 minutes. Stir in 1/4 teaspoon of the salt, transfer the mixture to a bowl, and let cool.

2 In a food processor, combine the beans, onion mixture, brown rice, pecans, green onion, cumin, tomato paste, vinegar, jalapeño, and the remaining 1/4 teaspoon salt. Pulse several times until the mixture is coarsely pureed. Fold in the eggs and bread crumbs. Form the mixture into 6 patties, each about 3/4-inch thick.

3 In the same pan used for the onion mixture, heat the remaining 1/2 tablespoon canola oil over medium-high heat. Add the patties to the pan and cook, turning once, until nicely browned on both sides and heated through, 7–9 minutes total.

Makes 6 patties.

Sherwood Forest Bed and Breakfast is located in the state of Michigan. One of their signature dishes, a tasty veggie burger with a spicy kick, can easily be modified to serve a reunion-sized crowd. It's one of the best black bean recipes I've found.

Easy Pot Pie

1 Preheat oven to 350 degrees.

2 Generously butter a 9 x 13-inch casserole dish.

3 Toss together chicken and vegetables; add mixture to the baking dish.

4 Whisk together soup and milk and pour over vegetables.

5 Unroll crescent roll dough but do not separate into triangles. Cover top of casserole with dough.

6 Bake 20–25 minutes until heated through and crescent roll top is golden brown.

Serves 6–8.

INGREDIENTS

2 cans (10 ounces each) turkey or chicken, well drained

1 package (16 ounces) frozen mixed vegetables (peas, carrots, corn, and beans), thawed

2 cans (10.75 ounces each) cream of chicken soup

1/2 cup milk

1 container (8 ounces) refrigerated crescent rolls

Minnesota Tater Tot Hotdish

Judie Ramsey, www.minnesota-visitor.com

INGREDIENTS

1 pound ground beef

1 medium onion, chopped

1 can (10.75 ounces) cream of mushroom soup

1 can (10.75 ounces) cream of chicken soup

1/2 cup milk

1 package (16 ounces) frozen mixed vegetables

1 package (16 ounces) frozen tater tots

1 1/2 cups shredded cheddar jack cheese

1 Preheat oven to 350 degrees.

2 Brown the ground beef with the onion; drain off any fat. Stir in the soups, milk, and the vegetables. Transfer the mixture to a 9 x 13-inch baking dish. Arrange the tater tots on top.

3 Bake 30 minutes, or until the mixture is bubbly and the tater tots are brown and crisp. Sprinkle the cheese over the tater tots, return the dish to the oven, and bake an additional 10–15 minutes, or until the cheese is melted.

Serves 8.

Minnesota cuisine is as varied as its residents' origins, with dishes based on traditional German, Swedish, and Norwegian fare as well as dishes representative of the state's large population of Vietnamese, Laotian, and Mexican immigrants. Native berries—chokecherries, lingonberries, blueberries, and raspberries—fresh-water trout from the state's lakes, and wild rice are also staples of Minnesota cuisine.

Also popular at the Minnesota table are hotdishes and salads (sometimes for dessert, sometimes not). Hotdishes are what the rest of the country calls casseroles. Judith Ramsey, a lifelong resident of Minnesota, and author of Minnesota State Parks: From Afton to Zippel Bay, *has been serving up hotdishes in Minnesota for years. From family gatherings to church suppers, Judith says this Minnesota Tater Tot Hotdish ranks among the most famous of Minnesota recipes.*

Minnesota Hotdish with Wild Rice

Judie Ramsey, www.minnesota-visitor.com

INGREDIENTS

1 cup Minnesota wild rice, uncooked

4 cups water

1 pound lean ground beef

1/2 pound fresh mushrooms, sliced

1/2 cup chopped green pepper

1/2 cup chopped onion

1 1/2 cups chopped celery

3 tablespoons low-sodium soy sauce

2 teaspoons low-salt beef bouillon

1 1/2 cups water

1. Rinse and soak wild rice in hot water for up to 3 hours. Drain.
2. Preheat oven to 350 degrees.
3. In a 4-quart saucepan, cover rice with 4 cups water; bring to a boil and simmer for 20 minutes. Drain any excess water.
4. Brown ground beef in a non-stick skillet. Drain off any fat or juices. Combine cooked ground beef with remaining ingredients in a large casserole dish. Mix thoroughly.
5. Cover and bake 1 hour. Uncover and bake 15 additional minutes.

Serves 4–6.

Wild rice grows abundantly in Minnesota and is native to the area. This recipe pairs wild rice with the famous hotdish for another delicious casserole.

Mississippi Wild-Caught Gulf Shrimp and Eggplant Casserole

Created by Jan Boyd

INGREDIENTS

1 cup diced green bell pepper

1 cup diced onion

1 cup diced celery

4 cups eggplant, peeled and cubed

2 cloves of garlic, crushed

2 tablespoons butter

1 pound Mississippi wild-caught shrimp, cleaned and peeled

2 cups rice, cooked

1 tablespoon Worcestershire sauce

2 teaspoon salt

1/2 teaspoon black pepper

1/2 teaspoon thyme

3/4 cup mayonnaise

1 cup bread crumbs

1. Preheat oven to 350 degrees.
2. Sauté bell pepper, onion, celery, eggplant, and garlic in butter.
3. In a large bowl, combine sautéed mixture, and remaining ingredients, except bread crumbs, and mix well.
4. Place in well-greased 2-quart casserole dish. Spread bread crumbs over the top and bake 45 minutes.

Serves 10–12.

Missouri Crockpot Beef Brisket

Art Ozias, Breezy-Hill-Farm

1 Combine liquid smoke, garlic powder, onion salt, and celery salt. Pour mixture over meat and rub in. Put meat in a gallon-sized zipper-top bag and refrigerate overnight.

2 Place meat in slow cooker and sprinkle with Worcestershire sauce and black pepper to taste. Cook on slow all day.

Serves 4–6.

A general rule of thumb for cooking brisket is low and slow, meaning low heat for a long time. When making this recipe, I prefer to lay the brisket on a shallow bed of celery slices and diced yellow onion. In additional to the Worcestershire in this recipe (about 1 tablespoon) I like about to add a cup of good smoke-flavored barbecue sauce that has been thinned with 1/4 cup of beef broth. Cover and slow cook 6–10 hours, depending on your slow cooker.

INGREDIENTS

3 tablespoons liquid smoke

1 teaspoon garlic powder

1 teaspoon onion salt

1 teaspoon celery salt

One 5- to 7-pound trimmed fresh beef brisket (not corned)

Worcestershire sauce

Ground black pepper

Barbecue sauce (optional)

For more than 130 years, the Ozias family has farmed in Centerview, Missouri, at Breezy Hill Farm. Current owner, Art Ozias, grew up on the farm and, after attending Texas A&M, served twenty years in the United States Air Force. He worked in research and development during his Air Force career and later developed digital weather instruments. He then served as a high school math and physics teacher before finally turning his extensive talents to studying bovine genetics and the production of pasture finished beef.

Art's beef brisket recipe takes advantage of a slow cooker's ease. With several slow cookers, this recipe can easily be adapted to feed a crowd.

Toni's Wild Woman Beans

Created by Toni Bowen

INGREDIENTS

8 slices bacon, cut up

3 large onions, cut in half and sliced

1 cup brown sugar

1 teaspoon dry mustard

1/2 teaspoon garlic powder

1 teaspoon salt

1/2 cup cider vinegar

2 cans (15 ounces each) lima or butter beans, drained

1 can (16 ounces) dark red kidney beans, drained

1 can (16 ounces) Baked Beans, undrained

1. Preheat oven to 350 degrees.
2. In a large Dutch oven, fry bacon pieces until crisp and crumbled. Remove bacon from pan with slotted spoon; reserve grease.
3. Place onions in bacon grease, then add brown sugar, mustard, garlic powder, salt, and vinegar. Cover and cook for 20 minutes.
4. Add beans and crumbled bacon. Move pot to oven and bake 1 hour.

Serves 12.

May be frozen and heated when ready to use.

Real estate broker Toni Bowen and her husband, Don, have lived in Montana's Madison Valley since 1993. They call it home, but Toni is quick to add it feels more like heaven. Her Wild Woman Beans are a keep-everybody-coming-back-for-more mainstay for any barbecue—she advises making a double batch because they'll be in demand!

Grilled Corn on the Cob

1 Line grill with aluminum foil.

2 Peel husks back to remove silk from corn; pull husks back into place.

3 Place corn on grill. Cover grill and turn cobs every 5–7 minutes until corn is tender when pierced with a fork (husks should be slightly charred).

4 Slather cobs with butter and desired amount of dressing.

INGREDIENTS

Corn on the cob

Melted butter

Dorothy Lynch Home Style Dressing

In 1940s Nebraska, Dorothy Lynch and her husband ran the kitchen at the local Legion Club in St. Paul. It was there that Dorothy Lynch Home Style Dressing was created. Legion Club members loved it so much that they started buying it in bottles from the club and bringing it with them to other restaurants to top their salads. Eventually, the recipe and name were purchased by Tasty-Toppings, Inc., and mass produced. Today, it still serves as a much-loved topping for many foods. In this recipe it transforms simple corn on the cob, a staple in the Corn Husker State, into a savory treat.

Buffet Casserole

From the files of Minnie Jensen

INGREDIENTS

4 tablespoons butter

5 tablespoons all-purpose flour

1 cup chicken stock

1 1/2 cups evaporated milk

1 teaspoon salt

3 cups cooked white or brown rice

1 1/2 cups diced cooked chicken

1 can (3 ounces) or 3/4 cup broiled mushrooms, sliced

1/4 cup chopped pimento

1/3 cup chopped green bell pepper

1/2 cup slivered almonds

Pineapple (optional)

Watercress (optional)

1 Preheat oven to 350 degrees. Grease an 8 x 8-inch baking dish and set aside.

2 To make sauce, melt butter in a medium saucepan over medium heat. Add flour and blend well. Whisk in chicken stock and milk and cook over low heat until thickened, stirring constantly. Add salt.

3 In prepared pan, alternate layers of rice, chicken, and vegetables. Pour sauce over the top and then sprinkle with almonds. Bake 30 minutes.

4 Garnish with pineapple slices and watercress if desired.

Serves 8–10.

Santa Fe Pasta

Created by Richard Bock, Owner of Guiseppe's on 28th, Phoenix, Arizona

1 Bring a large pot of salted water to a boil over medium heat. Add the penne pasta and cook until al dente.

2 Roast the green chiles over a flame until blackened. Let cool in a paper bag (this steams them and makes it easier to remove the skin), then peel. Do not rinse. When cool enough to handle, chop and set aside.

3 Toast the pine nuts until golden in a dry pan over low heat.

4 Dice the roast chicken and the sun-dried tomatoes. Add the olive oil to a large pan and sauté the onion and garlic until golden. Stir in the chicken, sun-dried tomatoes, and green chiles and cook for 1 minute. Season with plenty of salt and pepper, to taste. Drain the penne and add it to the pan. Toss until all of the ingredients are evenly mixed. Transfer to a serving bowl and garnish with toasted pine nuts.

INGREDIENTS

1 pound penne pasta

2–3 green chiles, slit lengthwise and seeds removed (yields 1/2 cup chopped)

1/2 cup pine nuts

1/2 pound boneless roasted chicken thighs

3 tablespoons chopped sun-dried tomatoes in oil

2 tablespoons olive oil

1/2 yellow onion, chopped

6 cloves of garlic, chopped

Salt and freshly ground black pepper

Serves 2.

One of the most frequently asked questions at New Mexico restaurants is, "Red or Green?" Red or green chile sauce, that is. The question is so ubiquitous, it's been named the official state question! New Mexican chile sauce is used in everything—enchiladas, eggs, even ice cream.

This dish from Richard Bock holds up the green chile as its star. Richard is a gifted cellist and played with Frank Sinatra's orchestra for five years. He first attended Juilliard at the age of twelve. He also studied cooking in Italy for nearly a decade and has been featured on the Food Network Channel. Those who know him—including legendary trumpet player Doc Severinsen and noted composer/conductor Marvin Hamlisch—agree that his cooking prowess equals his exceptional musical talent.

For this recipe, Richard, notes his preference for New Mexico's Hatch green chiles. Intensely hotter than Anaheim or California chiles, they're grown in New Mexico's Hatch Valley. An annual festival held each Labor Day in the town of Hatch, New Mexico, draws chile connoisseurs from all over the world. Their answer to New Mexico's state question is definitely, "Green!"

Chicken and Sour Cream Enchiladas

Created by Connie Buttle

INGREDIENTS

1 can (10 ounces) cream of chicken soup OR cream of mushroom soup

1 carton (16 ounces) sour cream

1 dozen flour tortillas

1 can (3 ounces) chopped green chile peppers

1/4 cup black olives, chopped

1 medium onion, chopped

3 cups chopped cooked chicken

1 pound shredded cheddar cheese

1. Preheat oven to 375 degrees.
2. Whisk together soup and sour cream.
3. Wet each tortilla with mixture on both sides and stack tortillas on a plate.
4. Into soup mixture, stir chile peppers, olives, onion, and chicken. Put a half cup of the mixture into each tortilla shell and fold like an enchilada.
5. Place enchiladas in a well-greased 9 x 13-inch pan and top with shredded cheese. Bake 15 minutes.
6. Serve with sour cream, salsa, or guacamole.

Makes 12 enchiladas.

Chicken with Glazed Apples

Courtesy Molly B. Golden, New York Apple Association

1 Sprinkle the chicken breast halves with nutmeg and salt. Heat the oil in a 10-inch skillet over medium-high heat until hot. Add the chicken and cook for 15–20 minutes, turning once, until juices are no longer pink and centers are cooked through.

2 Stir in the apples and wine or apple juice. Cook about 4 minutes, stirring occasionally, until apples are tender.

3 Stir in the jelly; cook and stir until jelly is melted.

Makes 4 servings.

INGREDIENTS

4 boneless, skinless chicken breast halves (approximately 1 pound)

1/2 teaspoon ground nutmeg

1/4 teaspoon salt

1 tablespoon vegetable oil

2 medium sized New York State Crispin apples, peeled and sliced

1/2 cup dry white wine or apple juice

1/2 cup apple jelly

There are few things as delicious as a freshly picked New York State apple, and there are dozens of varieties to choose from. The apple is New York State's official fruit. The New York Apple Association is so nuts about apples that their web site even allows users to find out what kind of apple suits their personality (http://www.nyapplecountry.com/personalityprofiles.htm). If you're "as sweet as pie" and "always willing to help a friend," you're a Cortland Apple. If you're "sharp and fun," you're a Macoun Apple. And if you're "down to earth and 'rooted,'" you're a Crispin Apple.

Crispin apples have Japanese origins and were once referred to as Mutsu. As their name now implies, green skinned Crispins are very crisp. These large apples are also wonderfully sweet and juicy; they're the perfect apple for the New York Apple Association's Chicken with Glazed Apples, as well as for pies and salads.

If you don't have access to Crispins, try a Golden Delicious or Granny Smith variety.

Crispy Baked Sweet Potato Fries with Blue Cheese Dressing

Courtesy the North Carolina Sweet Potato Commission, www.ncsweetpotatoes.com

INGREDIENTS

Sweet Potato Fries

5 pounds sweet potatoes (about 7), cut into 1/2-inch matchsticks

1/3 cup olive oil

1/2 cup flour

1 tablespoon salt

Blue Cheese Dressing:

1 cup sour cream

1/2 cup buttermilk

1/2 pound blue cheese, divided

2 tablespoons minced yellow onion

1 tablespoon fresh lemon juice

1 tablespoon Worcestershire sauce

1 teaspoon minced fresh garlic

1/2 teaspoon salt

1/4 teaspoon hot sauce

1. Preheat oven to 450 degrees. Line 2 baking sheets with aluminum foil; spray with non-stick cooking spray.
2. In a large bowl, combine sweet potatoes, oil, flour, and salt; toss until well-coated.
3. In a single layer, spread sweet potatoes on foil without overcrowding. Bake until cooked and crisp, about 20 minutes, stirring halfway through. Repeat with remaining sweet potatoes.

Blue Cheese Dressing

1. In a blender, place sour cream, buttermilk, half of the blue cheese, onion, lemon juice, Worcestershire, garlic, salt, and hot sauce; whirl until smooth. Remove to bowl. Add remaining cheese; mix with spoon.

Serves 8–10.

Do you know the difference between a sweet potato and a yam? The folks at the North Carolina Sweet Potato Commission do. The sweet potato is the official vegetable of North Carolina, and the Commission hopes to spread the word that nearly all the vegetables labeled as yams in US grocery stores are actually sweet potatoes. Ranging in color from white and mild tasting to a deep, super-sweet tasting red, sweet potatoes come in hundreds of varieties. North Carolina produces more of the sweet, colorful vegetable than any other state, and the uses for sweet potatoes are nearly endless.

Eastern North Carolina Chopped Turkey Barbecue

Created by Carrie Forbes, www.gingerlemongirl.com

1 Place turkey legs in a 4–6 quart slow cooker. Cook on low 8–10 hours, until meat is falling-off-the-bone tender.

2 Carefully remove turkey legs from the slow cooker and place on a large platter. Remove fat surrounding turkey meat. Remove bones and tendons from the turkey meat (this can be a bit tedious depending on the turkey leg).

3 Chop meat as fine as you prefer. (In eastern North Carolina, the meat is often chopped quite fine.) Place in a large bowl for storage.

4 To make the sauce, place remaining ingredients in a large mason jar. Place the lid on the jar and shake vigorously to combine. Pour desired amount of sauce over the prepared turkey barbecue and stir to combine. Use as little or as much as desired. Store any remaining sauce in an airtight jar or container in the refrigerator for up to 2 weeks.

Serves 4.

INGREDIENTS

3–5 pounds turkey legs (about 3–4 large turkey legs)

1 cup white vinegar

1 cup apple cider vinegar

3 tablespoons brown sugar

1 tablespoon cayenne pepper

1 tablespoon hot pepper sauce (like Tabasco)

1 teaspoon salt

1 teaspoon ground black pepper

1 tablespoon red pepper flakes

Carrie's Tip: Make sure to strain and save all the broth leftover in the slow cooker from the turkey. It's instant bone broth you can use in recipes through the rest of the week.

Carrie Forbes is a gluten-free food writer, recipe creator, cookbook author, home baker, and cook, who is passionate about sharing and eating healthy, whole, and nourishing foods. One of the first foods Forbes tried when she moved to eastern North Carolina from Virginia was chopped pork barbecue—it's a perennial favorite at locally owned restaurants throughout the region, which surely makes Jim Early and his North Carolina Barbecue Society happy. The sauce there is primarily vinegar-based—which Carrie prefers—while in the western part of the state, and states that are located west of North Carolina, the favored sauce seems to be a sweeter tomato-based sauce. According to Carrie, her turkey barbecue recipe is one of the most "ridiculously easy" recipes you'll ever make.

Swedish Meatballs

Adapted from a recipe by Alton Brown

INGREDIENTS

2 slices fresh white bread

1/4 cup milk

3 tablespoons butter, divided

1/2 cup finely chopped onion

3/4 pound ground beef

3/4 pound ground pork

2 egg yolks

1 teaspoon kosher salt

1/2 teaspoon black pepper

1/4 teaspoon ground allspice

Pinch nutmeg

1/4 cup all-purpose flour

3 cups beef stock

1/4 cup heavy cream

1 Preheat oven to 200 degrees.

2 Tear the bread into pieces and place in a small mixing bowl along with the milk. Set aside.

3 In a large sauté pan over medium heat, melt 1 tablespoon of the butter. Add the onion and sweat until the onions are soft. Remove from the heat and set aside.

4 In the bowl of a stand mixer, combine the bread and milk mixture, ground beef, pork, egg yolks, kosher salt, pepper, allspice, nutmeg, and onions. Beat on medium speed for 1–2 minutes.

5 Using your hands, shape the meatballs into 1-inch rounds and place on a baking sheet.

6 Heat the remaining butter in the sauté pan over medium-low heat, or in an electric skillet set to 250 degrees. Add the meatballs and sauté until golden brown on all sides, about 7–10 minutes. Do this in batches so the meatballs are not crowded in the pan. Remove the meatballs to an ovenproof dish using a slotted spoon and place in the warm oven. Repeat until all meatballs are cooked and in the warm oven.

7 Decrease the heat under the sauté pan to low and add the flour, whisking until lightly browned, approximately 1–2 minutes. Gradually add the beef stock and whisk until sauce begins to thicken. Add the cream and continue to cook until the gravy reaches the desired consistency.

8 Remove the meatballs from the oven, cover with the gravy, and serve.

Makes 24–30 meatballs.

Minot, North Dakota, is home to the largest Scandinavian festival in the United States. Food plays a huge part of the festival, with samplings from Sweden, Denmark, Norway, German-speaking Europe, the Netherlands, Iceland, Finland, and Estonia. One of the most popular food offerings at the festival is always Swedish meatballs. This recipe is an adaptation of Alton Brown's Swedish meatballs.

Hanky-Pankies

INGREDIENTS

1 pound spicy Italian sausage

1 pound ground beef

1 pound Velveeta cheese, cubed

1 teaspoon–1 tablespoon Worcestershire sauce

1 teaspoon Dijon mustard (optional)

1 teaspoon dried oregano (optional)

Dash ground pepper

1 In a large skillet, brown the sausage and beef. Crumble. Drain excess fat.

2 Stir in the cheese until melted. Add Worcestershire and other selected seasonings; stir until combined.

3 Serve open faced on either cocktail rye, pumpernickel, or sourdough slices, over tortilla strips or chips, or on baguettes.

Makes about 6–8 cups.

Cincinnati is home to the nation's longest running culinary arts festival, and if you ever have a chance to go, you won't want to miss sampling some of the uniquely Cincinnatian fare on hand, like Cincinnati Chili, Bourbon Bacon Caramel Popcorn, and Hanky-Panky Crouqets. The latter is an upscale version of the wildly popular Hanky-Panky, sometimes called a Hanky-Pank. No one seems to know where the name came from, but everyone in Cincinnati seems to love the way they taste. The Cincinnati Enquirer's *food and dining critic, Polly Campbell, writes enthusiastically about these "snacks made of ground beef, sausage, and processed cheese, piled on squares of cocktail rye and broiled or baked," adding that "they have a special place in Cincinnatians' hearts and at Cincinnatians' parties."*

"There's even a band named for the snack, The Hanky-Panks," Campbell writes. "Their slogan, according to lead singer Billy Scott, is 'Sausage, ground beef and Velveeta on party rye. Emphasis on the party.'" For your big family party, try partying like you're from Cincinnati and make this recipe.

Cooperative Meatloaf for One Hundred

Provided by Sarah Whitten, Oklahoma Food Cooperative

1 If making homemade sauce, drop 10 pounds fresh vine ripened tomatoes into boiling water. Leave tomatoes in water several minutes to help remove skins. Lift out tomatoes with a slotted spoon, remove skins, core, and chop. Place tomatoes in a small amount of water in a saucepan and simmer for 2 hours.

2 Preheat oven to 325 degrees.

3 In a large bowl, thoroughly blend meat, seasonings, onion, and crumbs by hand. (Machine mixing will harden the loaf.)

4 Add beaten eggs, milk, and tomato sauce and mix thoroughly. Bake in large loaf pans 1–1 1/2 half hours, until internal temperature registers 170 degrees.

INGREDIENTS

8 cups tomato sauce, homemade or canned

30 pounds ground Oklahoma beef

8 pounds ground Oklahoma pork

1 1/2 pounds finely minced onions

6 1/4 quarts fine bread crumbs

16 beaten eggs from pastured chickens

9 1/2 cups goat milk

Seasonings **per pound of meat:**

- 1/2 teaspoon salt
- 1/4 teaspoon pepper
- 1/8–1/4 teaspoon garlic powder
- 1/4 teaspoon dry mustard
- 1/8 teaspoon cayenne or crushed red pepper flakes (optional)
- 1/2–1 teaspoon Worcestershire sauce (optional)

Oklahoma ranks fifth in cattle production in the United States and is said to be one of five states where cattle outnumber people. The Oklahoma Food Cooperative promotes the cattle industry and advocates using crops and agriculture produced in the state. Their recipe for meatloaf is perfect for big crowds at family reunions and is based on a recipe from the book Quantity Cooking *by Nola Treat and Lenore Richards. First published in 1922, the book was used by the United States Army in World War II.*

You'll need several large mixing bowls and loaf pans, lots of willing hands, a good dose of patience—along with the ability to delegate specific tasks—and a bevy of hungry people to make this one.

OREGON

Dee's Spanish Chicken

Created by Dianne Buchanen

INGREDIENTS

4 boneless, skinless chicken breasts

1 jar (16 ounces) medium salsa

3 tablespoons brown sugar

1 tablespoon prepared mustard

2–3 cups cooked white rice

1 Preheat oven to 400 degrees.

2 Place the chicken in a shallow, well-greased baking dish.

3 Mix salsa, brown sugar, and mustard. Pour over chicken; cover with foil.

4 Bake about 45 minutes. Remove the chicken from the sauce when done, and add the sauce to cooked rice for Spanish Rice as a side dish.

Serves 4.

This recipe comes from my cousin Dee. She's been using the recipe for a couple of years. The simple ingredient list and preparation make it a quick and easy option for a potluck dish.

PENNSYLVANIA

Dillner Family Farm Broccoli Casserole

Courtesy Dillner Family Farm

INGREDIENTS

1 medium onion, diced

2 cups fresh mushrooms, sliced

1 large bunch broccoli, diced

1 jar (16 ounces) Cheez Whiz

2 cups cooked rice

1 can (10.75 ounces) cream of mushroom soup

1 Preheat oven to 350 degrees.

2 Sauté mushrooms and onions in butter until soft. Remove from heat.

3 Cook broccoli until tender, drain.

4 Warm Cheez Whiz on low in microwave, or in a small sauce pan on the stove top, until melted.

5 In a large bowl, mix cooked onions and broccoli with cooked rice. Fold in soup, Cheez Whiz, and mushrooms. Stir to combine. Pour into prepared 9 x 13-inch baking dish.

6 Bake for 35–45 minutes or until well heated through.

Serves 8.

Charleston Red Rice

1 Cook bacon in a large sauté pan over medium-high heat until crisp. Use a slotted spoon to remove bacon pieces to a paper-towel lined bowl. Do not drain off grease.

2 Sauté onions in bacon fat until softened, about 5 minutes.

3 Stir in tomato paste, salt, sugar, pepper, and water. Bring to a boil and then add rice. Stir and bring mixture to a simmer. Cover and reduce heat to low. Allow rice to cook until most of the liquid is absorbed, following directions on the package (do not remove the lid).

4 When rice is cooked, stir in reserved bacon pieces and serve.

Serves 6–8.

INGREDIENTS

1 pound bacon, coarsely chopped

2 medium onions, finely chopped

1 can (6 ounces) tomato paste

2 teaspoons salt

2–3 teaspoons sugar

1 teaspoon pepper

3 cups water

2 cups long grain rice

In Charleston, South Carolina, red rice is a Low Country favorite. Soulful and filling, the dish marries long grain rice with the flavors of pork and tomatoes.

Roasted Garlic and Root Vegetables

Courtesy Jessica Miller, Dakota Rural Action

INGREDIENTS

2 pounds mixed root vegetables (potatoes, carrots, parsnips, turnips, beets, sweet potatoes, small onions or whole shallots)

1–3 heads garlic, cloves separated but unpeeled

3 bay leaves

Olive oil

Salt and freshly milled pepper

Several fresh rosemary, thyme, oregano, or sage leaves (or a few teaspoons dried, any combination)

1 Preheat oven to 450 degrees.

2 Peel the vegetables and cut into similar sized pieces—parsnips, turnips, and sweet potatoes can be larger. Toss the garlic and vegetables to coat well with olive oil and herbs, then season with salt and pepper. Place the mixture in a large and roomy pan and bake uncovered for 30 minutes, stirring once or twice.

3 Reduce heat to 375 degrees and continue baking until vegetables are tender when pierced with a knife. Remove bay leaves and serve.

Serves 4.

Garlic can be eaten right out of the peel or spread onto crusty bread.

Root vegetables, such as carrots, parsnips, beets, potatoes, and more, grow well deep in eastern South Dakota's fertile soil. Agriculture is a crucial element of South Dakota's economy. In addition to vegetables, cattle, corn, soybeans, wheat, and hogs are the state's most important commodities.

At Dakota Rural Action, families, ranchers, and farmers work together to conserve and protect the state's natural resources and agricultural way of life. The group works to promote local eating, farm networking, and energy fairness. Local food co-ops and farmers' markets draw in residents eager to make a difference in their communities and share in the state's natural abundance. Here, Dakota Rural Action shares a simple yet satisfying dish that can easily be multiplied. Consider shopping your state's local markets before your reunion and gathering seasonal vegetables for a similar dish.

June Halverson's Best Sloppy Joe's Ever

Created by June Halverson

1 Combine all ingredients in a very large pot and warm through.

Makes enough for approximately 100 sandwiches.

INGREDIENTS

20 pounds ground beef or venison, browned and crumbled

4 onions, chopped

2 bottles (64 ounces each) ketchup

2/3 cup prepared mustard

2 1/2 cups brown sugar

1 cup white vinegar

*Years ago, the late Tony Dean, outdoor enthusiast and host of his own award-winning TV show—*Tony Dean Outdoors*—visited Steve Halverson's hunting lodge in Kennebec, South Dakota. Halverson Hunts offers full-service, guided pheasant hunts. During Tony's stay, he joined other guests in the lodge for meals prepared by Steve's mother, June. A favorite on the menu was Mrs. Halverson's Sloppy Joe's. Tony tried them out one day at lunch and declared that they were "the best Sloppy Joe's ever." The name stuck. This recipe feeds a crowd but can be easily reduced or frozen in batches for later use.*

Real Texas Tamales

Created by and used by permission of Ramona Werst, www.ramonasbasilgarden.com

INGREDIENTS

Meat Filling:

One 5-pound pork roast

Salt, to taste

Garlic pepper, to taste

1 dried red poblano pepper

1/8 cup chopped Spicy Globe Basil

Chile Pepper Paste:

12 dried chile pepper pods (heat of the pepper is your preference)

2 tablespoons minced garlic

1 teaspoon crushed oregano

2 teaspoons salt

2 tablespoons oil

2 tablespoons all-purpose flour

1 package corn husks

1 Place the pork roast in a slow cooker with the fat side up. Sprinkle roast with salt and garlic pepper to taste. Place poblano chile pepper to the side of the pork roast. Place the spicy globe basil leaves on top of the pork roast. Cover and cook on low 8–10 hours. The pork roast should be cooked until it falls apart when tested with a fork. You do not have to add any water; the pork roast will cook in its own juices.

2 While roast cooks, make the chile pepper paste. Slice off chiles' stems, rinse the chiles in water, and remove the seeds. Place chiles in a small pot and cover with water. Cook the chile pepper pods over medium heat until they become very soft. Remove chile pepper pods with a slotted spoon and place them in a blender, reserving chile-infused liquid. To the blender, also add minced garlic, oregano, and salt. Start blender, adding a little reserved liquid at a time. Blend to make a paste with a smooth but not watery consistency.

Heat the oil in a large skillet. Stir in flour and whisk until mixture turns brown. Add the blended sauce and stir well so that no lumps form. Simmer 2–3 minutes. Once paste has simmered, let it cool a bit and then store in the refrigerator until pork is ready.

3 When pork can be shredded easily with a fork, remove it from the slow cooker to a large bowl. Shred with 2 forks. Stir in chile pepper paste and mix well. Cover bowl and refrigerate overnight to allow flavors to meld.

4 Several hours before you'd like to serve the tamales, separate the corn husks and soak them in hot water for about an hour, or until softened. This will prevent them from breaking apart.

5 In the meantime, prepare the masa. Place lard and vegetable shortening in a large pot and melt over medium heat. Stir to ensure that fats are completely blended and melted. Stir in salt and chili powder. In a separate bowl, stir together chicken broth, garlic powder, and baking powder. Place fresh masa in a large container or bowl. Stir in lard and vegetable-shortening chili powder mixture. Using an electric mixer, blend in the broth mixture until masa is light and fluffy. To test the masa's readiness, fill a small cup with old water. Take a pinch of the masa and place it in the water. It's ready when the masa floats.

6 To assemble the tamales, remove the soaked corn husks and dry with paper towels. Place them on the counter or a large baking sheet, smooth side up, and spread the masa over them. Take approximately 1–2 tablespoons of pork mixture and spread on each masa-covered corn husk. Fold the sides of the husks toward the center. Pinch the end that looks open and fold the other longer end. Place aluminum foil at the middle of the tamale steamer pan. Place the tamales into the pan with the folded ends down. Stack against the foil to stand the tamales upright.

7 Cook over medium-high heat until water boils. Reduce heat to medium low or low and cook the tamales about 2 hours. Test tamales to make sure they are cooked. You can check by opening a tamale to make sure the masa is spongy and doesn't stick to the corn husk.

8 If freezing the tamales, divide into quantities of one dozen, place in aluminum foil and wrap tightly. To freeze, place foil-wrapped tamales in a freezer-safe zipper-top plastic bag.

Makes 15–20 dozen tamales.

Masa (traditional version):

1 pound lard

1/2 cup vegetable shortening

1/8 cup salt

1/4 cup chili powder

2 cups chicken broth

2 tablespoons garlic powder

2 tablespoons baking powder

5 pounds fresh masa

Mertzon, Texas, food blogger Ramona Werst is a talented cook and gardener. Born in Saigon, Ramona was raised in Arizona. She then married a Texan. Her interests range from growing basil to preparing her native Vietnamese food to experimenting with spicy Texas cuisine. Texas Tamales are her specialty. She infuses the meat filling with spicy globe basil she grows herself. It grows in a tidy bush the shape of a globe and is perfect for growing in pots in home kitchens. If you can't find the variety, any fresh basil will do.

Making tamales is time-consuming. But it's well worth the effort. For a memorable bonding experience with delicious results, engage several family members in the preparation.

Simple Seafood Paella

Use by permission of Blake Groomer, Groomer Seafood

INGREDIENTS

1 pound unpeeled, medium-large shrimp

4 cups chicken broth

1 tablespoons vegetable oil

1/2 pound Spanish chorizo, removed from casing and sliced

1/2 leek or onion, chopped

1/2 green bell pepper, diced

2 teaspoons minced garlic

3 strands saffron

1/2 teaspoon red pepper flakes

1/2 teaspoon freshly ground pepper

1 1/2 cups uncooked white short grain rice

1 chicken breast, cooked and shredded

1 cup frozen peas

1 pound fresh mussels, cleaned and debearded

1 pound fresh clams, scrubbed clean

1/2 red bell pepper in strips (for garnish)

2 lemons, zested

1 Peel shrimp, reserving shells; set shrimp aside.

2 Bring shrimp shells and chicken broth to a boil in a large saucepan over medium-high heat. Reduce heat and simmer 5 minutes. Remove from heat, and let stand 10 minutes. Pour mixture through a fine wire-mesh strainer into a bowl; discard shells.

3 Heat oil in a paella pan or heavy, large skillet over medium heat. Add Spanish chorizo, leek or onion, and bell pepper and sauté until vegetables are tender. Add garlic, saffron, red pepper flakes, and black pepper. Cook 1 minute. Stir in rice and cook, stirring to coat, 1 minute. Stir in shrimp broth in small amounts. Cover, reduce heat, and simmer 15 minutes.

4 Remove pan from heat; stir in shrimp and shredded chicken. Sprinkle peas evenly over mixture; arrange mussels and clams around outside of pan, hinge ends down. Arrange the red pepper strips decoratively on top.

5 Cook, covered, over medium-low heat 20 minutes or until liquid is absorbed and mussel and clam shells are open. Discard any unopened clams or mussels. Sprinkle lemon zest on top and serve with lemon wedges.

Makes 5–7 servings.

For four generations, Blake Groomer's family has been taking its nets to the Gulf Coast to catch what the waters have to offer. In the late 1800s the venture was a small family business based in Port Isabel, Texas. Today, Groomer Seafood is San Antonio's largest fish and fresh seafood processor and is considered the foremost fresh seafood expert in the state.

Cornburgers

INGREDIENTS

1 pound ground beef

3 tablespoons pine nuts

Salt and pepper to taste

1/3 cup canned whole kernel corn, well drained

4 teaspoons chili sauce

1/4 cup crumbled blue cheese

6 hamburger buns

1. In a large bowl, combine beef, pine nuts, salt, and pepper. Shape into 12 thin patties.
2. In a small bowl, combine corn, chili sauce, and blue cheese. Spread 1 tablespoon of mixture in the center of each of 6 patties. Cover with a second patty and pinch edges shut to seal.
3. Grill cornburgers for 10–15 minutes or until done. Place on hamburger buns and garnish as desired.

Makes 6 burgers.

Legend has it that in 1900 a customer in a hurry informed Louis' Lunch owner Louis Lassen he needed something to eat—fast. The quick-thinking Louis concocted a mix of ground steak trimmings and nestled it between a couple of slices of toast. The rest, as they say, is history!

This recipe from my Grandma Minnie's files combines ground beef, blue cheese, and pine nuts for a truly unique and delicious burger. The following burger recipe comes from her files as well.

Coney Island Burgers

INGREDIENTS

1 pound ground beef

Salt and pepper to taste

1–2 tablespoons fresh or dried minced onion

Chili sauce to taste

Sliced American cheese

6 slices bacon, uncooked

6 hamburger buns

1. Combine beef, onion, and chili sauce. Shape into 12 thin patties. Top 6 patties with a slice of American cheese and cover with second patty. Pinch to seal.
2. Wrap a slice of bacon around the edge of each burger and secure with a wooden pick. Grill for 10–15 minutes or until done as desired. Place on buns and garnish as desired.

Makes 6 burgers.

Tuna Fish Pie

Created by Virginia Hill

INGREDIENTS

2 eggs, separated

1/2 teaspoon salt

1/4 teaspoon pepper

1/4 teaspoon ground cardamom

2 cups soft bread crumbs

1 1/4 cups mayonnaise

2 cans tuna, well drained and flaked

1 package (16 ounces) frozen peas and carrots, cooked and drained

1 cup finely chopped celery

1/4 cup chopped pimento

2 tablespoons finely chopped onion

2 cups mashed potatoes

Melted butter or margarine, to taste

1. Preheat oven to 350 degrees. Grease a shallow 1 1/2-quart casserole dish.
2. In a large mixing bowl, beat egg yolks with salt, pepper, and cardamom. Stir in bread crumbs and 1 cup of the mayonnaise. Stir in tuna and vegetables. Turn into prepared casserole dish; level the top. Bake uncovered 15 minutes or thoroughly heated.
3. Meanwhile, beat egg whites until stiff peaks form. Fold in remaining 1/2 cup mayonnaise; spread on top of casserole to 1 inch from edge.
4. Add butter or margarine to mashed potatoes. Using a pastry tube, pipe potatoes along outer edges of casserole to make a border, or spoon them around the edge. Broil about 2 minutes or until golden brown.

Makes 6 servings.

Potato Wedges with Cilantro Lime Sauce

Used by permission of Jennifer Jacobsen, Teton County Extension

INGREDIENTS

Potato Wedges

3 tablespoons olive oil

3/4 teaspoon ground cumin, or more to taste

3/4 teaspoon dried oregano, or more to taste

1/2 teaspoon garlic powder, or more to taste

3/4 teaspoon salt

2 pounds red or baking potatoes, cut into small wedges

1 recipe Cilantro-Lime Sauce

Cilantro-Lime Sauce

1/2 cup light mayonnaise

1/2 cup reduced-fat sour cream

2 tablespoons finely chopped cilantro

2 teaspoons grated lime zest

2–3 teaspoons fresh lime juice

1/4 teaspoon salt

**Source Jackson Whole Grocer*

1 Preheat oven to 450 degrees. Line baking sheet with foil.

2 Stir oil, spices, and salt into large bowl. Add potatoes; toss.

3 Arrange potatoes, cut sides down, in 1 layer and roast, turning once, until golden, about 40 minutes.

4 Serve with Cilantro-Lime Sauce.

Cilantro-Lime Sauce

1 Stir together mayonnaise, sour cream, cilantro, lime zest, juice, and 1/4 teaspoon of salt in a small bowl.

Serves 4.

Cowboy Milk Can Dinner

1 In bottom of milk can, layer cabbage leaves. Pour in water and add bouillon cubes.

2 Layer remaining ingredients in the order listed, ending with meat and optional garlic.

3 Pour 1/2 gallon more water on top. Put lid on loosely, or drill holes in lid to allow steam to escape. Place over medium-high heat source.

4 When can is steaming well (approximately 1 1/2 hours), the dinner is done. Ensure meat or meats are fully cooked; do not overcook the dinner. Drain excess liquid before serving.

A 10-gallon can packed full will serve approximately 30–35 people.

INGREDIENTS

1/4 head cabbage

1/2 gallon water

3–4 beef or chicken bouillon cubes

1 medium red potato per person, washed but not peeled

2–3 large carrots per person, peeled and cut into 5-inch sections

1 quarter small onion per person, peeled

1 wedge green cabbage per person, cored

1/2 green pepper per person, sliced (optional)

1/2 cup fresh, crisp green beans per person (optional)

1 ear fresh ripe corn per person, shucked and broken in 2

2 bratwursts, Polish sausages, or Italian sausages per person, quartered

1/2 cup 3-inch cubes of steak or pork per person (optional)

2 slices bacon per person, halved (optional)

5 raw shrimp per person, shelled and deveined (optional)

1 clove of garlic, per person (optional)

In Wyoming the state sport is rodeo and the state code is The Code of the West. Meals still include many traditional cowboy favorites, this hearty dish included. Kids will love the idea that it is prepared in a milk can and are sure to want to help fill up the can. Serve with a green salad and biscuits for a memorable family reunion meal.

Before trying this recipe, obtain a large milk can that is clean, in very good condition, and totally rust free. The Ogallala Cream Can Supper Company (www.ogallalacreamcansupper.com) is a good source for quality, brand-new stainless steel cans. New cans are pricey. Old cans can be sandblasted to remove rust. To avoid accidents, ensure any rust or corrosion has not compromised the structure of the can. For older cans without lids, use several layers of heavy duty aluminum foil.

The can creates a pressure cooker of sorts full of hot steam. Use extreme caution when removing the lid, and never seal the lid tightly as the can could explode or lid blow off and cause injury. Always allow ventilation for steam. Use insulated gloves to handle the can to pour contents into large aluminum pots or bowls for serving.

This recipe can also be cooked in a Dutch oven.

SOUPS, *Stews,* SALADS, & SANDWICHES

Brown Jug Soup

Original recipe created by Dorothy Shank, adapted by Nick Williams

INGREDIENTS

3 cups chopped, cooked turkey

1 can (14.5 ounces) chicken broth

4 chicken bouillon cubes

1 quart water

2 cups diced celery

2 cups diced onions

3 cups diced carrots

1 package (10 ounces) frozen whole kernel corn

2 cans (10.75 ounces each) cream of chicken soup

1/2 pound Velveeta cheese, cubed

1 Combine all ingredients except cheese in slow cooker.

2 Cover and cook on low 10–12 hours, or until vegetables are tender.

3 Just before serving, add cheese. Stir until cheese is melted.

Makes 10–12 servings.

Try crusty artisan breads or sourdough with this soup. Sourdough made its way to Alaska during the Klondike Gold Rush. Pouches of sourdough starter were highly prized by miners and early settlers to the area. Frequently, old-timers in the state are still referred to as "sourdoughs."

When you think of Alaska, you likely never also think of turkeys, but free range turkeys are just what Alaska native Nick Williams raises on sixteen acres north of Fairbanks. The enterprising eighteen-year-old credits the 4-H program in his area for giving him the knowledge and resources to start his own business; he's also currently attending a firefighter academy in the state. Nick describes his family's favorite turkey soup recipe as, "Awesome."

If you roast a turkey or two for your reunion or grill turkey breasts for barbecue, the leftover meat not only makes for great sandwiches but is also ideal for this easy-to-throw-together slow cooker soup. This soup freezes well; freeze up to a week in advance and place frozen portions in crock pots or slow cookers to heat for a hearty quick-fix.

Taco Salad Bar

1 For baked tortilla bowls, use room-temperature flour tortillas. Invert 6–8 emptied, washed, and dried bean and/or olive cans (15 ounces or larger, labels removed) on a cookie sheet. Lightly oil or butter both sides of tortilla. Gently mold tortillas around cans; arrange cans on cookie sheet, ensuring edges of tortillas aren't touching. Bake 5–8 minutes at 400 degrees. Allow to cool slightly and then remove can and fill.

2 On warmed tortillas or in baked tortilla bowl, layer meat, cheese, and other desired ingredients. Top with salsa, guacamole, sour cream, or dressings. Sprinkle with crushed tortilla chips or strips and cilantro. Garnish with limes.

INGREDIENTS

Large flour tortillas, warmed

Taco salad bowls/tortilla shells, optional

Iceberg or Romaine lettuce, washed and torn into bite-sized pieces

Lean ground beef, seasoned, cooked, and crumbled

Chicken, beef, or pork; seasoned, cooked, and shredded (see Sweet Pork for Taco Salad on next page)

White or brown rice, cooked and seasoned

Canned chili, warmed

Sharp cheddar cheese, shredded

Pepper Jack cheese, shredded

Canned kidney beans, drained and rinsed

Canned black beans, drained and rinsed

Canned chili beans, drained and rinsed

Canned pinto beans, drained and rinsed

Canned black olives, drained and sliced

Green bell pepper, washed and diced

White or yellow corn kernels, frozen and thawed, canned, or cut fresh from the cob

Grape tomatoes, sliced tomato sections, or diced tomatoes

Cucumber sections, sliced or diced

Sweet onion, chopped

Green onion, sliced

Roasted green chiles, chopped

Salsa

Guacamole

Sour cream

Ranch or French dressing

Crushed tortilla chips or tortilla strips

Fresh cilantro, washed and chopped coarsely

Fresh limes, halved or quartered

Scottsdale, Arizona is home of The Arizona Taco Festival, an annual event filled with friendly competition and festive food. Dozens of teams compete to serve up the best specialty tacos in four categories: beef, pork, chicken, and seafood. The taco-making challenge is judged by officials of the National Taco Association and includes a "sidecar throwdown," featuring such items as salsa and guacamole.

For a crowd pleaser with a south-of-the-border twist, there's nothing more simple than a potluck salad bar featuring festive ingredients for taco salad. Adjust the amounts of each item to fit your needs. For a delicious pork topping, try Sweet Pork for Taco Salads (see next page). It's a copycat version of the delicious Sweet Pork Barbacoa from Café Rio.

Sweet Pork for Taco Salad

INGREDIENTS

One 3–5 pound boneless pork butt or shoulder roast

Salt and pepper, to taste

1 clove of garlic, minced

1 bottle (16.9 ounces) Dr. Pepper (don't use Diet Dr. Pepper)

1 bottle (16 ounces) Pace red taco sauce, mild or medium

1 teaspoon cumin

1 cup brown sugar

1 small can diced green chiles (optional)

1. Put roast, salt, pepper, and garlic in crock pot with just enough water to cover the top of the roast. Cook 5 hours on low.
2. Remove roast, drain water, cut roast into four or five chunks and return to crock pot. Add Dr. Pepper and cook on low 3 more hours. Transfer roast and any liquid to large pot or skillet. At this point you should be able to easily pull it apart and shred it.
3. Add taco sauce, cumin, and brown sugar. Add optional chiles. Warm through.

Makes 12–18 servings.

Wonderful as well for burritos and enchiladas!

Fried Catfish Poor Boy Sandwich Minis

INGREDIENTS

1 cup buttermilk

1/2 cup mustard

2 cups cornmeal

2 teaspoons garlic powder

1/2 teaspoon cayenne

1/4 teaspoon lemon pepper seasoning salt

2 pounds catfish, cut into approximately twelve 2- by 3-inch sections

Olive oil, for frying

Twelve 3–4-inch sections of cut French bread (for open-faced sandwiches) or twelve crusty rolls

Pickles, for garnish (optional)

1 Whisk together buttermilk and mustard in a small bowl. Combine cornmeal, garlic powder, cayenne, and seasoning salt in a shallow dish or pie plate. Dip each piece of fish in the buttermilk mixture, then dredge in cornmeal mixture, pressing cornmeal firmly into fish.

2 Add oil to a large skillet over medium to medium-high heat. Place fish sections in oil (don't overcrowd) and cook 3–4 minutes per side until browned and done in the center. Drain fish on a paper towel-lined platter.

3 Place fish sections on bread sections, add a generous scoop of Tangy Coleslaw (see below), and pickles if desired.

Makes 10–12 appetizer-size sandwiches.

Tangy Coleslaw

INGREDIENTS

1 medium head cabbage, shredded

2 teaspoons celery seed

1 cup mayonnaise

1/4 cup mustard

1/4 cup apple cider vinegar

1 Place cabbage in a large bowl.

2 In a separate bowl, whisk together remaining ingredients until well blended. Pour over cabbage and toss well to combine.

Serves 6.

Potato and Smoked Sausage Chowder

Kylie Helm, Absolutely Arkansas

INGREDIENTS

4 links smoked chicken sausage

Two 1-gallon freezer bags

5 potatoes, peeled and chopped into large chunks

1 large onion, chopped

4 cups chicken stock

2 bay leaves

4 ounces low-fat cream cheese

1 cup fat-free sour cream

Salt and pepper to taste

1 cup shredded cheddar cheese, or more according to taste

1 Cut open the chicken sausages to let the meat out of the casings; put two sausages into each freezer bag. Divide the potatoes and onions between the two freezer bags. Add two cups chicken stock per bag, along with one bay leaf each. Compress to let air out of the bags, seal, and freeze.

2 When ready to use, transfer the ingredients from the freezer bag to a slow cooker. Cook on low for eight hours or on high for five hours.

3 Before serving, add in the cream cheese and sour cream; mix thoroughly and warm through. Season with salt and pepper. Sprinkle on grated cheddar cheese.

Each freezer bag makes 4 adult dinner servings and 2 lunch servings. You can adjust the recipe however fits best for your family gathering.

San Diego native Kylie Helm, now a resident of northwest Arkansas, describes herself as a true country girl at heart. "I love everything having to do with keeping a tidy, beautiful home, anything to do with a fantastic recipe."

She also loves the ease and convenience of freezer meals. Her recipe for potato and sausage chowder is an ideal make-ahead dish to add to a slow cooker for a fuss-free family gathering.

Healthy Summer Quinoa Salad

Created by Kristie Rosset, Lookout Point Lakeside Inn

1 Cook the quinoa in the chicken broth according to package directions. Set aside and allow to cool. Remove corn from the cobs.

2 In a large bowl, combine quinoa, corn, black beans or chickpeas, cheese, leeks, onion, basil, and parsley.

3 To make the dressing, whisk together olive oil, lemon juice, salt, and pepper. Add to quinoa mixture and toss. Cover and refrigerate for at least 1 hour and up to 24 hours.

4 Bring to room temperature before serving. Stir in beets just before serving. Serve in bowls robustly lined with arugula.

Arkansas innkeeper Kristie Rosset says that when she was growing up her father was the real cook in the family; she looked forward to his holiday and Sunday dinners. As the owner of Lookout Point Lakeside Inn, Kristie's culinary talents and confidence have soared, and cooking has become her creative outlet. Kristie is a proud member of 8 Broads in the Kitchen, a group of bed and breakfast owners from across the country who delight in sharing their love of food.

Kristie explains that throughout summer in the South, supper consists of something grilled or a salad. Packed with protein, her healthy quinoa salad is low calorie. "I don't like beets," she says, "but in this recipe the beets add a lovely flavor and color. Don't let the beets scare you!"

INGREDIENTS

1 cup uncooked quinoa

2 cups organic chicken broth (or vegetable broth)

2 ears fresh corn, cooked (or 1 cup frozen corn)

1 can (15 ounces) black beans or chick peas, rinsed and drained

1/2 cup crumbled feta cheese

1/4 cup chopped leeks, using only the white and lightly green parts

1/4 cup chopped sweet onion

3 tablespoons fresh basil, snipped

2 tablespoons fresh parsley, snipped:

1/4 cup extra virgin olive oil

2 tablespoons lemon juice

1/2 teaspoon sea salt

1/2 teaspoon pepper

1 cup diced canned beets, rinsed and drained

Arugula

Slow Cooker Barbecue Chicken Sliders

Created by Amanda Kuzak, www.kuzakscloset.com

INGREDIENTS

4–6 boneless chicken breasts

1 bottle your favorite barbecue sauce

1 can (10 ounces) pineapple chunks (optional)

1. Place the chicken breasts on the bottom of a slow cooker.
2. If using 6 chicken breasts, pour the entire bottle of barbecue sauce on top. If using 4 breasts, pour 3/4 of the bottle on top.
3. Cook on high for 3–4 hours or low for 6–8 hours, depending on your schedule. Towards the end of the cooking process, add the pineapple chunks if you want more of a Hawaiian barbecue flavor. When the chicken is cooked to perfection it will almost fall apart.
4. Shred the meat into small pieces with two forks, and it is ready to be served. If there is extra liquid with the chicken, spoon it out with a soup ladle.

Makes 12–18.

Amanda's Tip: Buy little slider buns at the store and set up a sandwich bar with pickles and coleslaw.

Amanda Kuzak, Silicon Valley's premiere professional organizer, is an energetic go-getter and has a passion for helping people lead more efficient and organized lives. Her barbecue slow-cooker chicken is one of the easiest dishes she makes, requiring only 2–3 ingredients. The chicken is perfect in salads and sandwiches. Amanda loves making a big batch so she has leftovers to stick in the freezer for days she doesn't feel like cooking. These easy wonders are ideal reunion fare.

Chicken Salad Sandwiches

INGREDIENTS

4 cups (32 ounces) cooked, diced chicken

1 cup mayonnaise

1 cup sliced almonds

2/3 cup sliced water chestnuts (optional)

1 teaspoon celery salt (optional)

Salt and pepper to taste

Sandwich bread of choice or hard rolls

1 Combine chicken and mayonnaise in a medium bowl until combined. Add almonds and salt and pepper. Refrigerate until ready to use.

2 Assemble sandwiches when ready.

Makes approximately 8 standard size sandwiches.

Tuna Salad Sandwiches

INGREDIENTS

2 cans (6 ounces) tuna in water, well drained

1/2 cup red onion, finely chopped

2 teaspoons red wine vinegar

2 hard cooked eggs, chopped

1/2 cup mayonnaise

Salt and pepper to taste

1 teaspoon finely chopped fresh dill (optional)

Sandwich bread of choice or hard rolls

1 Combine tuna, onion, and vinegar. Fold in eggs. Add mayonnaise and stir gently until well combined. Refrigerate until ready to use.

2 Assemble sandwiches when ready.

Makes 4–5 standard sized sandwiches.

Smoked Salmon Salad Sandwiches

INGREDIENTS

4 pieces (16 ounces) smoked salmon, flaked

12 cucumber slices, diced

1/4 cup mayonnaise

1 tablespoon minced green onion

2 teaspoons minced fresh dill

1 teaspoon prepared horseradish

Salt and pepper to taste

Pumpernickel bread or rolls

1 Combine all ingredients and mix well. Refrigerate until ready to use.

2 Assemble sandwiches when ready.

Makes 6–8 standard sized sandwiches.

Fran's Easy Vegetable Soup

Created by Fran Nawyn

1 In a large pot, brown ground beef with grated onion over medium heat.

2 While beef is browning, grate or shred vegetables in a food processor or handheld grater.

3 When burger is cooked, drain off fat. Stir in V8 juice, water, and bouillon cubes. Stir in grated vegetables and frozen peas, corn, green beans, or mixed veggies if using.

4 Cook over medium-high heat, until fresh vegetables are tender and liquid is simmering.

Serves 24–30.

INGREDIENTS

1–2 pounds ground beef

1 large yellow onion, peeled and grated

1 can (64 ounces) V8 juice

6–8 cups water

2–3 each chicken and beef bouillon cubes

8–10 carrots

6–8 potatoes, peeled or unpeeled

1/2 head cabbage

1/2 cup diced celery (optional)

2 cups frozen peas, corn, or green beans or 1 bag (16 ounces) frozen mixed veggies (optional)

Pepper to taste

Growing up in Colorado, my husband and his brothers loved extreme sports like rock climbing, racing fast cars, and all the other stuff boys can get themselves involved with. Theirs was a single-parent household, and their mother, Fran, worked full-time. The element that held everyone together was family mealtime. Fran was and is a wonderful cook. Her simple, homemade dishes, like spaghetti and meatballs, lasagna, and a vegetable soup that was often more beef than vegetables, kept her sons coming back for more.

If you have leftover browned ground beef from a meal, you can use it in this soup. Cooked and shredded chicken or pork will also work well or, as the name implies, use only vegetables and no meat.

Marinated Corn and Pea Salad

Courtesy Delaware Farm-to-School Advisory Board

INGREDIENTS

6 cups chopped fresh green peppers

10 cups thinly sliced red onions

25 cups frozen cut green beans, cut

25 cups frozen kernel corn

25 cups frozen green peas

12 cups granulated sugar

9 1/2 cups white vinegar

2 tablespoons table salt

2 tablespoons ground black pepper

2 tablespoons + 1 teaspoon granulated garlic

6 cups soybean oil

1 Place peppers in a large bowl. Slice red onions and toss with peppers.

2 Steam frozen vegetables until tender and crisp. Rinse with cold water.

3 In saucepan or steam table pan, heat sugar, vinegar, salt, pepper, and granulated garlic until sugar is completely dissolved. Remove from heat and whisk in oil. Pour over vegetables and stir to coat.

4 Cover and refrigerate overnight.

Serves approximately 100.

Some family reunions draw huge crowds. This vegetable salad is a fast and easy fix for the masses: fresh peppers and onions, frozen beans, corn, and peas for one hundred hungry guests! If your gathering doesn't demand such quantities, try the Six Bean Salad with Corn (see opposite page). It's become a favorite at some of my family gatherings where it is most commonly used as a dip for tortilla chips. We've even used it on taco salad and as a garnish for burritos.

Six Bean Salad with Corn

INGREDIENTS

1 can (15.25 ounces) kidney beans, drained

1 can (15 ounces) garbanzo beans (chickpeas), drained

1 can (14.5 ounces) green beans, drained

1 can (14.5 ounces) wax beans, drained

1 can (15 ounces) baby lima beans, drained

1 can (15 ounces) black beans, drained

1 can (15.25 ounces) corn, drained

1 small red onion, chopped fine

1 bottle (8 ounces) zesty Italian dressing

1 green bell pepper, chopped fine (optional)

1 Combine all the beans, the corn, and the onions in a large bowl; mix until well combined.

2 Add Italian dressing, tossing until beans, corn, and onion are well coated. Refrigerate overnight.

3 Before serving, season with salt and pepper and optional green pepper.

Serves approximately 20.

Nancy's Holiday Salad

Created by Nancy Leila Green

INGREDIENTS

2 pounds sharp cheddar cheese

4 stalks celery, washed

2 large green peppers, washed

2 (4 ounces each) jars diced pimentos, drained

10 sweet pickles, diced

1 cup mayonnaise

1 1/2 teaspoons salt

1/8 cup granulated sugar

1 Cube all ingredients into 1/4-inch squares; mix together.

2 Refrigerate overnight before serving.

Serves approximately 10.

Florida native Martha Wilkes Harrison raves about a traditional holiday salad, passed down from her father's mother's family. Her grandmother, Nancy Leila Green, from Marianna Florida originated the dish in the early 1900s. Today, many family members continue to fix it every Thanksgiving and every Christmas.

Martha's salad, as colorful as it is quick and easy, is a fantastic addition to any family gathering and tastes delicious with turkey or ham.

Potato Mac Salad

Created by Chef Keoni Chang
Used by permission of Foodland Super Market, Hawaii

1 Place potatoes in a large bowl. Add garlic salt, vinegar, and pepper; mix until potato cubes are well coated.

2 Add macaroni; combine.

3 Fold in peas and carrots. Fold in mayonnaise; mix well. If desired, add other optional ingredients and additional garlic salt to taste.

4 Add in almost all the eggs, reserving some for garnish. If desired, garnish with green onion curls. Refrigerate until ready to serve.

Serves 8.

Fresh pineapple, lomi lomi salmon, poi, poke, kimchi, kalua pork, laulau, shaved ice with a rainbow of fruit syrups—Hawaiian foods are definitely an adventure for your taste buds.

Until I began research for this book, I never knew that the state-side-produced canned meat Spam (from the Hormel Company based in Minnesota) is a staple for many meals on the islands—even McDonald's and Burger King franchises in Hawaii have it on their menus.

And potato mac salad? It's a beloved part of the state's iconic plate lunches. Hawaiians are absolutely passionate about the stuff! If you've never tried it, it's definitely worth your time. No matter where you live it might easily become a top favorite for your family. Chef Keoni Chang's recipe is the best I've found.

INGREDIENTS

4 russet potatoes, peeled, cubed large, cooked until well done (fork tender), cooled to room temperature

1 tablespoon garlic salt

1 tablespoon vinegar

1/2 tablespoon pepper

1/2 pound macaroni, cooked until very tender, drained and cooled

1 cup frozen peas, thawed and drained

1/2 cup shredded fresh carrots

2 1/2 cups Best Foods mayonnaise

Optional add-ins: crab, imitation crab, cucumber, tuna, bacon

3 hard-boiled eggs, cooled, peeled, and chopped

Green onion curls (optional garnish)

Chef Keoni's Tip: Bring the potatoes to a boil, then simmer until done so they don't fall apart.

April Cardenas' Mango Curry Shrimp Salad

Created and used by permission of Chef April Cardenas

INGREDIENTS

1 cup mayonnaise

4 tablespoons freshly chopped cilantro

3–4 tablespoons lime juice

1 tablespoon mango chutney

1–2 teaspoons Thai green curry paste (add more for more spice)

1 KING'S HAWAIIAN® bread round

1 1/2 pounds medium shrimp, cooked, tails removed, roughly chopped into bite-sized pieces

Cilantro and limes for garnish

1 Whisk mayonnaise, cilantro, lime juice, mango chutney, and curry paste in a bowl, set aside 10–15 minutes to marry flavors.

2 Cut a circle or cap from the top of the bread round; remove the soft bread from the center of the round to create a hollow bowl. Remove the middle of bread "cap" and slice it into pieces suitable for dipping.

3 Add shrimp to dressing and toss to coat. Season with salt and pepper. Adjust sweetness or tartness with more chutney or more lime juice.

4 Place bread bowl on serving platter and fill with shrimp salad. Surround bowl with slices of KING'S HAWAIIAN® Round Bread to use for dipping. Garnish top of salad with cilantro and limes.

Serves 4.

Lori's Tip: The main ingredients in most commercially prepared Thai green curry pastes are lemongrass and green chiles. If you can't find the paste at your local grocer, search online for recipes to make your own.

In the 1950s, Robert Taira, the Hawaiian-born son of Japanese immigrants, opened a bake shop in Hilo. The bakery moved to Honolulu in 1963 and was renamed King's Bakery. Today, three generations of Robert's family continue his legacy of making delicious breads and Hawaiian foods. KING'S HAWAIIAN® is now a national brand with products available throughout the country. They remain committed to bringing families together through sharing irresistible food and the Aloha Spirit.

April Cardenas is a self-taught chef specializing in organic food. She's worked and has been a part of many notable restaurants and catering companies like Waters Catering, Haggo's Organic Tacos, and most recently Cups Organic. Her passion and love for food was the driving force for April as she learned technique and recipes by simply being in the kitchen. Her recipe for this spicy shrimp salad was developed for KING'S HAWAIIAN® and makes use of one of their most popular bread products.

Breaded Pork Tenderloin Sandwiches

1 Place one tenderloin in a heavy-duty freezer bag. Flatten with a meat mallet to 1/4-inch thick. Repeat with remaining tenderloins.

2 Whisk eggs and buttermilk together in a shallow bowl. Blend in garlic powder, cayenne, salt, and pepper. Place bread crumbs in a separate shallow bowl or pie tin. Dip each tenderloin into milk mixture then dredge in crumbs, pressing crumbs firmly into pork.

3 Heat canola oil in a large skillet over medium-high heat. Fry tenderloins until golden brown, approximately 4–5 minutes per side. Ensure centers are no longer pink. Drain on paper towel.

4 Spread mayonnaise on buns. Add cooked tenderloins. Garnish with lettuce, tomatoes, mustard, and pickle slices.

Serves 4.

The Sechler family pickle business was founded in Indiana; the company's pickles are still made on the family farm in St. Joe. Across the state, breaded and fried pork tenderloins are used in delectable sandwiches.

INGREDIENTS

1 (about 1.25 pounds) pork tenderloin, cut into four slices across the grain

3 large eggs, beaten

1 1/2 cups buttermilk

1/2 teaspoon garlic powder

1/4 teaspoon cayenne pepper

Salt and freshly ground black pepper to taste

2 cups Italian bread crumbs or Panko crumbs

Canola oil, for frying

4 buns or Kaiser rolls, toasted

Mayonnaise

Lettuce

Tomatoes

Mustard

Pickle slices

Mr. Maytag's Salad Dressing

Created by Minnie Jensen

INGREDIENTS

1 1/2 cups cooking oil

1/2 cup red wine vinegar

1 teaspoon granulated sugar

2 teaspoons salt

1/2 teaspoon dry mustard

1/2 teaspoon pepper

1/2 teaspoon paprika

1 Place all ingredients in jar and shake well. Chill.

Makes 2 cups.

It was 1905 when Fredrick Louis Maytag introduced his first washing machine in Newton, Iowa. The model, named the Pastime, had a wooden tub and was operated by a hand crank. His son, L.B. Maytag, became president of the company in 1920; his son Elmer Henry Maytag in 1926. By 1927, the company had manufactured over one million washing machines. In 1941, a grandson of Fredrick began production of blue cheese with milk from a herd of Grand Champion Holstein cattle established by his father, E. H. Maytag, in 1919. The famous blue cheese along with others, including baby Swiss, Swiss, edam, white cheddar, yellow cheddar, and extra sharp cheddar are still made today by third and fourth generation family members in Newton at Maytag Dairy Farms.

My Grandma Minnie never traveled far from home, but during the late 1920s and early 1930s she worked as a cook at the Million Dollar Duck Club west of Brigham City, Utah. There she had the great pleasure of meeting people from around the world. Some thirty years later, when I was a child, she often told me stories of the famous guests she cooked for at the club. One she identified as the founder of the Maytag company. She often spoke of "Mr. Maytag" as a kind man. In one of her cooking journals, Grandma listed two versions of a recipe she created for salad dressing for Mr. Maytag.

In her blue Spiral Career Girl notebook, Grandma refers once to the dressing as "French Dressing—Maytag Salad." Her next entry is "Maytag Favorite." She noted that the dressing, per Mr. Maytag's preference, was served over lettuce wedges or tossed salad sprinkled with blue cheese.

Okra and Tomato Stew

1 Sauté onions and celery in butter until tender.

2 Cut okra in to 1/2-inch rounds. Add to skillet and fry until brown, about 2 minutes per side.

3 Add remaining ingredients, cover, and continue cooking for 15–20 minutes or until okra is tender.

Serves 6.

INGREDIENTS

1 large onion, chopped

2 celery stalks, chopped

1 tablespoon butter

2 cups fresh okra, trimmed

1 cup fresh, frozen, or canned corn

1/2 teaspoon salt

1/2 teaspoon paprika

2 1/2 cups fresh tomatoes, diced

1 can (16 ounces) diced tomatoes

1/4 teaspoon curry powder

2 teaspoons brown sugar

Easy Kentucky Burgoo

INGREDIENTS

3 pounds chicken breasts, cubed

2 pounds beef sirloin, cut into 1/2-inch cubes

6 cups beef broth or stock

3 cups chicken broth or stock

1 medium onion, chopped fine

3 cloves of garlic, chopped

1 green pepper, chopped

1 can (28 ounces) crushed tomatoes

1–2 tablespoons Worcestershire sauce

1–2 dashes Tabasco sauce

1 package (28 ounces) frozen vegetable gumbo mix, thawed

1 can (6 ounces) tomato paste

Salt and pepper to taste

1 In a large soup pot, combine chicken and beef cubes with broths, onion, garlic, green pepper, crushed tomatoes, Worcestershire sauce, and Tabasco sauce. Bring to a boil over high heat. Reduce to medium-low and cover loosely. Simmer for 1 hour stirring occasionally.

2 Add gumbo vegetables and tomato paste. Return pot to a low boil. Boil 30 minutes or until thickened.

Serves approximately 24.

Piping hot blueberry cobbler, hush puppies, fried catfish, fried chicken, cheese grits, burgoo—Kentucky food will leave you dancing for more!

Burgoo (BUR goo)—a spicy stew with roots in Irish or mulligan stew—is a tradition at the Kentucky horse racing tracks. Historically, the stew was comprised of whatever meats and vegetables were in good supply. There are many variations, and communal preparation can be elaborate, often taking days. The effort involves cooking and deboning meat, reserving stock, peeling, dicing and cooking multiple vegetables, roasting the meats, putting everything together and continuing to cook until peak flavor is achieved. Cornbread or corn muffins usually accompany the dish.

This recipe is a far cry from traditionally prepared burgoo, but the much simplified version lends itself to quick preparation.

Original "Hot Brown" Sandwich

From the Brown Hotel in Louisville, Ky.

INGREDIENTS

1 1/2 tablespoons salted butter

1 1/2 tablespoons all-purpose flour

1 1/2 cups heavy cream

1/4 cup Pecorino-Romano cheese, plus extra for garnish

Pinch of ground nutmeg

Salt and pepper

14 ounces roasted turkey breast, sliced thick

4 slices Texas toast, crust removed and sliced in half diagonally

4 slices bacon

2 Roma tomatoes, halved

Paprika

Parsley

1 In a two-quart saucepan, melt butter and slowly whisk in flour until combined to form a thick paste or roux. Continue to cook roux for 2 minutes over medium-low heat, stirring frequently. Whisk heavy cream into roux and cook over medium heat until cream begins to simmer, about 2-3 minutes. Remove sauce from heat and slowly whisk in Pecorino-Romano cheese until sauce is smooth. Add nutmeg, salt, and pepper to taste.

2 For each Hot Brown, place one slice of toast in an oven safe dish and cover with 7 ounces turkey. Take the two halves of Roma tomato and two toast points and set them alongside the base of the turkey and toast. Pour half of the sauce over the dish, completely covering it. Sprinkle with additional cheese.

3 Place entire dish under a broiler until cheese begins to brown and bubble. Remove and cross two pieces of crispy bacon on top.

4 Sprinkle with parsley and paprika and serve immediately.

Makes 2 Hot Browns

In the 1920's, The Brown Hotel drew over 1,200 guests each evening for its dinner dance. In the wee hours of the morning, the guests would grow tired of dancing and retire to the restaurant for a bite to eat. Diners were rapidly growing bored with the traditional ham and eggs, so Chef Fred Schmidt set out to create something new to tempt his guests' palates. His unique creation was an open-faced turkey sandwich with bacon and a delicate Mornay sauce. The Hot Brown was born!

Louisiana Sweet Potato Salad

Created by Holly Clegg, Courtesy Rene Simon, Louisiana Sweet Potato Commission

INGREDIENTS

6 cups chopped, peeled sweet potatoes

1/2 teaspoon ground ginger

1/2 teaspoon ground cumin

3 tablespoons olive oil, divided

1/2 cup chopped green onions

1/4 cup dried cranberries

1/4 cup chopped pecans, toasted

2 tablespoons pure maple syrup

2 tablespoons orange juice

1 tablespoon lime juice

1/2 teaspoon ground nutmeg

1. Preheat oven 425 degrees.
2. Line baking sheet with foil and coat with non-stick cooking spray.
3. On prepared pan, toss together potatoes with ginger, cumin, and 1 tablespoon olive oil. Roast about 30 minutes or until potatoes are crisp. Cool and transfer to a large bowl. Add green onions, cranberries, and pecans.
4. In a small bowl, whisk together maple syrup, orange and lime juices, nutmeg, and remaining 2 tablespoons olive oil.
5. Toss with potatoes. Serve or refrigerate.

Serves 10.

This sweet potato dish—a tasty twist on potato salad with a hint of spice, toasty pecans, and tart cranberries—is topped with a maple citrus dressing. The salad is wonderful for picnics; a fun change from potato salads with mayonnaise.

Creamy Blueberry Salad

1 Dissolve Jell-O in boiling water. Beat in the cream cheese in 2-ounce portions until smooth. Fold in pineapple and blueberries.

2 Pour into a 9 x 13-inch baking dish. Chill until set; cover top with Cool-Whip and sliced bananas.

Serves 12.

INGREDIENTS

1 package (6 ounces) blueberry Jell-O

2 cups boiling water

1 package (8 ounces) cream cheese, room temperature

1 can (13.25 ounces) crushed pineapple, undrained

1 pound fresh blueberries

1 carton (12 ounces) Cool-Whip

1 banana, peeled and sliced

Summertime in Maine is blueberry season. The wild blueberry is the official state berry of Maine, and blueberry pie is the state dessert. If your reunion includes a picnic, consider making it all about summer's fresh bounty of berries. Serve up carved-out watermelons full of berries. Share favorite blueberry pie or cobbler recipes. Hold a contest to see who can create the best berry-centered salad recipe. This is a classic recipe to get you started.

Chicken and Dumplings

Created by Megan Viox, Viox Farms

INGREDIENTS

Chicken

3 quarts water

One 3–4 pound whole chicken

2 teaspoons salt

1 teaspoon pepper

1 onion, chopped

1 clove of garlic, peeled and chopped

1 bay leaf

1 tablespoon chopped fresh parsley

1 tablespoon lemon juice

Dumplings

2 cups all-purpose flour

1 tablespoon baking powder

1 1/4 teaspoons salt

1 cup + 2 tablespoons milk

1 Bring the water to a boil. Add the chicken, salt, pepper, onion, garlic, bay leaf, and parsley. Simmer uncovered for 2 hours or until the chicken is thoroughly cooked.

2 Remove the chicken from the pot and strain the stock. Pour 6 cups of stock back into the pot. If you have extra, freeze it for another use. Return the stock to a simmer and add the lemon juice.

3 Meanwhile, mix the dumpling ingredients. The dough will be slightly sticky. Let it rest for 5 minutes, then roll it out on floured surface to 1/4-inch thickness. Cut the dough into 1/2-inch squares and drop into simmering stock. Simmer 25–30 minutes, stirring occasionally, until stock is thickened.

4 While the dumplings are cooking, tear the cooled chicken into bite-sized pieces. Add the chicken to the stock and dumplings and cook until the chicken is heated through.

Serves 6.

An hour south of St. Louis, Viox Farms is nestled in the rolling hills of Ste. Genevieve County. Family owned and operated for more than one hundred years, it is now run by third- and fourth-generation family members. Megan Viox, who oversees the business end of the farm, also assists with actual farming and is a full-time mom. For her delicious dumplings, Megan suggests using a pizza cutter to cut the dough. Her family prefers to have their vegetables as a side dish, but she notes that vegetables (peas, carrots, and so on) can also be cooked right in the pot.

Dutch Oven Bison Stew

Created by Jay Bentley, reprinted from Open Range *by Jay Bentley and Patrick Dillon*

1 Add oil to a hot Dutch oven, pot, or braising pan. Brown the bison until nicely seared and then set aside.

2 Add the onions, and when translucent, add the flour. Stir well. When the flour has browned, add the seared meat. Pour in stock, beer, and tomato paste, stirring well to dislodge the cooked meat, flour, and onions from the bottom. Add the thyme, bay leaves, allspice, and garlic, cooking over low heat for three hours.

3 When the meat is tender, add the potatoes and carrots and cook until they are done, but not mushy. Salt and pepper to taste. At this point, the gravy should be fairly thick. If it is too thick, thin with water or beef stock. Add fresh chopped parsley for a garnish.

Serves 6–8.

Jay Bentley, author of Open Range: Steaks, Chops, and More from Big Sky Country, *loves Montana, its lifestyle, and its foods. At his new restaurant, Open Range, the menu features artisan-crafted food and beef from, you guessed it, the open range. Jay has a particular fondness for buffalo tenderloins, which are served at market price in the restaurant when available. He shares one of his favorite Montana-inspired recipes here.*

Jay advises, "You don't have to cook this dish in a Dutch oven over an open fire for it to be outstanding. And you don't have to serve it steaming hot on tin plates in a hunting camp pitched by the side of a rushing mountain stream—but it helps."

INGREDIENTS

1 cup olive oil

4 pounds bison meat, cut into 1 1/2-inch cubes

2 large onions, coarsely diced

1/3 cup all-purpose flour

2 cups beef stock or water + 2 tablespoons beef base

1 cup dark beer (porter or stout)

1 small can tomato paste

3 tablespoons thyme

3 bay leaves

1 teaspoon ground allspice

3 tablespoons granulated garlic

4 baking potatoes, cut into 1 1/2-inch cubes

2–3 medium carrots, cut into 1-inch pieces

1/2 cup chopped fresh parsley (optional)

Salt and pepper to taste

Open Range *by Jay Bentley and Patrick Dillon is available from Running Press, an imprint of The Perseus Books Group. Copyright © 2012.*

Berry Walnut Salad

Courtesy Kurt Alstede, Alstede Farms

INGREDIENTS

Salad

Large bowl mixed salad greens

1 pint fresh blueberries, raspberries, and/or strawberries

1/2 cup walnut pieces, toasted

1/2 cup Raspberry Vinaigrette

1/4 cup crumbled feta cheese

Raspberry Vinaigrette

1/2 cup fresh raspberries

1/4 cup extra-virgin olive oil

2 tablespoons apple cider vinegar

1 tablespoon honey

Pinch salt

Freshly ground black pepper

1 In a large bowl, toss the salad greens with the blueberries, walnuts, and Raspberry Vinaigrette. Top with feta cheese to serve.

Raspberry Vinaigrette

1 Pour all ingredients into a blender. Blend until smooth. Add a pinch of kosher salt and a little fresh pepper.

Serves 4.

Founded by Kurt Alstede in 1982, Alstede Farms utilizes sustainable and certified organic farming methods. The farm harvests one hundred different home grown fruits, vegetables, and flowers. Along with apples, peaches, strawberries, raspberries, currants, gooseberries, and pumpkins, many specialty vegetables are sold at their market on Route 513 in Chester, New Jersey. The Alstede Family Farm takes great care to preserve and promote quality of life, which they feel involves how they give back to their community, nation, and God for all the blessings they have collectively received.

Though Kurt notes he's uncertain of the original source of this recipe, he and his family have enjoyed it for many years. It's a great, light salad for summer that incorporates a medley of flavors.

Napa at the Waldorf

Created by Lynnette Schofield, William Henry Miller Inn

INGREDIENTS

1/2 head Napa cabbage, shredded thinly

1/2 cup dried cranberries

1/2 cup vanilla yogurt

1 tablespoon lemon juice

2 Granny Smith apples, cored and chopped coarsely, unpeeled

1/2 cup mayonnaise (more if you wish)

1 Toss all ingredients together. Chill and enjoy!

Serves 4.

New York native Lynnette Schofield grew up on the North Side of Syracuse, New York, which she describes as a food lover's dream. "Homemade sausages from the neighborhood butcher; tomato sauce from the house down the street whose fabulous perfume permeated the entire block; and clam chowder sales at the local church where the chowder was chock full of fresh clams and vegetables. I still have the blue enamel container that my family used for chowder take out! Dinnertime at our home was such a special time that I would pay thousands to have just one more dinner like we had every night."

Now Lynette, a member of 8 Broads in the Kitchen, owns her own bed and breakfast in Ithaca. The stunning Cascadilla Gorge is only a stone's throw away. Lynnette prides herself on making most everything from scratch—all the inn's breads are homemade, as are the pretzels and even the marshmallows! Back in 2011, finding herself in possession of a head of Napa cabbage from a local farmer's market, Lynnette decided to whip up a combination of cabbage salad and Waldorf salad (a New York specialty created in the 1890s at the New York City Waldorf Hotel). Lynette's guests love her creation!

Minnie Jensen's Million-Dollar Duck Club Coleslaw

INGREDIENTS

1 cup Miracle Whip salad dressing

1 teaspoon Kraft salad-style mustard

1/4 cup heavy cream

1/2 teaspoon salt

Dash seasoned salt

Dash black pepper

4 cups shredded raw green cabbage

1 Mix all ingredients well. Chill before serving.

Serves 4.

My Grandma Minnie's coleslaw recipe makes a great side dish for Carrie's Chopped Turkey Barbecue (see page 104). A more traditional version of North Carolina coleslaw follows.

Traditional North Carolina Coleslaw

1 Toss together cabbage, onion, and carrot if using.

2 Combine remaining ingredients in a medium bowl and then toss with cabbage mixture.

3 Refrigerate several hours to allow flavors to meld.

Serves 6.

In North Carolina, coleslaw and barbecue pork are inseparable. This version is a good option for gatherings held on warm summer days when you don't want to worry about refrigeration issues with mayonnaise based coleslaw.

A staple in the state is red slaw. It's served not only with barbecue dishes but is also great with other foods. It's wonderful on burgers and hot dogs. A fast and easy version of red slaw is use about 1 1/2 cups of barbecue sauce (such as the Lexington Style Dip on page 17) and mix it with a small head of finely shredded cabbage. Refrigerate overnight for the flavors to blend.

INGREDIENTS

1 head green cabbage, cored and finely shredded

1 large sweet onion, coarsely grated or very thinly sliced

1 coarsely shredded carrot (optional)

1/8 cup apple cider vinegar

1/4 cup distilled white vinegar

1/4 cup extra-virgin olive oil

1/4 cup granulated sugar

1 teaspoon salt

2 teaspoons dry mustard

1–1 1/2 teaspoons celery seed

Tony Geary's Aunt's Stew

INGREDIENTS

3–4 pounds stew meat

2 1/2 cups chopped celery

7 cups chopped carrots

2 medium onions, chopped

7–8 potatoes, peeled and cubed

1 package Lipton Dry Onion Soup mix

4 tablespoons dry tapioca pearls

1/2 teaspoon salt

1/2 teaspoon pepper

1 can (28 ounces) stewed tomatoes

1 tablespoon Worcestershire sauce

1/4 tablespoon sugar

2 tablespoons dried parsley

6 beef bouillon cubes

1 Preheat oven to 375 degrees.

2 In a large pot, brown stew meat in hot oil until seared on all sides.

3 Transfer to large baking pan. Add celery, carrots, onions, and potatoes. Mix. Sprinkle with dry soup mix, tapioca, salt, and pepper.

4 Pour stewed tomatoes over top. Add Worcestershire sauce, sugar, parsley, and bouillon cubes or granules.

5 Mix well and bake 3–5 hours, stirring 2–3 times an hour. Add a little water if necessary.

Serves approximately 20–24.

Well over a decade ago, I attended a cooking class at a local school. There, a charming woman with dark hair spoke of family mealtimes and family-sized meals. The last recipe she presented to the class was for a hearty stew. Shortly thereafter she replied to a question from one of the attendees about her roots. She told a little about herself, mentioning her northern Utah hometown of Tremonton and that she was Tony Geary's aunt. That got a gasp and a smile from some of the women in the audience. Tony, also a Utah native, plays Luke Spencer on the daytime soap opera General Hospital, *a role he's filled for more than twenty-five years (1978–1984 and 1993–present). I jotted the fact down next to the stew recipe. The stew subsequently became known to my family and friends as Tony Geary's Aunt's Stew.*

Tony Geary's aunt, wherever you are, I regret I never got the chance to thank you for your wonderful and informational cooking class and your savory stew recipe, which has become a favorite in my family for large gatherings.

Sharee's Jell-O Salad Delight

Created by Sharee Wanner

INGREDIENTS

2 cartons (16 ounces each) cottage cheese

2 packages (6 ounces each) orange Jell-O

2 large cartons non-dairy whipped topping, thawed

1 can (15 ounces) mandarin oranges, drained

1 In a large bowl, mix together the cottage cheese and gelatin. Stir until the gelatin is dissolved.

2 Fold in the whipped topping and then add the mandarin oranges.

3 Refrigerate at least 2 hours before serving.

You can change the flavor of the gelatin and add different fruits—lime with pineapple, strawberry with fresh strawberries, and so on.

Serves 25–30.

Jell-O salads, Funeral Potatoes (a cheesy potato casserole named because of its frequent appearance at funeral luncheons), and homemade bread made from wheat ground at home are common in Utah at community and religious gatherings. Recipes are passed down from generation to generation with revisions and additions to reflect the time and setting.

When the Winter Olympics were held in Salt Lake City, Utah, in 2002, one of the most sought-after collectible pins for sale depicted a bowl of green Jell-O. Boxes of the powdered gelatin are easy to store and extremely versatile, which is likely why recipes for Jell-O salads and molds were abundant in Utah in the 1950s and '60s. Today, Utahans do not consume the most Jell-O per capita (that honor belongs to Iowa), but nearly everyone has stories of Grandma's favorite green Jell-O with shredded carrots or Aunt Beth's recipe for orange Jell-O with mandarin oranges and cottage cheese. Here, Sharee Warner of Brigham City, Utah, shares a family favorite.

Vermont Cheddar Cheese Soup

From the recipe files of the kitchen at Rabbit Hill Inn, Lower Waterford, Vermont

1 Melt butter in a soup pot. When hot, add onions, celery, carrots, and garlic. Sauté for 5 minutes over medium heat. Sprinkle flour on top and stir constantly for another 5 minutes.

2 Add chicken stock, one cup at a time. Whip to incorporate each time. Bring to a boil, then reduce heat and simmer for 45 minutes.

3 Strain soup through a mesh strainer into another soup pot, pushing through as much liquid and vegetable as possible.

4 Place soup on a very low heat and add cheese, mustard, cream, sundried tomatoes, Worcestershire sauce, salt, and pepper and other optional ingredients. Do not return the soup to a boil.

Serves 10.

INGREDIENTS

Soup

6 tablespoons unsalted butter

1 cup diced onion

3/4 cup diced celery

1/2 cup diced carrots

2 teaspoons minced garlic

4 tablespoons flour

4 cups chicken stock

Add-Ins

1 pound grated cheddar cheese

1 teaspoon dry mustard

1 cup heavy cream

1 cup chopped sundried tomatoes

1 teaspoon Worcestershire sauce

Salt and pepper to taste

Cooked bacon, pancetta, or smoked chicken to taste (optional)

Vermont is home to all things maple: maple syrup, maple butter, maple taffy. As America's leading producer of maple syrup, this small-sized state produces more than 900,000 gallons of maple syrup each year. But maple isn't the only treat you'll find in Vermont. The state boasts a wonderful apple crop, lots of vegetable crops, and a thriving dairy industry.

Full of flavor, this cheddar cheese soup recipe is destined to become a family favorite.

Brunswick Stew

Adapted from Tested Recipes, circa 1927

INGREDIENTS

1 whole chicken, or 3 1/2 pounds chicken parts

1–2 teaspoons salt

2 cups canned butter (lima) beans, drained

1 large onion, chopped

2 cups chopped new potatoes

3 cups crushed tomatoes

2 cups whole kernel corn, fresh or canned, drained if canned

Salt and pepper to taste

1 cup sliced okra (optional)

Poultry seasoning to taste (optional)

1 Place chicken in a large pot on the stove. Sprinkle with 1–2 teaspoons salt and cover with water. Bring to a boil, cover, and reduce heat. Simmer until chicken is cooked through and falling off the bones. Remove chicken to a large bowl to cool slightly.

2 Pour broth through a mesh sieve, reserving liquid. When chicken is cool enough to handle, remove skin and bones and discard. Chop or shred chicken and refrigerate until called for.

3 Skim off any fat that has risen to the top of the broth. Pour broth into a large Dutch oven and bring to a simmer. Let broth simmer until liquid has reduced to about 2 cups (more broth than this will make the stew too thin).

4 Add lima beans, onions, potatoes, and tomatoes. Simmer 10–15 minutes, until potatoes are tender. Stir in corn and reserved chicken meat. Season with salt and pepper to taste and, if using, add okra and poultry seasoning as desired.

5 Simmer another 15 minutes to meld flavors.

Serves 8–10.

Southern favorite, Brunswick Stew—a thick vegetable soup loaded with meat—has dozens of variations and several origin stories. Folks in Brunswick County Virginia claim the stew was invented in 1828 by a state legislator's chef on a hunting expedition. North Carolina, Georgia, and even Germany also lay claim to the recipe's beginnings. What can't be disputed, though, is Lilli Pearl Fearnow's famous recipe for the hearty stew. Mrs. Fearnow began making the stew in her Mechanicsville, Virginia, kitchen in the 1920s. Eventually, she started entering the stew in Virginia's State Fair. It's said that Lillie's famous recipe won forty ribbons in state fairs. It was so popular that she started bottling it and shipping it off to demanding customers. Today, Mrs. Fearnow's Brunswick Stew is produced by Boost Distributing Company and available all throughout the South. This recipe is similar to Mrs. Fearnow's.

Grilled Shrimp and Scallop Salad with Dijon Lemon Vinaigrette

Adapted from a recipe at www.virginiaseafood.org

INGREDIENTS

2/3 cup olive oil

1/3 cup lemon juice

1/4 cup Dijon mustard

2 tablespoons capers (optional)

2 tablespoons chopped fresh dill (or 2 teaspoons dried)

Salt and black pepper to taste

1 1/2–2 pounds extra-large shrimp, peeled and deveined, or sea scallops (or a combination of both)

1 bag (10 ounces) mixed greens

1. In a large mixing bowl whisk together olive oil, lemon juice, mustard, capers, and dill. Season to taste with salt and pepper. Hold in the refrigerator (for up to two weeks) until ready to use.
2. Place 1 1/4 cups of the marinade in a large zipper-top bag. Add shrimp and/or scallops and seal. Marinate 30 minutes.
3. Thread marinated shrimp and/or scallops on skewers and grill over hot coals for 1 minute on each side, until scallops and shrimp are just opaque. (If using wooden skewers, soak skewers in water for an hour before grilling.)
4. Toss 1/4 cup remaining vinaigrette marinade with mixed greens and top with grilled shrimp and/or scallops.

Serves 4.

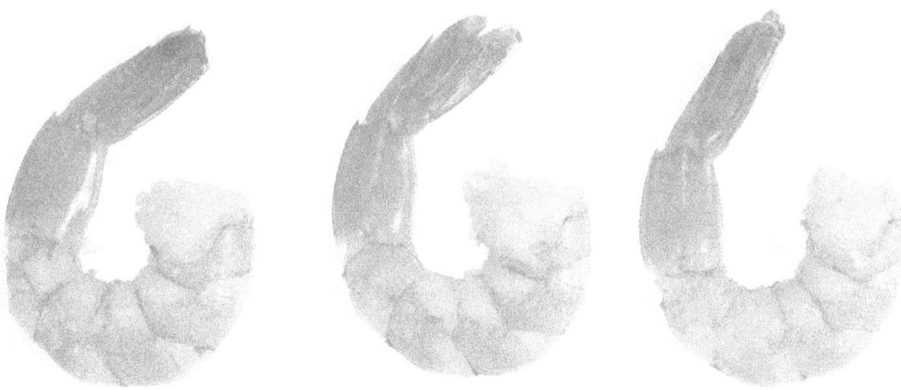

Hood River Salad

Courtesy David H. Dean, Washington State Creamery, Pullman, Washington

INGREDIENTS

1/4 cup olive oil

6 tablespoons ketchup

6 tablespoons red wine vinegar

2 tablespoons soy sauce

1/2 teaspoon sugar

1 package bacon, sliced cross-wise, fried crispy, and set aside to cool

1 cup hazelnuts, toasted and set aside to cool

1 package grape tomatoes, cut in half

2 avocados, chopped

1 large head Romaine lettuce, washed, dried, and torn into bite-sized pieces

1 cup Cougar Gold® cheese, grated

1 In a large bowl, whisk together oil, ketchup, red wine vinegar, soy sauce, and sugar. Add remaining ingredients and toss to combine. Serve immediately.

Serves 6–8.

Tip: Cougar Gold is an aged white sharp cheddar with a creamy, somewhat nutty, flavor. The distinctive flavor of the cheese is indeed best for this recipe; however, if it's not carried in your area, you can order it from the Internet; or substitute another white, sharp cheddar, such as Swiss or Gouda.

The creamery at Washington State University is a state treasure. In the 1930s researchers at Washington State and employees of the creamery began experimenting with methods of storing cheese. The results were so successful, and tasty, that a new cheese was born—Cougar Gold! The canned cheese is still in production today and sold all over the globe.

Apple Blue Cheese Slaw

Courtesy Molly Simpson, Washington Apple Commission

INGREDIENTS

2 Red Delicious apples (about 6 ounces each), cored and thinly cut or julienned

1/4 cup thinly sliced red onion

1/4 cup dairy sour cream

1/4 cup mayonnaise

3 tablespoons chopped parsley

1 ounce crumbled blue cheese

1 tablespoon lemon juice

1/4 teaspoon sugar

Salt and pepper to taste

1 Combine all ingredients; mix well. For optimum flavor, refrigerate 6 hours or overnight.

Serves 6–8.

Washington is known for its fresh catch of salmon, and the sweet Walla Walla onions that grow in the town named for them. Apples are plentiful in many states across the nation, but none so much as Washington. Nearly two-thirds of the nation's apples come from Washington state.

WEST VIRGINIA

Grandpa Hill's Favorite Fruit Salad

INGREDIENTS

1 cup coconut

1 cup mandarin oranges, well drained

1 cup mini marshmallows

1 cup sour cream

1 cup crushed pineapple, well drained

1 Combine and refrigerate overnight.

Serves 6.

Pioneer Soup

Created by Virginia Hill

INGREDIENTS

1 1/2 pounds ground beef

1 large onion, chopped

1 quart water

1 quart whole tomatoes

2–3 large potatoes, diced

5 large carrots, diced

1/2 head cabbage, chopped

3 beef bouillon cubes

1 tablespoon butter

1 tablespoon sugar

1 1/2 teaspoons salt

1/2 teaspoon pepper

2 zucchini, diced

1 Brown ground beef with onion in a large skillet over medium-high heat.

2 Transfer beef and onion mixture to a large soup pot. Add water, tomatoes, potatoes, carrots, cabbage, bouillon, butter, sugar, salt and pepper.

3 Cook 3 hours on medium heat, stirring occasionally. Add zucchini during last hour of cooking.

Serves approximately 8.

Broccoli and Cranberry Salad

Courtesy Mindy Hart

INGREDIENTS

5 cups broccoli florets, cut into 1/2-inch pieces

1/2 cup chopped green onions

1 cup shredded sharp cheddar cheese

1 cup sunflower seeds

1 cup dried cranberries

1 cup cooked and crumbled bacon pieces (optional)

1 cup low-fat mayonnaise

1/2 cup granulated sugar

2 tablespoons red wine vinegar

1/2 teaspoon salt

1/4 teaspoon pepper

1 Combine broccoli, green onions, cheese, sunflower seeds, cranberries, and bacon in a large bowl and mix well.

2 Process in a blender (or use a whisk and a bowl) the mayonnaise, sugar, vinegar, salt, and pepper until thoroughly mixed.

3 Pour dressing over salad mix and mix well. Refrigerate at least 1 hour before serving.

Serves approximately 20.

Potatoes and tomatoes, sausages and cheese, bratwurst, fresh-water fish, strudel, maple syrup, diverse ethnic foods, a rainbow of fresh produce, a bevy of beautiful berries. America's Dairy Land offers up much more than just milk! Whether it's in a local cafe with small-town comfort food, at a church supper, or at a community gathering rich with cultural diversity, Wisconsinites love food! The state's number-one fruit crop is the nutrient-rich cranberry, featured here in a healthy broccoli salad.

SNACKS, *Treats,* & DESSERTS

Alaska Blueberry and Peach Crisp

INGREDIENTS

4 cups fresh blueberries, washed

2–3 cups fresh peaches, diced

4 tablespoons butter, melted and still hot

3 teaspoons sugar, or more to taste

2 cups rolled oats

6 tablespoons flour

1 cup brown sugar, packed

4 tablespoons butter, melted

1 cup pecans, chopped (optional)

1 Preheat oven to 350 degrees.

2 Add fruits to a 9 x 13-inch baking dish. Pour hot butter over top of fruits and toss to coat. Sprinkle sugar over fruits.

3 Mix together oats, flour, brown sugar, and remaining butter until mixture resembles coarse crumbs. Fold in optional pecans.

4 Distribute the oatmeal mixture evenly over the fruit. Bake for 40–45 minutes, or until golden brown and bubbly.

5 Serve with vanilla, blueberry, or peach ice cream. If desired, garnish with fresh peach slices and/or fresh blueberries.

Serves 12–16.

Berry picking is popular in Alaska—among both bears and residents of the state—and there are several varieties to choose from including cranberries, crowberries, salmonberries, raspberries, and blueberries. Even if you don't have access to Alaska berries, find them in season in your area and enjoy them for breakfast or desert along with other fruits in a cobbler or crisp.

Mor's Sur Flode Kager (Mother's Sour Cream Cookies)

Adapted from a recipe created by Lyla G. Solum, from For Danish Appetites

1 Preheat oven to 350 degrees.

2 Cream together sugar, butter, eggs, sour cream, and vanilla.

3 In a separate bowl, sift together flour and baking powder. Gradually add to first mixture to form a soft dough that is easy to roll out to a 1/4-inch thickness.

4 Cut dough into circles. If desired top cookies with a teaspoonful or two of Danish Raisin Filling; top with another circle of dough and press edges gently together to seal.

5 Bake 12–15 minutes or until lightly browned.

Makes approximately 7 dozen single cookies, 3 1/2 dozen filled cookies.

Danish Raisin Filling

1 Boil sugar, water, chopped raisins, and vanilla in a medium pan stirring frequently until thickened.

INGREDIENTS

Dough

2 cups sugar

1 cup butter, soft

2 eggs, beaten

1 cup thick sour cream

1 teaspoon vanilla

4–4 1/2 cups flour

1 teaspoon baking soda

1 recipe Danish Raisin Filling

Danish Raisin Filling

2 cups sugar

1 1/2 cups water

2 cups seedless raisins, chopped

1/2 teaspoon vanilla

Italian Rice Pie Dessert

Giuseppe Asaro, passed down to her granddaughter Diega Greene, Courtesy Sharon Cote Merritt

INGREDIENTS

3/4 cup uncooked jasmine rice

1 1/2 pounds (2 2/3 cups) ricotta cheese

6 eggs, beaten

1 cup heavy cream

1 cup granulated sugar

1 tablespoon vanilla

Cinnamon to taste

Toasted bread crumbs (optional)

Whipped cream, for topping

1 Preheat oven to 325 degrees.

2 Cook rice and drain. When cool, mix in cheese, eggs, cream, sugar, vanilla, and cinnamon to taste with a wooden spoon.

3 Pour into an 8 x 8-inch glass baking dish. Bake 45 minutes. Refrigerate.

4 When completely cooled, sprinkle with cinnamon and cut into small squares (approximately 1 x 1 inch). If desired, garnish with toasted bread crumbs and whipped cream.

Serves 4–6.

Giuseppe Fiella was born in Sicily. She came to the United States alone by ship in 1915 when she was a young woman; she spoke no English. After arriving at Ellis Island, she lived in New York briefly then traveled to Torrington, Connecticut, where she knew a family that sponsored her. At a local dance hall, she met her husband, Antonio Asaro, who was also a Sicilian immigrant. Food was scarce, but Antonio devised his own methods of obtaining it. He was known to carefully watch squirrels as they cached away their winter supply of nuts; he would then take their larder for his own. He was also proficient at hunting rabbits. Together he and Giuseppe cultivated a half acre of land with over fifty fruit trees. The couple took great care to store precious root vegetables and wines in the sand in their basement. Antonio's family remembers him saying, "If people only knew what was in the woods, they would never go hungry."

Giuseppe's family often looks to her and Antonio's legacy of hard work and determination. Her descendant's enjoy her special holiday desert, usually served at Easter or Christmas, and regard it as traditional Connecticut fare. The custard-based dish is as delicious as it is simple.

Orange Cake

INGREDIENTS

Cake

1/2 cup butter, softened

1 cup sugar

2 eggs

2 cups cake flour

3 teaspoons baking powder

1/2 teaspoon salt

2/3 cup buttermilk

1 teaspoon orange zest

1/4 teaspoon orange extract

1 teaspoon vanilla extract

Orange Frosting

1 package (8 ounces) cream cheese, softened

2 tablespoons orange juice

2 tablespoons butter, softened

1 tablespoon candied orange peel and/or orange zest

4 cups powdered sugar

1. Preheat oven to 350 degrees. Prepare two 8-inch round layer pans.
2. Cream butter and sugar. Blend in eggs one at a time.
3. Sift together flour, baking powder, and salt. Add alternately with buttermilk to sugar mixture.
4. Mix in orange zest, orange extract, and vanilla. Beat for 3–4 minutes on medium speed until well blended.
5. Pour into pans. Bake for 25–30 minutes or until centers are firm. Cool before removing from pans.
6. Place first layer on cake plate or serving platter. Frost top with Orange Frosting and add second layer. Frost top and sides of entire cake with remaining frosting.

Orange Frosting

1. Cream together the first five ingredients.
2. Gradually beat in the powdered sugar until frosting is smooth.

Serves 12–16.

Fun with Florida Orange Juice

When most people hear "orange juice" they think of Florida—and rightly so! The state's bumper orange crop is used for world-famous juice; Florida also produces the most citrus fruits in America. Orange juice can be used in baking (substituted for water) for wonderful flavor in cakes and cookies. Splash fresh-squeezed orange juice on salads, or juice-it-up with these cool orange treats on hot summer days:

- *Spritz a glass of orange juice with fresh lime juice; add mint leaves.*
- *Add 1 part Sprite or other lemon-lime soda to 2 parts orange juice.*
- *Pulse orange juice with ice cubes in the blender for a frosty cooler.*
- *Add a scoop of vanilla ice cream to orange juice for an orange float; garnish with orange slices.*
- *Add a banana and equal parts mango juice and orange juice for a tropical twister; pulse until smooth.*
- *Pulse 1 part frozen orange juice concentrate to 5 parts milk for a smooth, frozen treat.*
- *Combine 1 cup vanilla yogurt with 1/2 cup frozen orange juice concentrate and 1/4 cup milk; pour into popsicle molds for homemade creamsicles.*
- *Stir in 1 part orange soda to 1 part orange juice; add a scoop of orange sherbet.*

Grilled Bacon, Bananas, and Oranges

INGREDIENTS

1/2 cup firmly packed brown sugar

1/2 teaspoon cinnamon

4 bananas, peeled

Lemon juice

4 strips bacon

3 oranges, peeled and halved

1 Stir together sugar and cinnamon. Roll bananas in lemon juice and then in sugar mixture. Spiral bacon strips around bananas; secure with toothpicks.

2 Place on rimmed foil-lined grill over medium-high heat. Place oranges next to bananas and sprinkle with remaining sugar.

3 Grill until bacon is fully cooked.

Easy Key Lime Pie

INGREDIENTS

4 large egg yolks

2 teaspoons grated lime zest

1/2 cup fresh lime juice

1 can (14 ounces) sweetened condensed milk

1 9-inch prepared graham cracker pie crust

1 Preheat oven to 350 degrees.

2 In a medium mixing bowl, beat eggs and zest until fluffy. Gradually add the condensed milk and beat until smooth and thick.

3 Fold in lime juice just until combined. Pour into crust. Bake 15 minutes.

4 Cool to room temperature and then refrigerate until thoroughly chilled. Garnish with sweet whipped cream, lime slices, and lime zest.

Serves 6–8.

Florida is well-known for its Key limes. The small version of the fruit has a distinct, tart flavor. This creamy, easy pie is a must have at Florida gatherings.

Dickey Farms' Sugar 'n' Spice Grilled Peaches

INGREDIENTS

2 teaspoons lemon juice

4 tablespoons butter, melted

4 tablespoons brown sugar

1/4 teaspoon salt

1 teaspoon cinnamon

1/4 teaspoon ginger

1/8 teaspoon nutmeg

4 peach halves, pits removed

1 Stir the lemon juice into the melted butter.

2 In a separate bowl, combine the brown sugar, salt, cinnamon, ginger, and nutmeg.

3 Brush all surfaces of the peach halves with half of the lemon-butter mixture.

4 Place the peaches cut side down on a grill over hot heat.

5 Grill for 3–4 minutes or until the peaches begin to brown; turn cut side up.

6 Brush tops with remaining lemon-butter. Sprinkle with brown sugar mixture; cover the grill.

7 Grill an additional 2–4 minutes, or until the peaches are soft and lightly browned.

Serves 4.

Georgia Sweet Potato Pie

Adapted from The Pocket Cookbook by Elizabeth Woody

INGREDIENTS

1 1/2 cups cooked sweet potatoes, mashed well

1/2 cup firmly packed brown sugar

1 teaspoon vanilla

1 teaspoon cinnamon

1/2 teaspoon salt

3 eggs, separated

3/4 cup evaporated milk

2 tablespoons butter, melted

1/2 cup chopped walnuts

9-inch unbaked pie shell

9 tablespoons brown sugar

1 Preheat oven to 425 degrees.

2 To a large bowl, add sweet potatoes and stir in brown sugar, vanilla, cinnamon, and salt. Beat egg yolks well and stir into sweet potato mixture. Add milk, butter, and walnuts, and mix well. Pour into pastry shell. Bake for 10 minutes.

3 Reduce heat to 350 degree and continue baking for 30 additional minutes.

4 Meanwhile, beat egg whites stiff, but not dry. Gradually add remaining sugar, beating constantly. Swirl onto pie.

5 Reduce oven temperature to 325 degrees and bake 20 minutes more.

Serves 6–8.

Georgia Pecan Popcorn with Rosemary and Thyme

Courtesy the Georgia Pecan Commission

INGREDIENTS

2 tablespoons extra-virgin olive oil

1 1/2 tablespoons minced fresh rosemary

1 tablespoon minced fresh thyme

1/4 teaspoon crushed red pepper (optional)

1 1/2 cups Georgia pecan halves

1 tablespoon vegetable oil

1/3 cup popcorn kernels

Salt and pepper to taste

1. Preheat the oven to 350 degrees.
2. Combine the olive oil, rosemary, thyme, and crushed red pepper, if using, in a heavy small skillet over medium-low heat. Cook until the mixture is fragrant, about 5 minutes.
3. Remove from the heat. Place the pecans in a small baking pan and roast until toasted, about 7 minutes. Set aside.
4. Combine the cooking oil and 3 popcorn kernels in a heavy 4-quart saucepan or large pot. Cover and cook over medium heat until 2 or 3 kernels pop, about 5 minutes.
5. Add the remaining corn kernels. Cover and cook until the popping stops, shaking the pan frequently, about 5 minutes. Remove the pan from the heat. Add the pecans and olive oil mixture and stir until the popcorn and pecans are well coated. Season to taste with salt and pepper.

Makes eight 1-cup servings.

Georgia is the leading pecan producer in the United States, averaging 88 million pounds per year. Enough, says the Georgia Pecan Commission, to make 176 million pecan pies! A recent USDA study found that pecans contain even more antioxidants than almonds and walnuts, earning pecans the title of "antioxiNUT." Pecans also contain phytochemicals, which are protective against certain cancers, and they provide essential nutrients such as oleic acid.

This savory herbed pecan popcorn is well worth the extra minutes of preparation. A sure-to-please snack for family movie time or anytime, it's a unique and healthy treat.

Idaho Honey Peach Ice Cream

Adapted by Skylar Jett from a recipe by Dorie Greenspan, used by permission of Skylar Jett, Idaho Preferred

INGREDIENTS

4 ripe Idaho peaches

1/4 cup Idaho honey

1 1/2 tablespoons lemon juice

2 cups half and half or light cream

3 large egg yolks

1/2 cup White Satin sugar

2 teaspoons vanilla

1 Wash, peel, and pit 2 of the peaches; chop into small chunks and toss into a small saucepan. Add the honey and lemon juice and bring to a boil. Lower heat, cover, and cook, stirring occasionally, until the peaches are soft but not mushy—about 10 minutes. Puree the mixture using a food processor or blender. Set mixture aside.

2 In a medium, heavy-bottomed saucepan, bring the half and half or cream to a boil.

3 Meanwhile, in a medium bowl, whisk together the yolks and sugar. Still whisking, drizzle in about one third of the hot cream. Continue to whisk while slowly pouring in the remaining hot cream.

4 Pour the custard back into the pan and cook over medium heat, stirring without stopping, until the custard thickens slightly and coats the back of a spoon. The custard should reach at least 170 degrees, but no more than 180 degrees, on an instant-read thermometer. Immediately remove the pan from the heat, and pour the custard into a 2-quart glass measuring cup or clean heatproof bowl. Stir in the vanilla and peach puree.

5 Refrigerate the mixture until chilled before churning it into ice cream.

6 Add chilled mixture to ice cream maker and churn according to manufacturer's directions. Dice up the remaining two peaches and add to mixture just before the ice cream is thickened and ready; churn to blend. Pack the ice cream into a container and freeze for at least 2 hours, until it is firm enough to scoop.

Makes 1 quart.

Maytag Blue Cheese Cookies

Courtesy Lindsay Petermeir

INGREDIENTS

1 cup butter, softened

1/2 cup granulated sugar

1 1/2 cups pecans, chopped

1 cup dried cranberries, chopped

12 ounces Maytag Blue Cheese crumbles

2 1/2 cups flour

1 cup cornstarch

1/2 teaspoon salt

1/2 cup clear raw sugar

1. Mix all ingredients in a food processor or by hand until fully blended.
2. Roll onto wax paper in the form of a log. Refrigerate for 1 hour.
3. Slice thin and sprinkle with raw sugar. Bake for 15 minutes at 350 degrees.

Makes about 4 dozen.

Homemade Peanut and Molasses Popcorn

INGREDIENTS

24 cups popped popcorn

2 cups (4 sticks) butter

1 cup sweetened condensed milk

2 cups brown sugar

6 tablespoons light molasses

1/2 teaspoon salt

2 teaspoons vanilla

1 teaspoon baking soda

2 cups lightly salted peanuts

1. Preheat oven to 250 degrees. Line 2 rimmed baking sheets with parchment paper.
2. Pop the popcorn and place in 2 large metal bowls that have been lightly buttered.
3. Melt butter over low heat in a medium saucepan. Stir in condensed milk, brown sugar, molasses, and salt. When sugar melts, increase heat to medium-high. Stirring constantly boil no longer than 4 minutes until mixture begins to bubble and thicken, or until mixture reaches 250 degrees on a candy thermometer.
4. Remove from heat. Stir in vanilla and baking soda. Immediately transfer the caramel to the bowls of popcorn and stir with a rubber spatulas to coat well. Fold in peanuts.
5. Spread popcorn on baking sheets. Bake for 30–45 minutes to desired dryness, stirring every 10–15 minutes.

Makes about 26 cups.

The Illinois state snack food is popcorn, which seems appropriate since, in 1893, a mix of popcorn, molasses, and peanuts was sold at the first Chicago World's Fair. The popular treat became what is today known as Cracker Jack.

Oatmeal Cake

1. Preheat oven to 350 degrees.
2. Mix oatmeal and water. Let cool for 15–20 minutes.
3. In a large bowl, cream together butter and sugars. Beat in eggs and vanilla. Blend in the oatmeal mixture.
4. In a separate bowl, sift together the flour, cinnamon, cloves, nutmeg, soda, and salt. Gradually stir the dry ingredients into the oatmeal mixture.
5. When combined, pour into a prepared 9 x 13-inch pan. Bake 35–40 minutes. When cooled spread with coconut frosting.

Coconut Frosting

1. Place butter and brown sugar in a small saucepan over medium heat. Stir until butter is melted and sugar dissolves.
2. Mix in milk and bring to a low boil, stirring constantly. Reduce heat and add coconut and nuts.
3. Spread over warm cake.

Serves 12–16.

The Quaker Oats Company is based in Chicago. Different variations of this oatmeal cake recipe have been circulated among my friends and family for years. I often return to it as time-honored favorite for special gatherings.

INGREDIENTS

Cake

1 cup boiling water

1 cup oatmeal

1/2 cup butter

1/2 cup granulated sugar

1 cup brown sugar

2 eggs

1 teaspoon vanilla

1 1/2 cups flour

1 teaspoon cinnamon

1 teaspoon cloves

1/2 teaspoon nutmeg

1 teaspoon soda

1/2 teaspoon salt

Coconut Frosting

4 tablespoons butter

1 cup brown sugar

1/3 cup whole milk, cream, or half and half

2/3 cup coconut

2/3 cup chopped nuts, such as walnuts or pecans

Sugar Cream Pie

Courtesy Jean Anne Bailey, Nick's Kitchen

INGREDIENTS

2 cups heavy cream

1/2 cup all-purpose flour

1/2 cup brown sugar

1/2 cup + 3 tablespoons granulated sugar

1/2 cup whole milk

1 teaspoon vanilla

One 9-inch prepared deep-dish pie crust, unbaked

1 tablespoon unsalted butter

1 teaspoon ground cinnamon

1 Preheat oven to 350 degrees.

2 In a medium bowl, combine heavy cream, flour, brown sugar, granulated sugar, milk, and vanilla.

3 Fit crust into a deep dish 9-inch pie pan and dot with butter. Pour filling into crust. Combine cinnamon and remaining 3 tablespoons sugar and sprinkle on top.

4 Bake pie until set and center is firm to touch, about 1 hour. Cool on a wire rack.

Serves 8–10.

Indiana's state pie, sugar cream pie—also commonly called Hoosier Sugar Cream Pie—is a heavenly traditional dessert said to have its roots in early Amish and Shaker cuisine. As the name implies, sugar and cream are the main ingredients, a throwback to times when fruit was scarce. The pie is sought-after feel-good comfort food.

Jean Anne Bailey, the proprietor of Nick's Kitchen (home of Nick Freienstein's Original Breaded Pork Tenderloin) in Huntington, Indiana, generously shares her family recipe for the pies she bakes almost daily for the restaurant.

Real Hoosier Sugar Cream Pie

Courtesy Gayle Lane

INGREDIENTS

1/4 cup white sugar

1/4 cup brown sugar

2 heaping tablespoons flour

Prepared, unbaked pie crust

1 egg yolk

1–1 1/2 cups milk or cream

1 pinch salt

1 generous tablespoon butter

Cinnamon or nutmeg

1 Preheat oven to 410 degrees.

2 Mix white and brown sugars with flour. Sprinkle flour-sugar mixture over pie crust. Beat egg yolk with milk and salt. Fill pie shell. Take a spoon and swirl it through the milk mixture a couple of times. Dot with butter. Sprinkle with cinnamon or nutmeg.

3 Bake at 410 degrees for 10 minutes. Reduce temperature to 350 degrees and bake an additional 45 minutes. The filling should be bubbling. The center should still jiggle. Be careful not to overcook or the filling will not set.

Serves 6–8.

Indiana blogger Gayle Lane is an avid proponent of her state's official pie. She writes: "According to my grandmother, a good sugar cream pie has two layers. The top should be a light custard. The second layer needs to be rich and even a little syrupy. The result is a totally decadent blend of flavor and texture.

"When my grandparents owned the Wawasee Restaurant during the '40s (which is before I was born), my grandmother's 'old-fashioned cream' pie was the signature dessert. She also served it at family gatherings; as did my mother. When I was a new bride, this was the first recipe I copied into the blank pages of my brand-new cookbook.

"It was and always will be my favorite pie.

"Although sugar cream pie is associated with the Amish, the recipe has been traced back to 1816, the year Indiana became a state and long before the Amish came to this area. Virtually unheard of outside of Indiana, sugar cream pie officially became Indiana's State Pie on January 23, 2009.

"I definitely believe sugar cream pie is more than worthy of the honor.

"But, I think there is an over-abundance of gloppy (where you can really taste the flour) custard pies being passed off as Hoosier Sugar Creams. Basically, they are custard pies—only with a lot of flour substituted for the eggs. They don't do the dessert justice.

"If the recipe sounds a bit artery-clogging, my mother makes her pie with 2% milk instead of cream. It is still wonderful."

Unbelievable Cookies

Courtesy Patricia Wiles

INGREDIENTS

1 cup peanut butter (plain or crunchy)

1 cup sugar

1 egg, unbeaten

1 Preheat oven to 350 degrees.

2 Mix all ingredients together. Drop by teaspoons onto greased cookie sheet.

3 Bake 12–15 minutes. Don't overcook.

Makes 1 dozen cookies.

No-Bake Oatmeal Cookies

Courtesy Patricia Wiles

INGREDIENTS

2 cups sugar

1/4 cup cocoa

1/2 cup milk

1/4 pound butter

1 teaspoon vanilla pinch of salt

1/2 cup peanut butter

3 cups quick-cooking oats

1 In a medium-sized pot, cook sugar, cocoa, milk, and butter until mixture starts to boil. Remove from heat and cool one minute.

2 Add vanilla, salt, peanut butter, and oats. Stir well and drop by spoonfuls onto wax paper.

3 Allow to cool and harden slightly before eating.

Makes approximately 2 dozen cookies.

The Bluebird's Blueberry Lemon Cobbler

Courtesy Janna DeVore, Ballerina Cookbook

INGREDIENTS

Fruit Filling

6 cups fresh or frozen blueberries, thawed and drained

1 tablespoon freshly squeezed lemon juice

1/2 cup sugar

1/2 teaspoon ground cinnamon

1/4 teaspoon ground nutmeg

4 teaspoons cornstarch

Biscuit Topping

1 1/2 cups flour

1/4 cup + 2 teaspoons sugar

1 1/2 teaspoons baking powder

1/2 teaspoon baking soda

1/4 teaspoon salt

1/8 teaspoon ground nutmeg

1 1/2 teaspoons lemon zest

5 tablespoons butter, melted

3/4 cup cold buttermilk

1 teaspoon freshly squeezed lemon juice

1 Preheat oven to 400 degrees.

2 Prepare fruit filling by measuring blueberries into a large bowl. Sprinkle lemon juice over the top and set aside. In a small bowl, whisk together sugar, cinnamon, nutmeg, and cornstarch. Pour dry ingredients over berries and toss gently to coat berries. Transfer berries to a 2-quart casserole or similar baking dish. Set aside while preparing biscuit topping.

3 In a medium bowl, whisk together flour, 1/4 cup of the sugar, baking powder, baking soda, salt, nutmeg, and lemon zest. In a separate small bowl, stir together melted butter and cold buttermilk. Pour liquid mixture into dry ingredients and combine gently, using a rubber spatula.

4 Place spoonfuls of the biscuit dough evenly over top of berries. Brush the tops with lemon juice and sprinkle with remaining 2 teaspoons sugar.

5 Bake 25–30 minutes, until top is golden brown and fruit is bubbly.

6 Cool slightly, then serve warm with whipped cream or vanilla ice cream.

Serves 8–10.

Traditional Smith Island Ten-Layer Cake

Adapted from Mrs. Kitching's Smith Island Cookbook

INGREDIENTS

Cake

2 cups sugar

1 cup unsalted butter, room temperature, cut into chunks

5 large eggs

3 cups flour

1/4 teaspoon salt

1 heaping teaspoon baking powder

1 cup evaporated milk

2 teaspoons vanilla

1/2 cup water

1 recipe Smith Island Frosting

1 Preheat oven to 350 degrees. Lightly grease and flour ten 9-inch round cake pans or reuse 2–3 cake pans, cleaning and regreasing before baking each new layer.

2 In a large bowl, cream together sugar and butter. Add eggs one at a time and beat until smooth. Sift together flour, salt, and baking powder. Mix into the egg mixture one cup at a time.

3 Slowly blend in evaporated milk, vanilla, and water. Mix just until uniform. Put 3 large spoonfuls of batter into each prepared pan (use a serving spoon rather than a soup spoon for this). Use the back of the spoon to spread evenly.

4 Bake three layers at a time on the middle rack of the oven for 8 minutes. A layer is done when you hold it near your ear and you don't hear it sizzle.

5 Let the layers cool slightly in the pans, and then run a spatula around the edge of the pans to ease the layers out. While layers are baking, prepare the frosting.

6 To ice the cake, take one cooled layer and spread with frosting; use 2–3 large spoonfuls of frosting between each cake layer. Repeat for all ten layers. Cover the top and sides of the cake with the remaining frosting. Push the frosting that runs onto the serving plate back onto the cake.

Smith Island Frosting

Smith Island Frosting

1 cup butter

2 cans (12 ounces each) evaporated milk

8 heaping tablespoons unsweetened cocoa

2 pounds powdered sugar

1 Melt butter in a large saucepan; remove from heat. Stir in the evaporated milk.

2 Whisk in cocoa until smooth, return to heat, and cook for approximately 10 minutes, stirring frequently. Take care not to scorch, and do not allow the mixture to come to a boil.

3 Remove from heat and slowly whisk in the powdered sugar.

4 Cook slowly, stirring constantly, until thickened and frosting will stick to back of a spoon or to the whisk (it will form a ribbon when you drizzle a spoonful onto mixture while cooking).

Serves approximately 14–16.

Maryland may be small in area, but it's bursting with people—and flavors. The cities and suburbs just outside of Washington, DC, are teeming with people from all over the world and a huge number of ethnic restaurants dot the streets and corners of cities like Bethesda, Chevy Chase, and Baltimore.

In April of 2008, Smith Island Cake was designated the official dessert of Maryland. Located in the Chesapeake Bay, Smith Island is accessible only by ferry and is home to fewer than five hundred residents. Still, the town has its own unique cuisine. According to the Smith Island web site, "The most famous dish is a locally produced cake featuring eight to fifteen thin layers filled with crème, frosting and/or crushed candy bars. The cake is iced with a cooked chocolate icing. The cake is often made using a commercial cake mix but with unique additions such as condensed milk. It can also be made from scratch using flour. The most common flavor is yellow cake with chocolate icing but other flavors such as coconut, fig, strawberry, lemon, and orange are also common. Known simply as the Smith Island Cake, the dessert is baked for any occasion and not reserved only for holidays."

The recipe shared here is ten layers, and probably requires more than ten laps around the track to work off!

Fudge Brownie Pie

Created by Marie Rayner, The English Kitchen

INGREDIENTS

Brownie

3/4 cup all-purpose flour

1 cup extra-fine sugar

1/4 cup unsweetened cocoa powder, sifted

1 teaspoon baking powder

1/4 teaspoon salt

1/2 cup butter, melted

2 large eggs, beaten

2 teaspoons vanilla

1/2 cup chopped toasted pecans

2 handfuls mini marshmallows

1 recipe Chocolate Frosting

Chocolate Frosting

1/4 cup butter, melted

1/4 cup cocoa powder, sifted

1/4 cup evaporated milk

2 cups powdered sugar, sifted

1 Preheat oven to 350 degrees. Butter a 9-inch tart pan with a removable bottom, such as a flan pan or even a cheesecake pan; set aside.

2 Whisk together the flour, sugar, cocoa powder, baking powder, and salt in a bowl.

3 In a separate bowl, beat together the butter, eggs, and vanilla. Add to the dry ingredients and mix until smooth. Stir in the toasted nuts. Pour into the prepared pan.

4 Bake on the middle rack of the oven 25–30 minutes, or until a toothpick inserted in the center comes out clean.

5 Immediately sprinkle the marshmallows on top and return to the oven for a few minutes to melt the marshmallows. Remove from the oven and carefully spread the chocolate frosting over top. Let cool completely. Remove sides from the pan and cut into wedges to serve.

Makes one 9-inch pie.

Chocolate Frosting

1 Combine all ingredients together in a bowl, beating with an electric whisk until smooth and thick.

Lori's Tip: Toasting pecans adds to their crunchiness and brings out more of their wonderful nutty flavor. For use in baking, toss pecans with a thin coat of melted butter. Line a baking sheet with parchment paper and arrange the pecans in a single layer on the pan. Toast at 325 degrees for 10–15 minutes, turning once halfway through. Since they can scorch quickly, keep close watch. They should turn slightly dark; a subtle "toasted" aroma means they're done. Spread on paper towels to cool.

Aunt Thelma's Orange Carrot Cookies

Courtesy Lorie Roach, www.loriesmississippikitchen.com

INGREDIENTS

3/4 cup shortening

1 cup granulated sugar

1 egg

1 teaspoon vanilla

1 cup cooked, mashed carrots

2 cups all-purpose flour

1 teaspoon baking powder

1/2 teaspoon salt

1 cup chopped walnuts

1 tablespoon orange juice (or a little bit more for desired consistency)

1 cup powdered sugar

The zest of one orange

1 Preheat oven to 375 degrees.

2 Cream the shortening and sugar together on medium speed; add the egg. Mix in vanilla, carrots, flour, baking powder, and salt and beat until combined. Stir in the nuts.

3 Drop by rounded teaspoonfuls onto a lightly greased cookie sheet. Bake 12–15 minutes or until light golden brown on bottoms.

4 Meanwhile, whisk together orange juice, powdered sugar, and orange zest until smooth, adjusting the amount of orange juice to make frosting reach drizzling consistency.

5 When the cookies are done, transfer to a wire rack that has been placed over a baking sheet. Drizzle cookies with the frosting and let cool completely.

Makes about 3 dozen cookies.

Handwritten recipes, passed down through the generations, can be as treasured as the food itself. Blogger Lorie Roach tells the story of her Aunt Thelma's Orange Carrot cookies:

"A few years ago, my mother gave me a recipe that was given to her by my Aunt Thelma, my dad's sister, when I was just a little girl back in the seventies.

"The recipe is handwritten on paper that has yellowed with age, and the ink has bled and [run], probably because of the shortening that has been accidentally smeared on it from the many times it has been used. I can still remember being in my aunt's kitchen the day I first tasted these cookies. She was babysitting my sister and me and we eagerly watched as she made them for us. Her son, Shawn, our cousin, was also there and although I don't remember much, I do remember it being a really fun day.

"This recipe is very special to me, and the actual sheet of paper even more so. I guess it's silly to be sentimental about a piece of paper, but when I look at it, I can still see my aunt writing out the recipe along with a short note to my mother, and it takes me back to a pleasant and carefree place. For just a moment, I am a little girl again, anxiously waiting for cookies to cool, with no concerns of failing economies and financial bail outs. My biggest worry then was how many cookies I would be allowed to eat."

Twirling Toffee Bars

Used with permission of Heather Berry, Rural Missouri, www.ruralmissouri.coop

INGREDIENTS

1/2 cup butter or margarine, melted

1 3/4 cups chocolate Teddy Graham cookies, crushed

1 1/4 cups Werther's Original candies, crushed (about 50)

6 toffee candy bars (1.4 ounces), crushed

1 cup semi-sweet chocolate chips

1 cup pecans, chopped

1/2 cup walnuts, chopped

1 can (14 ounces) sweetened condensed milk

1. Preheat oven to 325 degrees. Line a 9 x 13-inch pan with aluminum foil, allowing foil to extend over ends of pan.
2. Pour melted butter into pan. Sprinkle crushed Teddy Grahams in bottom of pan; press firmly and bake for 5 minutes.
3. Layer crushed Werther's candies, crushed toffee bars, chocolate chips, pecans, and walnuts over crust. Press layers down firmly. Pour condensed milk evenly over the top.
4. Bake an additional 30 minutes or until edges are lightly browned. Cool completely in pan. Lift foil out of pan and cut into bars.

Makes approximately 18 bars.

Potato Chip Cookies

Courtesy Marlene Prichard

INGREDIENTS

1 cup vegetable oil

1 cup butter

1 cup brown sugar

1 cup granulated sugar

1 egg, beaten

1 teaspoon buttermilk

1 teaspoon vanilla

1 teaspoon almond extract

3 1/2 cups all-purpose flour

1 teaspoon cream of tartar

1 teaspoon baking soda

1 teaspoon salt

1 cup sweetened coconut flakes

1 cup quick oats

1 cup crushed potato chips

Granulated sugar

1 Preheat oven to 325 degrees.

2 Cream together oil, butter, and sugars. Add beaten egg, buttermilk, vanilla, and almond extract.

3 Add sifted dry ingredients, then fold in coconut, oats, and chips. Roll into balls and press down with fork dipped in water, then sprinkle with sugar.

4 Bake about 15 minutes on parchment-lined cookie sheet.

Makes 5–6 dozen small cookies.

Biscochitos

INGREDIENTS

1 1/2 cups lard, chilled

1 cup + 3 tablespoons sugar, divided

2 eggs

2 teaspoons anise seeds

4 cups all-purpose flour

2 teaspoons baking powder

1/2 teaspoon salt

About 3 tablespoons brandy, apple juice, or milk

2 teaspoons ground cinnamon

1. Preheat oven to 350 degrees.
2. Beat lard and 1 cup of the sugar in a bowl until fluffy. Add eggs and anise seeds, and beat until very light and fluffy.
3. Sift together flour, baking powder, and salt. Add to creamed mixture along with the brandy. Mix thoroughly to make a stiff dough.
4. Place dough on a long piece—about three feet—of waxed paper at one end. Bring the long end over the top and press to about one inch or slightly less in thickness and refrigerate until chilled.
5. Roll out dough between waxed paper to just under 1/2-inch thickness. Cut with flour dusted cutters into traditional fleur-de-lis shapes or into 3-inch rounds.
6. Combine the 3 remaining tablespoons sugar and the cinnamon in a shallow bowl; dip unbaked cookies into the sugar-cinnamon mixture on one side. Place cookies on ungreased baking sheets.
7. Bake 10–12 minutes or until tops of cookies are just firm. Cool cookies on wire racks.

Makes 4–5 dozen cookies.

New Mexico's state cookie, the biscochito, doesn't get its spicy flavor from red or green chile sauce but from anise seeds and cinnamon. Spanish in origin, these New Mexico favorites are a sweet, unique treat. Traditionally, the cookie is made with lard, but you can substitute butter or vegetable shortening. You may also substitute milk or juice for the brandy. Either substitution will work, but New Mexicans promise the cookies won't taste quite as good or be quite as crispy on the outside and soft on the inside.

Grandma Esther's Applesauce Cake

INGREDIENTS

2 cups sifted all-purpose flour

2 teaspoons baking soda

3/4 teaspoon salt

1 teaspoon cinnamon

1/4 teaspoon nutmeg

1/4 teaspoon ground cloves

1 tablespoon cocoa

1/2 cup vegetable oil

1 cup granulated sugar

1 1/2 cups unsweetened applesauce, heated

1/2 cup raisins (optional)

1/2 cup chopped walnuts (optional)

1 Preheat oven to 350 degrees. Grease and flour a 9 x 13-inch pan.

2 Sift together flour, baking soda, salt, cinnamon, nutmeg, cloves, and cocoa.

3 In a large mixing bowl, combine the oil and sugar. Beat until well blended. Stir in hot applesauce, blending thoroughly.

4 Add in dry ingredients, blend well. Stir in optional raisins and walnuts.

5 Turn batter into prepared pan and bake 30 minutes. Cut into small squares.

Serves approximately 18.

Pennsylvania Dutch Soft Sugar Cookies

Created by Kathryn White, The Beechmont Inn Bed and Breakfast

INGREDIENTS

3 1/2 cups all-purpose flour

1 teaspoon baking soda

1 teaspoon baking powder

1 teaspoon salt

2 cups sugar

1 cup butter

2 eggs

1 tablespoon vanilla

1 cup buttermilk

1. Preheat oven to 375 degrees.
2. Sift together flour, baking soda, baking powder, and salt. Set aside.
3. Cream together sugar and butter. Add eggs one at a time and beat. Add vanilla and beat.
4. Stir flour mixture into sugar mixture alternating with the buttermilk. Stir until smooth.
5. Drop by tablespoonfuls (or use a small ice cream scoop) onto greased cookie sheet (or for best results, use cookie sheet lined with parchment paper).
6. Sprinkle tops with sugar. Bake 8–10 minutes.
7. Remove from cookie sheet and cool on rack. Store in an air-tight container.

Makes 2–3 dozen cookies.

Hanover resident, innkeeper, and 8 Broads in the Kitchen member, Kathryn White loves to bake. She notes that south central Pennsylvania is rich farm country. Locally grown fruits, vegetables, eggs, and breakfast meats from the butcher are integral to her inn's breakfasts. So is the influence of the Pennsylvania Dutch. Kathryn's sugar cookies are second to none!

Pumpkin Spice Bars

Created by Debbie Mosiman, Swiss Woods Inn

1 Preheat oven to 350 degrees. Grease a 15 1/2 x 10 1/2-inch jelly roll pan, or a half sheet pan.

2 In a large bowl with an electric mixer, beat eggs, sugar, oil, and pumpkin together. Stir in flour, baking powder, cinnamon, baking soda, ginger, and cloves. Mix in orange rind and raisins.

3 Pour batter into the prepared pan and bake until light brown and the middle springs back to touch, about 25–30 minutes. Cool completely on a rack. Frost with Cream Cheese Frosting. Keep refrigerated if not using immediately.

Cream Cheese Frosting

1 Mix cream cheese, butter, vanilla, and orange rind together.

2 Gradually add the powdered sugar, mixing until completely smooth.

3 Spread on cooled cake, sprinkle with remaining grated orange rind and refrigerate.

Makes approximately 3–4 dozen bars.

Swiss Woods Inn is tucked away along the back roads of Lancaster County. Debbie Mosiman of 8 Broads in the Kitchen grew up in a Pennsylvania Dutch family with deep roots in the area.

Debbie's pumpkin bar recipe is a hit with her guests and is very easy to make. The bars freeze well if you want to make them in advance and frost before serving. She notes that if you love walnuts you could add some to the recipe or chop them very fine and sprinkle over the top with the orange zest.

INGREDIENTS

Bars

4 eggs

2 cups sugar

1 cup vegetable oil

1 can (16 ounces) pumpkin

2 cups all-purpose flour

2 teaspoons baking powder

2 teaspoons cinnamon

1 teaspoon baking soda

1/2 teaspoon ginger

1/4 teaspoon ground cloves

1 teaspoon grated orange rind

1/2 cup golden raisins

1 recipe Cream Cheese Frosting

Cream Cheese Frosting

1 package (3 ounces) cream cheese, softened

1/3 cup butter, softened

1 1/2 teaspoons vanilla

1 teaspoon grated orange rind (plus some to sprinkle on the top)

2 cups powdered sugar

Chocolate Raspberry Truffle Cake

Created by Hannah Harris

INGREDIENTS

Cake

3 cups sugar

2 2/3 cups all-purpose flour

1 cup Hershey's Cocoa Powder

2 1/4 teaspoon baking powder

1/4 cup Hershey's Special Dark Cocoa Powder

2 1/4 teaspoon baking soda

3 teaspoons espresso powder

1 1/2 teaspoons salt

3 eggs (room temperature)

3/4 cup vegetable oil

1 1/2 cups milk (room temperature)

3 teaspoons pure vanilla

1 cup boiling water

Truffle Filling

2 cups Hershey's Semisweet Chocolate Chips

2 packages (8 ounces each) cream cheese, softened

1/2 cup powdered sugar

2/3 cup seedless red raspberry jam

2 teaspoons Hershey's Cocoa

1 teaspoon vanilla extract

1. Preheat oven to 350 degrees. Grease and flour three 9-inch cake pans.
2. Put all dry ingredients into a large bowl and mix for 20–30 seconds. Beat eggs in a small bowl and then add to the dry ingredients.
3. Next add oil, milk, and then vanilla. Beat on medium speed until well blended. Stir in boiling water until blended. Divide batter evenly between the 3 prepared pans and bake 30–35 minutes. Allow cakes to cool in pans on wire racks for approximately 15 minutes.
4. Take cakes out of pans and cool completely on wire racks.
5. Make Truffle Filling, Chocolate Glaze Filling, and Chocolate Frosting as directed.
6. Assemble the cake by filling the first and second cake layers with truffle filling topped by chocolate glaze filling. Add the third cake layer and frost the entire cake with chocolate frosting.

Truffle Filling

1. Melt chocolate chips in the top of a double boiler. While chocolate is melting, beat cream cheese until fluffy. To cream cheese add powdered sugar and raspberry preserves, beating until fluffy. Beat in melted chocolate, cocoa, and vanilla until well blended.

Chocolate Glaze Filling

1 Melt chocolate chips in top of a double boiler. Stir in heavy cream and cocoa.

Chocolate Frosting

1 Beat butter, sugar, and cocoa together. Stir in vanilla and milk and then beat until smooth.

Serves 14–16.

Chocolate Glaze Filling

1/2 cup Hershey's Semisweet Chocolate Chips

2 tablespoons + 2 teaspoons heavy cream

1 teaspoon Hershey's Cocoa

Chocolate Frosting

1/4 cup butter, softened

About 2 cups confectioner's sugar

1/3 cup Hershey's Special Dark Cocoa Powder

2 tablespoons milk

1 teaspoon pure vanilla

Just east of Harrisburg, Pennsylvania, is Hershey, often called Chocolate Town, USA. Hershey was founded by Milton S. Hershey as the home of his chocolate company and his employees. Today, people all over the world enjoy a taste of Pennsylvania whenever they taste some Hershey's chocolate.

This moist, luscious cake made with Hershey's chocolate garnered Pennsylvania resident Hannah Harris second place in the Oley Valley Community Fair Association contest. A chocolate lover's delight, this is one of the best chocolate cake recipes I've ever found—thank you, Hannah!

Shoo-Fly Pie

Linda DeVore, Lehighton Pennsylvania

INGREDIENTS

1 1/2 cups flour

1/2 cup brown sugar

1/2 teaspoon cinnamon

1/8 teaspoon ground cloves

1/8 teaspoon ground ginger

1/8 teaspoon ground nutmeg

1 teaspoon salt

1/4 cup vegetable shortening

One 9-inch unbaked pie shell

3/4 cup molasses

3/4 cup boiling water

3/4 teaspoon baking soda

1 Preheat oven to 450 degrees.

2 In a small bowl, mix flour, sugar, cinnamon, cloves, salt, and shortening together with a fork until crumbs form.

3 Pour crumbs into the bottom of the unbaked pie shell. In a separate bowl stir together molasses, boiling water, and baking soda. Pour hot liquid over crumbs.

4 Bake 10 minutes. Reduce oven temperature to 350 degrees and bake an additional 20 minutes.

Serves 6–8.

Among the many Pennsylvania Dutch recipes famous in the state is the cleverly named shoo-fly pie, a fluffy molasses-based dessert that is said to get its name because its sticky sweetness attracted flies as it cooled, thus necessitating that a watchful baker stay nearby to shoo away the flies.

Depending on the baker's preference the pie can have a wet or a dry bottom. The difference is in where the crumb "topping" is placed. If placed directly on the crust, before pouring in the molasses base, it becomes a dry bottom pie. When the crumbs are spread on top of the molasses base, it is considered a wet bottom. Everyone seems to have his or her preference. Linda DeVore, a transplant to Pennsylvania, has been making the dry bottom version for almost forty years for her Pennsylvania-born husband. Her mother-in-law passed it down with special directions for how to get it just right. The recipe is shared here.

Quick Coffee Cake

Created by Minnie Jensen

INGREDIENTS

3 cups all-purpose flour

1 cup sugar

2 teaspoons baking powder

1 teaspoon salt

1/3 cup shortening

2 eggs

1 1/2 cups milk

Brown sugar for sprinkling

8 pats of butter

1. Preheat oven to 375 degrees.
2. Sift together flour, sugar, baking powder, and salt. Cut in shortening until mixture is crumbly.
3. Beat eggs; add milk. Add this to flour mixture. Mix only until flour is moistened, then pour into well-greased pan.
4. Sprinkle with brown sugar and dot with pats of butter.
5. Bake in a 9-inch square baking dish for approximately 30 minutes or until a toothpick inserted in center comes out with just a few moist crumbs.

Serves 9.

Rhode Island coffee milk is simply milk with coffee syrup stirred in (about 2 tablespoons coffee syrup for every 8 ounces milk). Some Rhode Islanders like to go a step further and make Coffee Cabinet, a version of the drink with ice cream mixed in. (It's called a cabinet because the drink's originator kept his blender in his cabinet and pulled it out when he wanted to mix in ice cream.) Coffee Milk is so popular it's sold in nearly every Rhode Island grocery store and is also available in school cafeterias. If you're feeling adventurous, whip some up and try it—instead of a hot coffee—with this quick and easy coffee cake.

Cream-Filled Peach Brownie Cake

Adapted from Patty Bloomer, South Carolina Peach Festival

INGREDIENTS

Brownie Layer

1 box brownie mix

1/2 cup vegetable oil

1/4 cup water

3 eggs

Cake Layer

1 box vanilla cake mix

1 cup finely chopped peaches

1 teaspoon cinnamon

Dash nutmeg

3/4 cup water

1/3 cup vegetable oil

3 eggs

Filling

1 package (8 ounces) cream cheese, softened

1/4 cup butter

3 cups powdered sugar

3/4 cup heavy cream

3 cups sliced peaches, plus more for garnishing

1 Preheat oven 350 degrees. Grease 2 round cake pans.

Brownie Layer

1 In a large bowl, with a wooden spoon, stir together brownie mix, vegetable oil, water, and eggs.

2 Spoon 1 cup brownie batter into each prepared pan and smooth out with a rubber spatula.

Cake Layer

1 In a separate large bowl, beat together all cake layer ingredients with an electric mixer.

2 Pour and spread about 1 1/3 cup of mixture evenly over brownie batter in each pan.

3 Bake 20–30 minutes. Cool 10 minutes then invert cakes onto cooling racks.

Filling

1 To prepare filling, in a medium bowl beat cream cheese and butter until smooth, about 3 minutes.

2 Mix in 3 cups powdered sugar. In a separate bowl, whip 3/4 cup cream until soft peaks form.

3 Fold whipped cream into cream cheese mixture.

Frosting

1 Beat together cream and powdered sugar with electric mixer until cream is slightly stiff and spreadable.

Assembling the Cake

1 To assemble cake, place one cake layer, brownie side down, on a cake plate or platter. Spread filling over the cake-side of the layer and top with sliced peaches. Add second layer, brownie side down. Frost sides and top of cake with sweetened whipped cream. Garnish with peaches.

2 Refrigerate 1 hour before serving.

Frosting

1 1/2 cups heavy cream

1/3–2/3 cup powdered sugar

Serves 12–14.

Food in South Carolina has a number of fascinating influences. In the Low Country (made up of counties along South Carolina's lower coast), the cuisine features elements of African and Caribbean culture blended with a bit of French and Creole influence. Throughout the state, barbecue is hugely popular. Unlike most southern states, though—which tend to favor one particular barbecue sauce over all others—South Carolina embraces each of the four common sauce varieties: vinegar and pepper based, which was introduced by Scot-Irish settlers; mustard, introduced by German settlers and quite popular in the southeastern corner of the state; light tomato sauces, which add ketchup to the vinegar and pepper-based version; and heavy tomato-based sauces.

Hearty stews, bogs, and gumbos are also prevalent. A bog is a stew that includes rice cooked right along with the rest of the ingredients and not added later, like in a gumbo. Bogs tend to be more soggy than soupy.

Like much of the coastal south, seafood is a big industry in South Carolina. And, like much of the rest of the country, snacking is also big. Boiled peanuts are the official state snack. These raw, in-the-shell peanuts are boiled in brine for a long time and are sold all over the state at major grocery stores and at makeshift roadside stands scattered through the countryside. Also widely available at Carolina roadside stands are South Carolina peaches. South Carolina is among the top four producers of peaches in the country.

The South Carolina recipes included in this book celebrate the sweetness of a Carolina peach, the tang of slow-cooked barbecue, and the soulful feel of Carolina cooking.

Held every July in Gaffney, the South Carolina Peach Festival welcomes thousands of visitors. The festival includes a peach dessert contest and a barbecue event. This recipe is adapted from the prize-winning dessert entry at the 2012 festival.

Fresh Raspberry Shake

INGREDIENTS

1/2 cup whole milk or half and half

3 cups vanilla bean ice cream

1/4 cup raspberry jam

1 cup fresh raspberries

1 Add milk or half and half and 2 cups ice cream to blender; blend until well combined.

2 Add and blend in jam; add and blend in remaining ice cream.

3 Add 3/4 cup raspberries; pulse only a few times to combine. Top with remaining raspberries.

Serves 2.

When my grandfather wasn't designing, building, and racing snow planes, he spent time dry farming on Idaho's Pine Creek Bench and another fertile mountain bench beneath Swan Valley's Baldy Mountain. Dry farming remains an important part of agriculture in the state. My grandparents always raised most of what they ate. Grandma had a garden brimming with peas, carrots, strawberries, and, of course, potatoes! They raised pigs, cattle, and chickens. One of my tasks when staying on my grandparents' farm was gathering eggs. I remember Grandma's wonderful chokecherry juice, jam, and syrup; wild game including venison, elk, and bear (I never summoned the courage to taste the latter!); her famous fried chicken and potato salad, red Jell-O, and the salad she described as her "cabbage slaw."

One of the few store-bought items my grandparents enjoyed was Grandpa's favorite raspberry ripple ice cream. Grandpa and Grandma always kept at least a gallon of it in the freezer, along with a large box of cones at the side of an old desk in the kitchen. After supper, family members and visitors shared in the ritual of having a raspberry ripple ice cream cone: to me it was a sacred custom of bonding and belonging. Raspberry ripple ice cream remains one of the foods I delight in.

Plump, delicious raspberries are grown in many areas of the state, like Bear Lake where the raspberry shakes are world-renown. Sometimes I can't stop thinking about the Bear Lake Raspberry shakes. I have my own recipe to tide me over until I can make an annual summer pilgrimage to the area.

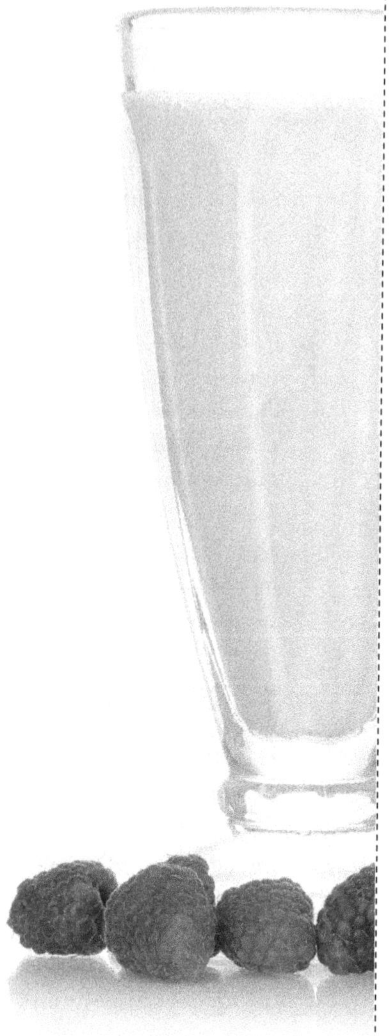

Marguerites

Mrs. F. E. Bradford, Corinne, Utah

INGREDIENTS

2 egg whites

1/2 cup sugar

1/2 cup water

5 marshmallows, cut into small pieces

2 tablespoons sweetened shredded coconut

1/4 teaspoon vanilla

1 cup walnuts, chopped

2–3 dozen soda crackers

1. Preheat oven to 325 degrees.
2. Beat eggs whites in a large, clean bowl until stiff peaks form. Set aside.
3. Boil sugar and water in a small pot over medium-high heat until syrup will thread.
4. Remove pan from heat and add marshmallow pieces; stir until smooth.
5. Pour hot mixture into beaten egg whites. Fold in coconut, vanilla, and nuts.
6. Spread soda crackers with 1–2 tablespoons of mixture and bake until brown, 3–5 minutes.

Makes approximately 2–3 dozen.

Utah native Bernice Gibbs Anderson was a tenacious historian. Among her most important efforts was her campaign to bring notoriety to the site where East and West came together and a golden spike was driven into a laurelwood railroad tie to commemorate the meeting of the Union Pacific and Central Pacific railroads. "This is sacred soil," she wrote to Congress, "dedicated to the sacrifices of thousands who labored in the great race to build the first transcontinental railway . . . . Will it take its rightful place in the heritage and traditions of America, preserved and protected by a grateful government, or will it remain desolate and forgotten to sink into oblivion?"

Bernice's secretary, friend, and staunch supporter in the effort to bring recognition to the historic site, was northern Utah resident Delone Bradford Glover. When I was working as a correspondent for a regional newspaper, I had the pleasure of meeting Delone, now in her late eighties. Recently, she came across a treasured recipe from her childhood that was often prepared by her mother for special gatherings. "I loved when Mother made Marguerites for us," she says with a sparkle in her eyes, "they were my favorite."

The Most Delicious Cake I Ever Ate

Created by Virginia Hill

INGREDIENTS

1 can soda pop (match with the flavor of the cake mix and the Jell-O)

1 package (6 ounces) Jell-O (match with the flavor of the cake mix)

Any flavor cake mix, prepared according to package directions and cooled.

1 package (3 ounces) vanilla instant pudding, prepared according to package directions

1 container non-dairy whipped topping, thawed

1 Bring 1 cup of the soda pop to a simmer in a small saucepan over medium-high heat. Remove from heat. Add Jell-O and stir until dissolved, 2–3 minutes. Pour in remaining soda pop. Refrigerate Jell-O mixture just until it begins to thicken.

2 Meanwhile, poke holes in the cake with a fork. When Jell-O has thickened slightly, pour it evenly over the cake.

3 Refrigerate to cool several hours. Spread prepared pudding over top of cake and chill until pudding is well set.

4 Layer whipped topping on top. Store in the refrigerator.

Serves 12.

*West Virginia has a special place in my heart because it was home to the Hill Family, from which my Grandma Minnie is a descendant and into which my Aunt Virginia "Virgie" Hill married. As I researched states and recipes for this book, I discovered many wonderful details about my family in Aunt Virgie's cookbook—*Grandma's Cookbook: Recipes and Remembrances of the Hill Family*—which was loaned to me by my cousin, Shirlee.*

Aunt Virgie had a zest for life and a love of hiking and backyard bonfires. She enjoyed roasting hot dogs and marshmallows. She had a great sense of humor and especially loved pushing her grandchildren on the tire swing and taking them out for ice cream. Family was her life. For your reunion, consider selecting menus from your own family's collected recipes.

Aunt Virgie named this recipe the most delicious cake she ever ate and recommended a strawberry cake mix from Betty Crocker to make the dessert especially fluffy.

Cranberry Pecan Cream Cheese Bars

Created by Margaret Paetow, Franklin, Wisconsin
Courtesy Wisconsin State Cranberry Growers Association

INGREDIENTS

1 cup butter, softened

1 cup firmly packed brown sugar

2 cups all-purpose flour

1 1/2 cups quick oats

1 cup chopped pecans

1 1/2 cups sweetened dried cranberries

1 package (8 ounces) cream cheese, softened

1 can sweetened, condensed milk

1 Preheat oven to 350 degrees. Grease a 9 x 13-inch pan.

2 In a large bowl, cream together butter and sugar. Gradually beat in flour and oats. Stir in cranberries and pecans. Reserve 2 cups of mixture. Press remaining mix into prepared pan and bake 15 minutes.

3 In a small bowl beat cream cheese and milk until smooth. Pour over hot crust and sprinkle remaining oat mixture over top.

4 Bake an additional 25–30 minutes. Cool completely on metal rack and then cut into bars.

Makes approximately 18 bars.

Wisconsin cranberries are second to none! The official state fruit, early settlers initially called them crane berries due to the perception that cranberry blossoms look much like tiny sandhill cranes. No longer merely a garnishment for Thanksgiving meals, the sought-after berry is a perennial year-round favorite across the county.

This fantastic cranberry recipe garnered Margaret Paetow a first place blue ribbon at the 2011 Wisconsin State Fair.

THEMED REUNION *Menus*

A STATE FAIR REUNION

The 1945 Rodgers and Hammerstein movie musical *State Fair* follows the Frake family to Des Moines where they spend three days at the Iowa State Fair. Mom and Pop Frake—Melissa and Abel—are hoping for blue ribbons. Teens Margy and Wayne are hoping for romance.

A state fair theme is easy to adapt to any size reunion—and you don't even need to be in Iowa!

When planning any reunion, it's great to have several activities in mind that family members can participate in throughout the event. A state fair theme makes for quite a few wonderful possibilities.

Games, Activities, and Decorations

* Make a family quilt.
* Create a photo booth from a refrigerator box. Decorate the box and assign a photographer. Using a digital camera and printer setup, make provisions to print photos on site and hang them with clothespins on a length of rope or twine.
* Go fishing—for prizes. Make fishing poles with sticks, using a string, yarn, twine, or ribbon for the fishing line. Tie a clothespin on the end of the string and have kids "cast" over the top of a suspended sheet. Volunteers behind the sheet clip small prizes or treats onto the clothespins such as a small bag of Goldfish crackers. After a tug on the line, kids pull the pole back to discover what they've received.

* Hold a baking contest. Make blue ribbon awards for the best cake, pie, cookies, homemade pickles, jams, jellies, or rolls.
* Hold an art or photography contest.
* Have a yodeling contest, or a pig calling contest.
* Invite musicians in your group to bring guitars, violins, harmonicas, or other instruments. Have them take turns providing background music during meals. Or have a family sing-a-long. Before the reunion, invite a family member to compose a family song. Learn and sing the song together at the reunion.
* Make pies together, followed by a pie eating contest.
* Hold a watermelon eating contest.
* Have a gunny sack race or three-legged race.
* Play tug-of-war. Pit the aunts against uncles, cousins against parents, and so on.
* Hold a hula hoop contest and see who can keep hoops spinning the longest, or who can spin the most hoops at once.
* Hold a shaving contest. Have wives or girlfriends create shaving foam mustaches and beards on their husbands or boyfriends. Then have them "shave" the foam off with a Popsicle stick—blindfolded!
* Make a ring toss. Toss canning jar rings at soda pop bottles. A ring around the neck of a pop bottle wins the soda.
* Play Tip the Can. Throw tennis balls at a stack of emptied tin cans. Whoever knocks over the most cans wins a full can of fruit (peaches, pears, etc.).
* Using a grouping of small sand pails, see who can get the most ping pong balls into the pails.
* If you have a relative with farm animals, see if it's possible for them to bring a bunny, chicken, or duck for a mini-petting zoo. Or provide farm animal coloring pages and a set of crayons for the younger kids to color. Have one of the grandmas judge a coloring contest and award prizes, such as small stuffed animals.
* Have a face painting booth.
* For older kids, provide beads so they can make bracelets and/or necklaces.

Food and Treats

* Rent a cotton candy machine or buy premade cotton candy.
* Make snow cones with shaved ice and various flavorings.
* Serve caramel apple bites—apple slices with a small cup of caramel dipping sauce. Use caramel ice cream topping for the sauce.
* Serve giant dill pickles, or make fried dill pickles.
* Make corn doggies. Mix packaged cornmeal muffin mix and pour batter into muffin tins according to package directions. Cut hot dogs into thirds or quarters (depending on the size of the muffins) and insert one piece into the center of each muffin. Bake according to package directions. Or, make and fry corn doggies with the recipe provided by Hazel James (see next page).
* Make grilled glazed donuts. Spray glazed doughnuts with cooking spray. Grill over medium low heat on well-seasoned grate until glaze is bubbly and the doughnut begins to brown. Serve with small cups of dipping sauce: chocolate ice cream topping, honey, fruit jams, or jellies.
* Set out large glass canisters with candy sticks, large gumballs, or all-day suckers.
* Purchase or rent a chocolate fountain. Cut up slices of bananas and other fruits and foods to dip in chocolate. Offer cups of chopped nuts or sprinkles to finish off your chocolate creations.

Corn Doggies

Courtesy Hazel James

1 Blend egg and milk. Stir in dry ingredients.

2 Cut hot dogs into thirds. Dip hot dogs into batter and fry in deep fryer set at 375 degrees for 2–3 minutes or until brown.

3 Serve with ketchup and mustard.

Makes 30.

INGREDIENTS

1 egg

1/2 cup milk

1 cup Bisquick

2 tablespoons yellow cornmeal

1/4 teaspoon paprika

1/2 teaspoon dry mustard

10 hot dogs

Iowa Girl Eats Clubhouse Turkey Burgers

Created by Kristin Porter, www.iowagirleats.com

INGREDIENTS

1 pound ground turkey

6 strips bacon, cooked and crumbled

1 cup shredded cheddar cheese

1/3 cup Panko bread crumbs

1/4 cup of your favorite barbecue sauce

Salt and pepper to taste

Buns

Toppings: red onion, tomato, lettuce, barbecue sauce

1 Mix together the turkey, bacon, cheese, Panko bread crumbs, barbecue sauce, salt, and pepper in a large bowl then divide into 4 parts and form into patties.

2 Brush or mist one side of the burgers with extra virgin olive oil or non-stick spray, then cook for 4–5 minutes on each side, or until cooked through, brushing or misting the uncooked side with more oil before flipping.

3 Top with toppings and serve on toasted buns.

Serves 4.

Kristin advises that whether you're using an indoor or outdoor grill, make sure you generously brush or mist the burgers with olive oil or non-stick spray before cooking since the cheese and barbecue sauce will make them stick.

Blue Ribbon Mandarin Chicken Salad

Created by Esther Wiese

1 In a medium bowl, combine first eight ingredients. Mix well.

2 Cover and chill 1–2 hours. Fold in pecans just before serving.

Makes 16 servings.

INGREDIENTS

9 cups diced cooked chicken

3 cups diced celery

6 tablespoons lemon juice

3 tablespoons finely chopped white onion

2 1/4 cups mayonnaise

3 cans (11 ounces each) mandarin oranges, well drained

3 cups seedless grapes, halved

3 teaspoons lemon pepper

1 1/2 cups chopped pecans, toasted (optional)

State Fair Bacon Corn

INGREDIENTS

Corn on the cob, shucked and cleaned

Raw bacon

Seasonings

Aluminum foil

1 Wrap each ear of corn with a slice of bacon; spiral the bacon down the length of the corn. Sprinkle with salt, pepper, garlic, or other seasonings.

2 Wrap corn cobs individually in heavy foil.

3 Grill over medium-high heat 15–20 minutes, or until bacon is fully cooked and corn is fork tender.

State Fair Raspberry-Lemonade

INGREDIENTS

Canned lemonade concentrate

Fresh lemons, washed and sliced into thin sections

Fresh raspberries, washed

1 Prepare lemonade according to container directions.

2 Add in desired amount of lemon slices and raspberries.

Grandma's Prize-Winning Cobbler

Created by Esther Wiese

INGREDIENTS

1/4 cup butter, softened

1/2 cup + 1/4 cup granulated sugar

1 cup sifted all-purpose flour

1/4 teaspoon salt

2 teaspoons baking powder

1/2 cup milk or half and half

1 can (29 ounces) sliced peaches or 1 quart fresh fruit slices, drained (reserve 1 cup juice)

1 Preheat oven to 375 degrees.

2 Cream together butter and sugar.

3 In a separate bowl, mix flour, salt, and baking powder and then blend into butter and sugar mixture. Stir in milk or half and half until well blended.

4 Pour the batter into a well-buttered 9 x 13-inch pan. Spoon fruit evenly over the top. Sprinkle with 1/4 cup sugar.

5 Pour 1 cup reserved juice over top of batter and fruit. Bake 25–30 minutes.

6 Serve piping hot with vanilla ice cream or whipped topping.

Serves approximately 12–16.

Homemade Eskimo Pies

INGREDIENTS

Brownies

Vanilla ice cream

Premade chocolate sauce or chocolate shell sauce

Premade caramel sauce (optional)

1. Bake brownies in desired quantity according to package directions and cool.
2. Allow ice cream to soften until spreadable. Spread ice cream evenly over brownies in baking dish or pan to a thickness of 1/2-inch. Freeze until ice cream is firm.
3. Remove from freezer and cut into individual servings. Top each serving with chocolate sauce or chocolate shell sauce and optional caramel.

If you don't choose to host a state fair themed reunion, you can still look to Iowa for recipe and meal ideas. Often referred to as America's Heartland, Iowa is home to fun foods such as the Eskimo Pie. You can make your own rendition of the popular treat with just four ingredients.

A PICNIC THEMED REUNION

I found the three following recipes, typed out on yellowed 3 x 5-inch index cards in an old tin recipe box passed down in my family; together they make for truly terrific picnic cuisine!

Also for picnic fare, consider the Muffaletta—the signature sandwich of New Orleans—which is made on round Sicilian bread of the same name. The bread is layered with provolone and mozzarella, ham, mortadella (a type of Italian sausage), salami, minced garlic, and a piquant prepared green and kalamata olive salad. True muffaletta sandwiches, which originated in the French Quarter at Central Grocery in 1906, are served at room temperature, as opposed to being toasted.

There are lots of fun ways to make your picnic themed reunion memorable. Consider some of these possibilities:

Games, Activities, and Decorations

* Make place mats out of bandannas.
* Serve food/sack lunches in brown paper lunch sack, or serve boxed lunches.
* Bring quilts to sit on.
* Dine under sunshades, canopies, or beach umbrellas.
* Light the picnic area with luminarias or votive candles set in sand in Mason jars.

* Buy checkerboard fabric, and use chocolate and vanilla cookies to play checkers.
* Make seating on the ground on old pillows; place lengths of boards on barrels, bricks, or cinder blocks to make low tables to dine at; or use crates for seating and/or tables.
* Use children's wagons to serve from or to group foods in.
* Have your family talent show during the picnic, or assign family members to preform musical numbers.
* Invite members to bring their best deviled/picnic egg dishes. Vote on a winner and award a "You're a Good Egg!" for the best tasting, most creative, etc.
* Purchase inexpensive lunch boxes for younger kids. Pack their picnic lunches inside; they can keep the box as a handy carrying case for crafts and other items.

Food and Treats

* Pour Jell-O into clear plastic cups; layer different colors if desired. Chill and top with fresh fruit.
* Cut lemons, limes, or oranges in halves. Remove centers and use in punch, lemonade, or ice cream. Use the hollowed out peels/cups to serve ice cream.
* Make brownie kabobs with 1-inch sections of brownies, alternating with berries and marshmallows. Or make angel food kabobs alternating 1-inch sections of angel food cake with berries; drizzle with chocolate.
* Make mini-fruit pies in muffin tins or small jam jars.
* Grill small sections of bacon-wrapped chicken and/or mushrooms over a small Hibachi grill.
* Serve pie-shaped sections of watermelon on Popsicle sticks.
* Serve salads in a medium-sized Mason jar. Layer the ingredients: veggies, greens, croutons, etc. with a small cup of salad dressing. Serve other salads in jars as well.
* Serve meats, cheeses, fruits, and veggies on sticks or toothpicks.
* Serve take-out fried chicken from small wicker baskets.
* For ease, buy large premade hoagies or sub-sandwiches; cut into lengths and let guests choose from three or four different kinds.

Tuna Salad Coneys

INGREDIENTS

1 cup American cheese, cubed

3 hard boiled eggs, chopped

1 can (7 ounces) tuna, flaked

2 tablespoons chopped green pepper

2 tablespoons chopped onion

2 tablespoons chopped stuffed olives

2 tablespoons chopped sweet pickles

1/2 cup mayonnaise or salad dressing

6 Coney (or sub sandwich) buns

1 Preheat oven to 250 degrees.

2 Combine all ingredients except buns; mix lightly.

3 Split buns and fill with generous amount of sandwich filling. Wrap each sandwich in aluminum foil.

4 Bake approximately 30 minutes. Serve hot.

Makes six 4-6 inch sandwiches.

Devil's Eggs

INGREDIENTS

6 hard boiled eggs

4 tablespoons mayonnaise

1/4 teaspoon salt

Dash pepper

3/4 teaspoon freshly minced marjoram

3/4 teaspoon freshly minced tarragon

1 Cut eggs into halves. Remove and mash yolks; add remaining ingredients.

2 Pile yolk mixture back into whites.

3 Chill well covered for several hours to blend flavors.

Makes 12.

Rocky Road

1 Place chocolate, salt, and butter in a heavy saucepan over low heat. Stir until chocolate and butter are melted and well blended.

2 Pour half of the chocolate onto a well-buttered 9 x 13-inch cookie sheet.

3 Arrange marshmallows in rows over the chocolate and sprinkle nuts between the rows.

4 Cover with remaining melted chocolate. Spread with the back of a knife dipped in butter. Chill well. Use a sharp knife to cut into squares.

Makes approximately 24 bite-sized pieces (or 12 larger squares, depending on how you cut them).

INGREDIENTS

1 pound semi-sweet chocolate pieces

1/8 teaspoon fine sea salt

1 tablespoon butter

24 miniature marshmallows

1/2-1 cup broken nuts

A GUYS-DO-ALL-THE-WORK COOK OUT REUNION

Curt Despres grew up in Texas but has called Wisconsin home for the past twenty-plus years. However, his days in Texas instilled a love of grilling and barbecuing that take center stage in his life as an expert griller—Curt operates www.smokedngrilled.com.

At your reunion, take some inspiration from Curt and have the guys in the family pull out their grills. The ladies can sit back and relax while the guys put together this smoky, delicious menu.

First up is the main dish, Curt's Grilled Sweet Soy Salmon. "We just can't get enough salmon around our house," he says. "We seem to choose salmon more than any other fish—or meat for that matter—when it comes to grilling time."

Curt credits his wife with creating the marinade using soy sauce as the base. She sweetened it up a bit with brown sugar and honey-infused vinegar.

Grilled Sweet Soy Salmon

Created and used by permission of Curt Despres, www.smokedngrilled.com

INGREDIENTS

1 1/2 pounds fresh salmon fillets

1/2 cup honey-infused vinegar (found in the Asian section of the grocery store)

2 tablespoons soy sauce

1 tablespoon brown sugar

1 teaspoon ground allspice

1. Rinse the salmon fillets and remove the skin. Place the fillets in a plastic container or a plastic bag.
2. Combine all the marinade ingredients and microwave on high for about 15 seconds. (Just long enough to help dissolve the allspice.) Whisk to mix.
3. Pour the marinade over the salmon fillets and marinate in the refrigerator 30 minutes.
4. Once marinated, remove and discard the excess marinade and set the fillets out at room temperature (no longer than a half hour or so) while you prepare your grill.
5. Grill over medium-high heat, turning the fillets once. For average-sized fillets, this should take about 5 minutes per side.

Serves 4.

Grilled Cinnamon Sweet Potatoes

Created and used by permission of Curt Despres, www.smokedngrilled.com

1 Slice the sweet potatoes into 1/2-inch thick slices and place in a pot of water. Bring water to a boil and cook 3–5 minutes.

2 With a slotted spoon, move the potatoes to a bowl of cool water, and let them sit for 10 minutes to cool. Remove the potatoes from the cool water and pat dry.

3 Lightly coat the potatoes with olive oil. Sprinkle one side of each potato with the salt and cinnamon.

4 Grill (spiced-side down) over medium-high heat, and sprinkle spices on the second side. Cook until tender, a few minutes on each side. Remove them from the grill and enjoy.

Serves 4.

INGREDIENTS

3 medium sweet potatoes, washed and unpeeled

Olive oil

Kosher salt, to taste

Cinnamon, to taste

Sweet Addictions Crisps

Created and used by permission of Curt Despres, www.smokedngrilled.com

INGREDIENTS

40 Club crackers (original)*

1 cup butter

1 cup brown sugar

8 ounces semisweet chocolate chips (about 1 1/3 cups)

1 Preheat oven to 425 degrees. Line a 15 x 10 x 1-inch baking pan with aluminum foil. Spread crackers along foil.

2 In a medium saucepan, melt butter and brown sugar and bring to a boil. Boil 5 minutes. Remove from the heat and pour over the crackers, covering them evenly. Bake 2–4 minutes, or until just bubbly, watching closely to avoid burning. Remove from the oven and pour chocolate chips over the crackers. When the chips melt a bit, spread them over the crackers with a knife.

3 Transfer the pan to the freezer for 15–20 minutes, or until completely cold. They will form one big sheet. Break up into pieces. Store in an airtight container.

Makes 20 servings.

**Substitute 24 graham crackers for the Club crackers for a sweeter snack and use 1/2 cup butter. Boil the brown sugar and butter mixture for 3 minutes.*

A FRONTIER REUNION

Once known as a lawless hangout for gun slingers, Dodge City is located in southwest Kansas. Cowtown fame was attained when cattle drovers started using the Texas Trail, a shorter route leading into the city than the famed Chisholm Trail. Tens of thousands of head of longhorn cattle were herded into rail cars. Cowboys came with them—as did outlaws. Without any form of law enforcement, Boot Hill Cemetery regularly accepted new arrivals!

Lawmen like Wyatt Earp, Bat Masterson, and Charlie Bassett attempted to turn the tide. Today the city is an ever-popular tourist destination. Its history makes the perfect background for a western-themed Kansas Cowboy Frontier dinner at your reunion.

Games, Activities, and Decorations

- Give people western themed invitations and t-shirts.
- Hang "Wanted" posters around the room.
- Let people sit on bales of hay or fruit crates.
- Use bandannas for table coverings or napkins.
- Use different colored bandannas for neckerchiefs or wristbands.
- Buy dollar store sheriff's badges and write names of guests on them in indelible marker.

* Have a family member read cowboy poetry.
* Hold a chili cook-off. Give awards for the best tasting, spiciest, most beany, etc.
* Have a campfire sing-a-long.
* Go on a hike or horseback ride together.
* Teach classes about western history and cooking.
* Have a pie plate throwing contest; see who can throw the farthest.
* See who can lasso a bale of hay.
* See who can roll a hula hoop the longest distance without it falling over. If it's too easy, try rolling it with a stick instead of your hands.
* Conduct old-fashioned relay races, such as carrying a raw egg on a spoon without dropping it.
* Hold a stick horse race.
* Suspend empty pop cans on lengths of twine. Provide small rocks or pebbles, and allot 10 chances (ten rocks or pebbles) to throw. Whoever is able to hit the most cans wins.
* Fill snack-sized zipper bags with beans. Place hula hoops on ground. Have children stand several feet away and take turns trying to get the most bags into a hoop. Or try and toss rubber snakes into the hoops.
* Use water pistols to see who can propel a balloon the farthest away from where they're standing. Or group family members with matching colored bandannas for a water pistol shootout.
* Play put-the-hat-on-the-cowboy. Blindfold players and have them try to make their way to the cowboy (Grandpa, Dad, or other willing participants) and put his hat on his head.

Food and Treats

* S'mores on a stick. Put marshmallows on bamboo skewers or craft sticks. Dip in chocolate and roll in crushed graham crackers.
* Roasted peanuts in galvanized buckets
* Peppermint sticks (or other candy sticks), rock candy
* Watermelon wedges on craft sticks

* Pickle spears
* A build-your-own trail mix bar with different kinds of nuts, pretzels, dried fruit pieces, pretzels, small candies, mini marshmallows, or various cereals like Chex.
* Spiral crescent roll dough around hot dog sticks. Sprinkle with cinnamon and sugar. Bake over coals.
* Kettle corn or caramel corn
* Rice Krispie treats in the shape of a star or cowboy boot (use cookie cutters) served on sticks.
* Decorated cowboy-themed cookies or cupcakes

"Best of the West" Burgers

INGREDIENTS

10 pounds lean ground beef

10 tablespoons (5 ounces) dry ranch dressing mix

5 eggs, beaten

4 cups crushed Club House Crackers

4 large white or yellow onions, chopped fine

2–3 tablespoons Tabasco or other hot sauce (optional)

Cheddar cheese, sliced thick

1. Preheat grill to medium-high heat and lightly oil.
2. Combine all ingredients except cheese slices and form into patties. Grill patties 5–7 minutes on each side, until centers are no longer pink. A few minutes before burgers are done, top with slices of cheese.
3. Serve on lightly toasted Kaiser rolls.

Serves 40–45 hungry cowboys and cowgirls.

Kansas Corn Salad

INGREDIENTS

4 cans (106 ounces each) corn, well-drained

20–25 large tomatoes, diced

8 large red onions, peeled and diced

1/2–1 large bunch green onions, chopped

2 cups extra virgin olive oil

1 1/2–2 cups Italian salad dressing to taste

2 cups chopped fresh basil

2–3 fresh red peppers, diced (optional)

Salt and pepper to taste

1. Combine all ingredients in a very large mixing bowl, pot, or turkey roasting pan. Refrigerate for several hours prior to serving.

Serves 35–40 people.

Buffalo Chips

1 Cover chips with cheese and other ingredients. Heat until cheese bubbles. Serve hot.

INGREDIENTS

Tortilla chips

Shredded cheese

Canned or prepared chili, refried beans, or black beans

Canned diced green chiles

Blue-Buffalo Chicken Dip

Courtesy Lindsay Petermeier, Maytag Dairy Farms

1 Preheat oven to 350 degrees.

2 Warm buffalo sauce and ranch dressing in a saucepan over low heat. Add cream cheese, shredded cheddar, and half of the blue cheese. Add shredded chicken to mixture and pour into oven-safe dish. Crumble remaining blue cheese on top.

3 Bake 12–14 minutes or until bubbly. Serve with pita chips or crackers.

Makes 6 cups.

INGREDIENTS

1 cup buffalo sauce

1 cup ranch dressing

1/2 cup shredded white cheddar

8 ounces blue cheese, crumbled

3 chicken breasts, boiled and shredded

4 ounces cream cheese

Frontier Root Beer

INGREDIENTS

5 cups granulated sugar

8 quarts cold water

1/4 cup root beer extract

3 pounds dry ice, broken into chunks

1 In a large plastic cooler, mix sugar and water until sugar is completely dissolved. Stir in root beer extract. Place dry ice into cooler; cover loosely. Ensure lid is *not* tight fitting. Allow to stand 50–60 minutes prior to serving.

Makes 2 gallons.

Cow Pies

INGREDIENTS

1 cup butter

1/2 cup cocoa

1 cup packed light brown sugar

1/2 cup granulated sugar

3 eggs, beaten

1 teaspoon vanilla extract

1 cup all-purpose flour

1 1/3 cup chopped pecans, divided

12 Reese's Peanut Butter Cup Minis

1 Preheat oven to 350 degrees. Line 12 large muffin tins with paper or foil liners.

2 Melt butter in a large, microwave-safe bowl. Add in cocoa and stir until smooth.

3 Stir in sugars and blend well. Stir in eggs and vanilla until combined.

4 Add flour and 1 cup pecans. Blend well.

5 Fill baking cups just under full. Insert a mini Reese's into the center of each cupcake. Sprinkle with remaining nuts.

6 Bake 20–25 minutes. Serve warm with a heaping scoop of ice cream.

Makes 12–16.

A MOUNTAIN CAMPOUT REUNION

The name Vermont is thought to have originated from the French term les Verts Monts, which translated means "the Green Mountains." Verdant, green conifers and northern hardwoods cover Vermont's mountain slopes. Camping and other outdoor activities are popular in the warm months and make ideal locations for family reunions.

Of course, if you want to rough it, you can find a wonderful campground in any state with all the facilities you need for all ages. Even if the weather or your location doesn't allow you to be outside, you can still have a camping theme. Here are some ideas.

Games, Activities, and Decorations

* Hang stars from the ceiling and use sleeping bags just like you would at a real camp site. Or, if your facility allows, set up a couple of tents.
* Use kerosene lanterns and pine cones for centerpieces. Battery-operated tea lights placed in paper bags can help set the mood.
* Tell family stories around a real or make believe fire.
* Hold a family sing-a-long. Do campfire karaoke or rounds of favorite verses (Row, Row, Row, Your Boat, etc.).
* Project a favorite camping or outdoor movie onto a homemade movie screen (a white sheet, large white canvas, or tarp). Serve popcorn.

* Have a scavenger hunt.
* Plan a hike to a certain destination.
* Create a family skit based on a story from an ancestor's native land or culture.
* Make a family band using pots and pans as "musical" instruments.
* Make a contest of throwing marshmallows into galvanized buckets.
* Have a cookie decorating contest.
* See who can come up with the most fabulous dessert using only a few basic ingredients.
* Have a three-legged race.
* If you need wood for the fire, make it a contest—see who can gather the most fire wood in the least amount of time.
* Using glow sticks and pop bottles, make a glow-in-the-dark ring toss game.
* If you're outside, search for things in nature that start with each letter of the alphabet.
* Create an obstacle course.
* Play flashlight tag and see who you can "catch" with your beam.
* Make paddles out of craft sticks and paper plates and play ping pong with balloons.

Food and Treats

* Peanut butter and jelly sandwiches cut into bite-sized pieces
* Carrot and celery slices served in a cup of ranch dressing
* Banana porcupines made by sticking small pretzel sticks into sections of banana
* Apple smiles made by filling 2 apple slices with peanut butter and adding mini-marshmallow "teeth."
* Happy Camper Trail Mix (see page 225).

The menu that follows is perfect for camp outs. The Under-the-Stars dinner is particularly fun because each person can make his or her own dinner, wrap it in foil, and choose the perfect spot on the fire to cook it (or in the oven if you're having an indoor campout).

"Under the Stars" Dinner

INGREDIENTS

1/4 pound ground beef, pork, or turkey per person

1 medium red potato, sliced, per person

1 carrot, sliced, per person

2 tablespoons chopped onion, per person

1 sheet heavy-duty aluminum foil, per person

Salt and pepper to taste

Dash Worcestershire sauce

1. Spray one side of foil with non-stick spray. Crumble meat into center of foil. Add vegetables and seasonings.
2. Bring right and left sides of foil up and crimp together at top (center) over food. Crimp remaining edges securely to seal well.
3. Bake in the oven (best done on a cookie sheet) at 350 degrees for 40–45 minutes. Or grill over medium-high or open coals for 20–25 minutes until meat is fully cooked and vegetables are tender. Serve with ketchup or steak sauce.

Orange Peel Cupcakes

INGREDIENTS

Oranges

1 box cake mix batter, any flavor, prepared according to package directions

Heavy-duty tin foil

1. Cut off top quarter of oranges; remove fruit (use at breakfast for homemade orange juice). Fill each orange cup a little over half full with cake batter. Replace tops, wrap entire orange in foil. Place in coals 15–20 minutes, or until centers of cupcakes are set.

Makes 10–12.

Mountain-Fresh Fruit Salad

1 Combine first six ingredients in a large bowl.

2 Prepare pudding according to package directions. Fold into first ingredients along with pecans.

3 Scoop into waffle cones to serve.

Serves 6–8.

INGREDIENTS

1 can (20 ounces) pineapple tidbits, well drained

1 can (11 ounces) mandarin oranges sections, well drained

1 Granny smith apple, diced

1 cup blueberries

1/4 cup sweetened shredded coconut

1 banana, sliced

1 package (3.4 ounces) instant vanilla pudding

Milk (amount according to pudding package instructions)

1/4 cup pecan pieces

6–8 small waffle cones

Wilderness Pretzels

1 Spiral the dough around the stick and sprinkle with salt.

2 Hold over coals, turning so the pretzel cooks evenly, until dough is golden brown. Dip in melted butter.

**For a sweet treat, use frozen cinnamon rolls. Apply glaze when cooking is complete. Yum!*

INGREDIENTS

Stick skewers 1/2 inch or more in diameter, bark removed

Frozen dinner rolls, thawed just until the dough is manageable

Coarse sea salt

Happy Camper Trail Mix

1 Combine all ingredients in a large bowl. Divide into individual paper cups or bags to serve on the go.

Makes approximately 18 servings.

INGREDIENTS

6 cups mini pretzels

4 cups mixed nuts

2 cups chopped dried apples or peaches

1 1/2 cups dried pineapple

2 cups dried cranberries or cherries

1 package (3.4 ounces) M&Ms candies

1 bag (4 ounces) Skittles

A FESTIVAL THEMED REUNION

From the blue hills of the Smokey Mountains to Music City and the stage at the Grand Ole Opry, Tennessee is bursting with things to do, see, hear, and, of course, eat! A long growing season—June through October—means that fresh produce is abundant. Tomatoes, green beans, and pumpkins are among the state's largest vegetable commodities. Blackberries, blueberries, and cantaloupe top the long list of fruits grown in the state. More than 45,000 producers raise one million cows for beef. And Tennessee farmers produce 323 million eggs a year from their plump chickens. In total, Tennessee has 10.9 million acres of farmland.

But it also has its sweets. A specialty in the Appalachian region, Tennessee Stack Cakes—sweet layer cakes infused with dried apples—are said to have been created as a substitute for more fancy and costly wedding cakes. Neighbors would each bring a layer of cake to the wedding to add to the stack. Tradition holds that the more layers in the stack the more popular the bride. The Stack Cake is still well-loved throughout the state at family gatherings and celebrations.

MoonPies also originated in Tennessee. The history of the MoonPie began in the 1910s as a treat dreamt up at the request of miners who asked Chattanooga Bakery salesman Earl Mitchell Sr. to make them something solid and filling. Mr. Mitchell asked how big this treat should be, and a miner held out his hands, framed the moon, and said, "About that big." According to the company's official history, "When Mr. Mitchell returned to the bakery, he noticed some of the workers dipping graham cookies into marshmallow and laying them on the window sill to harden. The idea of adding another cookie and a generous coating of chocolate was tried, and samples of this MoonPie were distributed." The response to the sweet treats was overwhelming. In the next two decades, their popularity grew. By the 1930s, MoonPies came to be known as the "working man's lunch." For a nickel each, a miner or laborer could get a MoonPie and large RC Cola and stay full the rest of the day. In the 1950s, the pie-and-soda duo landed on country music charts in the hit song, "Give Me an RC and MoonPie."

Food festivals are abundant in Tennessee, including The Annual National Cornbread Festival, The Annual Tennessee Strawberry Festival, The World Championship Barbecue Cooking Contest, and the RC Moon Pie Festival.

A festival theme is perfect for family reunions: good food, entertainment, arts and crafts, what could be better? In a nod to the varied foods and activities boasted by Tennessee, try creating your own festival with a buffet of offerings. Here are some ideas and recipes:

Popcorn Party

Serve bowls of popcorn with different toppings set out, such as cinnamon and sugar, grated cheeses, chocolate chips, nuts, candies, and a variety of fresh herbs and spices. Make popcorn balls and popcorn-themed crafts.

Cookies!

Include as many kinds of cookies as you can think of. Have cookie-making demonstrations. Hold a contest where the participant puts on a blindfold and then tests a bite of several different cookies and has to name each one. Let the kids roll out and decorate sugar cookies. Organize a cookie swap. Serve cookies and milk for a bedtime treat.

Ice Cream Social

Serve a variety of ice creams and toppings for an ice cream sundae bar: caramel, chocolate, marshmallow and butterscotch sauces, bananas, maraschino cherries, chopped nuts, whipped cream—the works! Teach everyone how to make homemade ice cream and hold a contest to see who can come up with the most unique but tasty flavor.

Marshmallow Madness

Serve large marshmallows on craft sticks with a variety of dipping sauces. Provide shredded coconut, chopped nuts, crushed cookies, and candies for dipping. Let the kids make snowmen out of marshmallows and toothpicks, with chocolate chips for eyes and coal buttons (secure with a dab of frosting). Teach guests how to make homemade marshmallows. Make marshmallow guns out of PVC pipes and have a marshmallow-shooting war.

Waffle Bar

Serve piping hot waffles with both sweet and savory toppings: fresh fruits and berries, canned pineapple and mandarin oranges, pie fillings, powdered sugar, cinnamon, cream cheese, peanut butter, grapes, chocolate chips, chocolate and caramel sauce, fruit cocktail, syrups, jams and jellies, puddings, whipped cream, ice cream, sprinkles, chopped nuts, scrambled eggs, cooked breakfast meats, gravy, and fried chicken. Use your family's favorite waffle recipe; or, use the Whole Wheat Waffle recipe or Townsend Tennessee's own Gracehill Bed and Breakfast's Wild Rice Pecan Waffle recipe, both included at the end of this section.

Cupcake Carnival

Have a cupcake bar with several different varieties of cupcakes. Let the kids decorate cupcakes. Have a cupcake walk instead of a traditional cake walk. Make crafts out of cupcake wrappers. Hold a cupcake decorating or baking contest. Perhaps teach a class on making and using fondant for decorations.

Hawaiian Haystack Luau

Hold a luau with Hawaiian Haystacks for food. Guests can build their haystacks over a bed of chow mein noodles and rice, with the following toppings: chicken or turkey gravy, diced cooked chicken or turkey, pineapple tidbits, water chestnuts, grated American or cheddar cheese, sliced black olives, sunflower seeds, sliced almonds, sliced green olives, mandarin oranges, shredded unsweetened coconut, chow mien noodles, and diced tomatoes. For an activity, make flower leis and serve slushy piña coladas for drinks. Teach the kids how to hula dance.

Chili or Soup Festival

Have an all-chili or all-soup potluck and let everyone bring their own creation. Award prizes for the best flavor, spiciest, knock-your-socks-off hot, most unique, creamiest, healthiest, and so on. Teach classes on the basics of making a roux or homemade chicken stock. Play off the song "Animal Crackers in My Soup," and find related stories, games, and crafts to entertain the kids.

Nachos

Bags of tortillas chips and a plethora of toppings make nacho bars a perennial favorite! Top chips with melted cheese, salsa, guacamole, diced tomatoes, shredded pork or chicken, browned ground beef, sliced green onions, chili, refried beans, black beans, pinto beans, grated cheeses, canned or diced green chiles, jalapeño peppers, diced onions, diced bell and red peppers, and queso. Teach guests how to make homemade salsa and guacamole. Give a primer on cheese and then let guests sample different cheeses to determine a family favorite.

Pita Party

Provide options for stuffing pita pockets with pizza sauce and pizza ingredients; deli meats, cheese, and lettuce; tuna fish salad and pickles; peanut butter and jelly; bacon, lettuce, and tomato; cooked sausages, onions, and cucumbers; egg salad; or chicken salad. Run a contest to see who can create the best filling, or use the recipe for Chicken Pita Pockets on page 231. Play games or activities that start with the letter P to entertain the kids, like a pocket relay, where each line of kids starts with a pocket full of change and has to empty the pennies one-by-one down the line into a piggy bank. The line that finishes first wins.

TENNESSEE

Gracehill Bed and Breakfast Wild Rice Pecan Waffles

Used by permission of Kathy Janke, Owner/Innkeeper, Gracehill Bed and Breakfast

1 Beat the first eight ingredients with an electric mixer just until well mixed.

2 Stir in rice and pecans. Bake in a waffle iron according to manufacturer's directions.

3 Serve waffles with butter and maple syrup or with honey butter.

Honey Butter

1 Mix equal amounts of slightly softened butter with honey. Refrigerate leftover honey butter.

Kathy's tip: When you take the waffles off the waffle iron, let them sit on a wire rack for 10–15 seconds before putting them on a plate. Doing so helps keep them crisp.

INGREDIENTS

2 eggs

1 1/2 cups all-purpose flour

1 3/4 cups milk

5 1/2 tablespoons melted butter

2 tablespoons packed brown sugar

4 teaspoons baking powder

1 teaspoon vanilla

1/4 teaspoon salt

3/4 cup cold cooked wild rice

1 cup pecans, chopped fine

Honey Butter

Butter, softened

Honey

Whole-Wheat Waffles

1. Separate egg yolks and whites into two separate bowls; set aside egg whites.
2. To the yolks, add milk or club soda, vegetable oil, and vanilla. Stir well to combine.
3. In a large, separate bowl, sift together flour, soda, sugar, and salt. Blend wet ingredients into dry.
4. Beat egg whites with an electric mixer until stiff. Fold into batter.
5. Bake in a hot waffle iron according to manufacturer's directions. Whole wheat waffles will take a little longer to cook than regular waffles.

INGREDIENTS

2 large eggs

1 1/4 cup milk or 1 1/4 cup club soda

3 tablespoons vegetable oil

1/2 teaspoon vanilla extract

1 cup sifted whole wheat flour

3 teaspoons baking soda

3 tablespoons brown sugar

3/4 teaspoon salt

Chicken Pita Pockets

Created by Lydia Stucki, www.family-reunion-success.com

1. In a bowl, combine chicken, cucumber, tomato, and onions.
2. In a separate bowl, combine lemon juice, oil, garlic powder, sugar, and basil; mix well. Pour over chicken mixture and toss to coat.
3. Cover and refrigerate for at least 2 hours. Just before serving, mix with lettuce, torn in small pieces.
4. Serve in pitas.

INGREDIENTS

8 cooked chicken breasts, cubed

4 cucumbers, cubed

4 tomatoes, cubed

12 green onions, sliced

1 cup lemon juice

3/4 cup oil

1 teaspoon garlic powder

4 teaspoons sugar

1 tablespoon dried basil

2–3 heads lettuce

Pita pockets

IDEAS & ACTIVITIES

Ideas for Your Family Reunion

To create the best possible experience for your guests, when planning your family reunion draw on the individual interests and talents of those who will be present. In this section are a few ideas and activities for how to make the best of your family reunion and bring everyone closer together.

A Touch of Family History

A Passion for Fashion

If you're having your first family reunion, getting to know everyone can be as uncomfortable as, well, Aunt Gladys's old girdle. There's nothing like a family fashion show to break the ice and get things going. Younger kids will have fun modeling clothes their parents and grandparents wore.

Have an MC introduce each model and tell a little about the person who originally wore the outfit. Pioneer era clothing and the wedding attire of ancestors can add an educational facet to the show, as can native costumes from countries where the family originated.

If your reunion has a theme, a theme fashion show from any culture or era can tie everything together. Styles from bygone eras can provide a smile and a chuckle as they give insight into the lives of ancestors and family members:

- a top hat or cowboy hat, spats or boots
- an old uniform
- a vintage Flapper dress or '40s-style Swing dress
- a muumuu or kimono
- pioneer or prairie attire
- a grass skirt
- a ball gown or Gibson Girl apparel
- the dusty tux from the attic
- the overalls from Grandpa's garage

A Day at the Museum

Visit a museum that contains artifacts or exhibits that give insight into the lives of ancestors. Discuss donating family artifacts or photos for display at the museum. Gather funds to make a monetary donation in the name of a loved one to the museum, a local charity, or a library.

You can also form a family history committee to find and keep track of family history, as well as current events such as newspaper clippings for weddings, births, graduations, and other honors.

A Class with Class

Learning first-hand about what life was like in the "old days" builds lasting memories. Utilize older family members to talk about and demonstrate crafts or skills from bygone eras. Ask them to discuss what life was like when they were young and what their favorite activities or foods were. Have someone teach a cooking class related to a treasured family recipe. Let attendees ask questions and share time-honored cooking tips.

Ode to Home

Verdant mountain valley, arid desert, or tropical paradise. Bustling city, quiet town, or remote rural hamlet. Ask someone in your family to write a poem paying tribute to your ancestral home. Print copies to distribute as keepsakes at your reunion.

Time Worn Comfort

Old shirts, ties, baby clothing, and jeans donated by family members can be cut and sewn together to make a memory quilt. The quilt can be displayed or given as a special gift.

A Sketch of Life

Have someone dress as an ancestor and give a life-sketch of the person they're depicting. Make sure the "actor" has genuine knowledge of their progenitor so the audience can ask questions. If the ancestor is unknown to most family members, pass out a few hints with trivia to get things started, for example, "What year did you first fly a plane?" Or "Who was your hero?"

Tell Me 'Bout the Good Old Days

Preserve family history while you hold your reunion. Enlist willing children or teens to interview the older set. Encourage youngsters to gather pertinent life-history facts and write them down in designated spiral notebooks. If available, arm your family history detectives with cameras or voice recorders. Make them official badges by cutting 3 x 5-inch index cards in halves and labeling them "History Hunter."

Visiting Those Who Have Gone Before Us

Visit a cemetery where your ancestors or family members are buried. Place flowers or seasonal wreaths on their graves. If the grave sites are overgrown, get permission to tidy up. Make a plan to repair broken or marred and aging grave markers. Take photos of headstones to document dates for family history work.

Take a Hike

If your reunion can't be held near where your forebearers lived, organize a walk or hike with stops that illustrate living conditions similar to those of your ancestors. Point out areas or buildings of interest: a field of grain like the one that your grandparents once farmed, a dairy similar to one once owned by your uncle, a little cozy corner café like one once owned by a favorite aunt.

Discuss the functions of horses and buggies, tractors, grain threshers, and other machines that children might not be familiar with. Visit an orchard, cattle ranch, textile factory, or other type of workplace that might be relevant.

Bridging Generations

This is a lovely idea from Idaho resident Sheila Anderson: "Have individual photos taken of your children with each blood aunt and uncle. We usually take pictures with the grandparents but forget the aunts and uncles. Over the years, I've taken a picture of my daughter with each of her aunts, uncles, great-aunts, great-uncles, great-great-aunts, and great-great-uncles. It will give her a personal sense of connection to her ancestors. I don't have any pictures of me with my great-aunts or uncles except with my Uncle Tom and Aunt Selma. I wish I had visual proof that I knew my other relations. It is a visual connection to the past; a way to bridge the generations."

Time Capsule

Add mementos, photos, newspaper clippings, or written sentiments to a moisture-proof container that will serve as a family time capsule. Find a place to either stash or bury the container. Set a prearranged date to either add to or open the capsule.

Recipe for Success

Appoint someone to be "cookbook chairperson" and ask family members to contribute favorite recipes, or recipes they've inherited from family members who've passed on. Create a family cookbook, or post the best recipes on the family blog or website. You can also plan for several recipe books with recipes to be collected for a new book each year: *Grandma's Favorites*, *Just Desserts*, or *Our Family's Best Cakes*. Another great idea is to start a monthly newsletter and share new recipes and cooking tips each month. Finally, consider scanning any handwritten recipes you receive or that other family members have in their collections. There's nothing that brings back memories like looking at an ingredient-smudged recipe card in Grandmother's hand, passed down through the years.

History Panel

Family reunions are genealogy prime-time. Arrange a special session for those interested in finding out more about their family tree so family history discoveries and collaborative projects can be discussed.

Smile Awhile

Appoint a techno-guru to record footage of family interviews to put on DVD. In addition, appoint one or two home videographers to take footage of various reunion activities. You can show the videos next year with popcorn as a family movie tradition.

Activities for All

On Your Mark, Get Set . . . Cook

Create teams and hold a cook-off! Provide simple ingredients and a recipe and see who can whip up a wonderful culinary creation in the shortest amount of time. Award aprons and chef hats as prizes or whisks tied with a festive bow for the "You're a Whisk in the Kitchen" awards, or egg-beaters for the "You Beat All!" award.

In the Limelight

Choose one family or group of individuals to spotlight. Let them strut their stuff in a talent show or magic show. Give awards like a block or bag of cheese for "The Big Cheese Award." Draw names out of a hat to find out whose turn it will be next year.

You Can't Climb It—Yet!

Find a location to plant a real family tree. Involve everyone in digging the hole and getting the tree off to a good start. Ask a relative or friend who lives nearby to help watch the tree's progress and ensure it gets ample water. Create a tradition of visiting the tree on a regular basis. Make the location a special place where you can share family stories or have a picnic.

I'll Take Uncle Hank for Five!

A couple of months prior to your family gathering or reunion send out questionnaires. Ask potential attendees for dates and information pertaining to specific events in their lives, such as when and where they were married, where they have lived, the kinds of employment they've had, what kinds of cars they have owned, their favorite colors, foods, movies, books, and so on. Compile the info and make up trivia questions such as "Who lived in Africa?" or "Who owned a blue Corvette?" Write questions and answers on opposite sides of 3 x 5-inch index cards and play Family Trivia. Various photos of relatives could also be used. For prizes, give bags of macaroni with "That's Using Your Noodle" awards.

May I Have Your Autograph?

Well in advance of the reunion, ask family members for individual or family photos. Photocopy the images, print pages, and staple them together. Give the booklets to young reunion goers and have them find the people in the photos and get their autographs. For the most autographs gathered, award a pair of inexpensive sunglasses for the "You've Got Stars in Your Eyes" award.

Road Rally, Anyone?

Divide family members into teams comprised of children and adults. Appoint drivers. Give prearranged clues to direct teams to specific destinations where more clues will be obtained. For instance, to the park where your grandparents first met, and from there to the church where they were married, then on to the first home they lived in.

A similar activity could be undertaken on foot or by bicycle with only one location visited.

Teaching Moments

Have a family member teach a class on the local flora and fauna, customs, culture, or language. Or hold a class to teach the basics of photography, videography, or a class on gathering family history.

Online puzzle creators can be used to make teaching games for children. Crossword puzzles, word matches, word searches, and other word games can incorporate family names and place names, important dates, events, special holidays, and other items of family trivia.

Hey, I Want to Kick the Can!

There isn't much that is better than ice cream and games. Combine the two for a delightful family reunion activity. Be sure to try the recipe prior to the reunion so you'll know what's involved and can gauge how much of everything you'll need. Also, to avoid salmonella bacteria, be sure to use pasteurized egg substitute, instead of real eggs.

This is what you'll need:

- Ice
- Rock salt
- #1 size coffee cans
- #3 size coffee cans
- Duct or electrical tape

Ingredients per can:

- 1 pint half and half or milk
- Pasteurized egg substitute equal to one whole egg
- 1/2 cup sugar
- 1 teaspoon vanilla or 2 tablespoons chocolate syrup or 1/4 cup jam, any flavor

Put milk, egg substitute, sugar, and flavoring into the #1 coffee cans. Stir well.

Secure the lids on the cans with tape. Place the #1 cans inside of the #3 cans. Pack alternating layers of ice and salt around the smaller cans. Secure the lids of the #3 cans with tape or rope. Let the kids have fun rolling the cans back and forth for ten minutes.

After ten minutes, check to see if the ice cream has reached the desired consistency. If not, drain the melted ice water and refill the cans with alternating ice and salt layers. Give the cans back to the kids for an additional ten minutes.

To make things even more deliciously exciting, have families or groups of individuals vie for the title of the "The Ice Cream Dream Team" in a taste testing contest. Or have a build-your-own sundae bar.

10K, 5K, 3K, OK?

Plan a Family Fun Run and run or walk for a worthy cause. Let those unable to participate take photos, cheer others on, or hand out water and snacks. Create medals of achievement for the fastest time, most enthusiastic runner, most encouraging to others, and so on.

Activities for Kids

Involve children and teens in personalizing dime-store picture frames. Have them add buttons, rocks, shells, or leaves, or paint the family name. An alternative is to make handmade frames from craft sticks, twigs, construction paper, or small squares of cardboard. Later, young crafters can use the frame to display their favorite reunion photo.

We Match!

Reunion t-shirts are a great way to celebrate family unity. Have a budding artist in your group design a graphic using the family name. Contact apparel printers for prices on shirts and printing, or make your own decals with computer transfers.

Long May It Wave

Prior to the reunion, have a family logo contest. Chose a winner and incorporate the logo on a family flag. The logo can be transferred to a large piece of fabric with a computer-generated iron-on or fabric paint. Proudly display the flag at each reunion.

Blog All about It

Check out options for creating a family blog. Sites such as Blogger.com offer a free and easy way to create blogs where family members can stay connected year round.

A Family Reunion Association

Set up a family reunion association with board members who can make command decisions for annual reunion planning. Appoint a family treasurer and secretary, plus representatives from each family group.

Once your reunion association is up and going, a quarterly newsletter (or blog post) can keep everyone apprised of new developments. Advertise for help with specific reunion activities, give would-be journalists a chance to write about family related topics, or give each family a column of their own.

You can also have the family secretary make a family directory that contains birth dates as well as contact info. A digital version will make sharing via email easy.

Address De-stress

Updating family information such as snail mail addresses, email addresses, and phone numbers can be daunting. At the reunion, gather everyone together for an update session and get it all done at once!

And the Gold Medal Goes to . . .

Hold a Family Olympics at your reunion. Baseball, football, golf, Frisbee, any individual or group sport will work. Simple "medals" can be made by gluing a length of ribbon to a canning lid. Play boys against girls, aunts against uncles, or moms against dads.

No Hands Allowed

Divide into equal groups of no more than ten. Sit in a straight line on the ground. On a signal, have everyone pass grocery items—canned goods, a box of crackers, a bag of chips, soda pop, a cake mix—from a brown paper grocery bag at the start of the line to an empty one at the end of the line. Players may use only their feet. The first team that successfully passes the groceries from one bag to the other wins. Give pairs of dollar-store flip-flops as prizes for the "Hot Footing It" award.

A Simply Delicious Dish!

Plan a potluck meal beforehand by asking family members to bring their most delectable appetizer, main course, or dessert, and let everyone vote for their favorite chef. Award an apron to the winner.

Tug-of-War

Put a new twist on an old activity and use a round of Tug-of-War to determine who gets clean up and garbage duty. Make it fun!

I'll Give You My Heart

Make a heart stick: a slender length of wood into which a heart has been carved. At the end of the reunion, pass the stick around and have each person tell their favorite part of their time together.

As things wind up, have families add a brief message of love and hope to a sheet of paper. Roll the paper and tie it to a helium-filled balloon. Release the balloon and its messages of goodwill.

Getting to Know You

Whose Are You?

Make a display of numbered baby photos. Have everyone identify as many as possible. If they're in attendance, have the relatives in the photos identify themselves. Award prizes for the most correct answers. Prizes could include such items as a baby bottle filled with jelly beans or gummy bears, a pacifier attached to a candy bar, or a small plush baby toy.

You can also use photos for decorations. Use them to make a photo wreath or a photo garland by clipping photos to twine or rope using clothespins, or place them on tables in frames or inside of inverted jars.

Another option is to invite someone in the family with artistic skills to draw or paint a tree on a large piece of paper. Have family members bring photos of themselves to place on the "branch" they belong to. Or, cut leaves from green construction paper, write each attendee's name on a leaf, and tape the leaves to the tree. Suspend individual or family photos with ribbon on a "family tree": a spray of twigs tied together and placed in a large flowerpot filled with gravel.

Family Circle

A fun getting-to-know-you game that can be played by everyone is Family Circle. First, have the players sit in a circle, either in chairs or on the ground. Appoint one person to start the game and ask them to state their name: "I'm John." The person to their right then states their own name and the name of the first person. For example, "I'm Kathy and that's John." Play continues to the right (counter clock-wise), with each person stating their name and the names of all the previous players. If someone misses, they're out of game. Play starts over again with the next person whose turn it is stating their own name.

To make the game more interesting, have everyone state his or her full name and the city and/

or state where they are from. For a real challenge, have players add their occupation, birth date, or the names of their spouse or children! Or have younger players state the name of their favorite food.

The last remaining person is the winner. Award the winner with a small bag of cookies and a certificate proclaiming them "One Smart Cookie."

Conversation Starters

Conversation Starters—simple questions written on large craft/Popsicle sticks—are another great icebreaker. Put the sticks in a jar and place the jar at the center of the table, or pass the jar from person to person. Have everyone take turns choosing a stick and asking a question.

A few sample questions are:

- What are some of your hobbies?
- Who does the cooking in your family?
- What is your favorite food?
- What is your least favorite food?
- What were the clothing styles like when you were growing up?
- What were/are your goals and dreams?
- Was there anyone famous you wanted to meet? Did you meet them?
- Did you have a pet when you were a child? What was the pet's name?
- Do you have a garden? What do you like to plant?

Remember When . . .

Have everyone write down favorite memories from childhood or other events, or memories of certain family members: A first time milking the cow with Grandpa. A trip to the corner store with a great-grandmother. First impressions of meeting a great-uncle or aunt. A special story of courage and bravery about a family member who served in the military.

Compile the memories in plastic sheaths inside a three-ring binder. Display the memory book at every reunion.

This Blue Belongs to You!

Make colored wristbands to help identify who belongs to whom. Give each family group a different color. Lengths of ribbon work as well. Colored bandannas or t-shirts can serve the same purpose.

About the Author

Lori Nawyn has worked as a freelance writer for regional and national publications and has produced numerous essays, articles, and short stories. Her work has been featured in six anthologies, and she is the author of one novel, *My Gift to You* (2010). Her book for girls and women, *Fill Your Day with Hope*, was released August 2013. *Simple Things*, her nonfiction book for women which includes inspirational essays and seasonal recipes and activities, was released January 2014.

The Great American Family Reunion Cookbook is her second cookbook with Familius, following *Peachy: A Harvest of Fruity Goodness* (2013). Her forthcoming books include *The Pear Aficionado* (August 2014), and a book featuring cherry recipes (2015). An artist and graphic designer, Lori is also the illustrator of the book *Love, Hugs, and Hope: When Scary Things Happen* (Familius, 2013) and the author/illustrator of the forthcoming travel series for children *Abbie & Jack* (Familius, 2015).

The wife of a fireman, mother of four, and grandmother of four, Lori is a contributor to KSL.com and the *Deseret News* and frequently writes about family relationships and family travel.

To learn more about Lori, her books, art, and adventures, please visit her website www.lorinawyn.com and www.lifedancestudios.blogspot.com, and follow her on Twitter: www.twitter.com/LoriNawyn and Pinterest: www.pinterest.com/lorinawyn. Lori's family reunion-themed decor, with printables and scrapbooking papers, can be found at her Etsy shop: https://www.etsy.com/shop/LifeDanceStudios.

About Familius

Welcome to a place where mothers are celebrated, not compared. Where heart is at the center of our families, and family at the center of our homes. Where boo boos are still kissed, cake beaters are still licked, and mistakes are still okay. Welcome to a place where books—and family—are beautiful. Familius: a book publisher dedicated to helping families be happy.

Visit Our Website: www.familius.com

Our website is a different kind of place. Get inspired, read articles, discover books, watch videos, connect with our family experts, download books and apps and audiobooks, and along the way, discover how values and happy family life go together.

Join Our Family

There are lots of ways to connect with us! Subscribe to our newsletters at www.familius.com to receive uplifting daily inspiration, essays from our Pater Familius, a free ebook every month, and the first word on special discounts and Familius news.

Become an Expert

Familius authors and other established writers interested in helping families be happy are invited to join our family and contribute online content. If you have something important to say on the family, join our expert community by applying at:

www.familius.com/apply-to-become-a-familius-expert

Get Bulk Discounts

If you feel a few friends and family might benefit from what you've read, let us know and we'll be happy to provide you with quantity discounts. Simply email us at specialorders@familius.com.

Website: www.familius.com

Facebook: www.facebook.com/paterfamilius

Twitter: @familiustalk, @paterfamilius1

Pinterest: www.pinterest.com/familius

The most important work you ever do will be within the walls of your own home.

CPSIA information can be obtained
at www.ICGtesting.com
Printed in the USA
JSHW041141020322
23490JS00003B/11

9 781938 301995